HITCHCOCK
IN PRIME TIME

HITCHCOCK IN PRIME TIME

EDITED BY

**FRANCIS M. NEVINS, JR. &
MARTIN HARRY GREENBERG**

WITH AN INTRODUCTION BY HENRY SLESAR

AVON
PUBLISHERS OF BARD, CAMELOT, DISCUS AND FLARE BOOKS

HITCHCOCK IN PRIME TIME is an original publication of Avon Books. This work has never before appeared in book form.

AVON BOOKS
A division of
The Hearst Corporation
1790 Broadway
New York, New York 10019

First Avon Printing, August 1985

AVON TRADEMARK REG. U. S. PAT. OFF. AND IN
OTHER COUNTRIES, MARCA REGISTRADA, HECHO EN
U. S. A.

Printed in the U. S. A.

OPB 10 9 8 7 6 5 4 3 2 1

Acknowledgments

"And So Died Riabouchinska" by Ray Bradbury. Copyright © 1953; copyright renewed 1981 by Ray Bradbury. Reprinted by permission of Don Congdon Associates, Inc.

"The Orderly World of Mr. Appleby" by Stanley Ellin. Copyright © 1950; copyright renewed 1978 by Stanley Ellin. Reprinted by permission of Curtis Brown, Ltd.

"Momentum" by Cornell Woolrich. Copyright © 1940 by Cornell Woolrich. Reprinted by permission of the agents for the author's estate, Scott Meredith Literary Agency, Inc., 845 Third Avenue, New York, New York 10022.

"The Better Bargain" by Richard Deming. Copyright © 1956 by Richard Deming. Reprinted by permission of the agents for the author's estate, Scott Meredith Literary Agency, Inc., 845 Third Avenue, New York, New York 10022.

"The Dangerous People" by Fredric Brown. Copyright © 1945 by Fredric Brown. Reprinted by permission of International Creative Management.

"Enough Rope for Two" by Clark Howard. Copyright © 1957. Reprinted by permission of the author.

"Suburban Tigress" by Lawrence Treat. Copyright © 1970 by

Contents

Introduction

by Henry Slesar

IN THE EARLY 1960s, the offices of Shamley Productions in Universal City were housed in a cozy bungalow nestled among well-tended flower beds. If it hadn't been for the roar of traffic on Lankersham Boulevard, you might have thought you were in an English suburb, an impression fortified by the accents of the people who worked in the building. The overall effect was peaceful and bucolic, despite Shamley's being in the business of murder, robbery, and larcenies of every description. It was the home of *Alfred Hitchcock Presents*.

One morning, having flown to Los Angeles from my home in New York, I arrived to attend a story meeting at Shamley. It was an unusual morning because of the weather; instead of the persistent sunshine that kept the tourists and the lizards happy, the skies were leaden with gray clouds. On my way to the bungalow, I met Gordon Hessler, then an associate producer of the Hitchcock show. He greeted me in his customary shy, affable way, and there was more than the usual width to his friendly smile. Strolling the twisty paths, we met Joan Harrison, the executive producer; her own smile had an extra pearliness and her step was lively. Their good mood was infectious, but I didn't understand its source until Gordon said, "Beautiful day, isn't it?" Joan echoed his opinion with enthusiasm. Then we all went into the bungalow, where Norman Lloyd, another English expatriate,

1

greeted us all with a jolly "good morning" that finally made the picture clear. They were overjoyed at the bad weather.

It may not be surprising that the producing staff of *Alfred Hitchcock Presents,* as well as the subsequent *Alfred Hitchcock Hour,* were bearers of British birth certificates. Hitchcock himself was English, of course, beginning his life and his long career in London. But looking back on the totality of the television programs they produced, on the mood they created and the mark they made on dramatic entertainment, the *Englishness* of the Hitchcock staff may be the most important factor in the show's long-running success and its claim to "classic" status. It has taken me almost a quarter of a century, and more than fifty teleplays, to realize that I wasn't involved in a strictly American television project. The people in that pretty bungalow were producing an exercise in British drollery.

Droll is the only word that explains to me why *Alfred Hitchcock Presents,* despite its dedication to mystery and crime, was probably the least violent program of the genre. It was never the crime itself that intrigued the shamans of Shamley Productions. It was the droll behavior of the people who committed crimes, the twists and turns that surrounded every criminal circumstance. It was the droll irony, the jests of fate, the mockery of the gods that they enjoyed depicting on the tiny screens of America. How much more English can you get?

This viewpoint resulted in that "special" *Alfred Hitchcock* story—a combination of suspense, irony, and dry humor that Shamley had increasing difficulty in finding. Especially since Shamley made a policy of buying *published* fiction to dramatize, a policy only rarely breached.

Fortunately for me, I was publishing a lot of suspense and mystery short fiction at the time when their need was greatest. As it happened, my stories also dealt only peripherally with crime. My interest, like Shamley's, was in the odd behavior of people who resort to extremes, and the ironic and sometimes comical consequences of their actions. I was also madly in love with the twist ending, probably due to a childhood infection named William

Sidney Porter, who called himself O. Henry. It was obvious that Shamley and Slesar were made for each other.

After a dozen sales of published stories, most of them in Hitchcock's namesake publication, *Alfred Hitchcock's Mystery Magazine,* my agent held his breath and gave Shamley an ultimatum. There would be no more sales unless the author was allowed to adapt his own material. I quaked at his boldness; he had only ten percent to lose. As it turned out, his strategy was the right one. I began to adapt my own material, and was soon a well-established regular, commuting almost bimonthly between my home and advertising job in New York to the sun-drenched flower beds of Universal City. It was my first television-writing experience, and a deceptive one. Everyone at Shamley was nice to me. The stories went on the air exactly as scripted. I was rarely to find such a paradise again. Maybe there are no more.

The stories I wrote and adapted were all typically "Hitchcock." But the story most fans of the show consider its prototype is one I didn't write. I can't count the number of times I've been asked if I was the author of "the one about the leg of lamb."

"Lamb to the Slaughter" is a Roald Dahl story. It can be summed up in one sentence. Woman kills husband with frozen leg of lamb, then serves the blunt instrument to investigating officers. Surely the ideal half-hour Hitchcock. Murder by an amateur. A cozy domestic setting. Suspense. Irony. And—oh yes, a droll twist at the end.

However, I don't want to give the impression that all Hitchcock's TV stories were based on a strict formula. For instance, not all the crimes had to be committed by amateurs; occasionally, the professionals did the dirty work. Two stories I supplied were prime examples. One was about a veteran armed robber. Another was about a cop-killer. The first was played by Walter Matthau. The second by Robert Redford. One thing Shamley knew how to do was cast future superstars.

The Hitchcock show was also a showcase of nostalgic performances. I watched with inordinate pleasure when I saw my story characters brought to life by people like Claude Rains, Judy

Canova, Claire Trevor, Shirley Booth, and Eduardo Ciannelli—the last a permanent part of my childhood psyche, if only for his portrayal of the mad Thuggee in *Gunga Din*. I also recall a special gulp of joy upon seeing Ed Gardner speaking *my words,* although only Trivial Pursuit players may remember him as Archie of radio's *Duffy's Tavern*.

But best of all the Hitchcock joys were the people who put the show together. In the sixties, women television producers were rarities, and Joan Harrison was even more unusual for the forthright way she worked with writers. I attributed it to the fact that she was married to one. He wasn't bad. His name is Eric Ambler.

Joan's associate producer, Gordon Hessler (now a very successful director), was impossibly cordial, with a boyish enthusiasm for the show which made him smile even when discussing ax murders. A few years later, I was to meet Gordon at his mews home in London, and work on a screenplay with him. (It was *Murders in the Rue Morgue,* and contained a few ax murders, too.)

Norman Lloyd, who became a noted producer himself, was as impish as the Devil he once portrayed in a Hitchcock Western episode. Norman, as every right-thinking moviegoer must know, was the man who fell from the Statue of Liberty in Hitchcock's *Saboteur,* to say nothing of his many other acting achievements, including a continuing role in TV's *St. Elsewhere*. His boundless talent and humor not only improved the morale of Shamley Productions, it improved the output.

Then there was Hitchcock. I never referred to him as "Hitch," even if everyone else did. He was too sacrosanct an image, even after I met him and took away the impression of a cordial, corpulent, comfortable man who enjoyed talking about stories as if he were a writer himself. In fact, it was apparent from the Shamley mailbox that there were hundreds and maybe thousands of viewers out there who believed that Alfred Hitchcock was the author of the tales he told. So much for credits.

It was within this tight little island of Shamley Productions that I and other writers flourished, at a time when Story was king, and when the word *anthology* didn't send shudders up and down the

INTRODUCTION 5

spines of television network executives. (But then, how many anthologies had an Alfred Hitchcock as a continuing character?)

But like that other tight little island, Shamley was only a demi-paradise. Producers and writers are born to disagree, it seems, and there was the customary amount of abrasion before a script was stamped FINAL. For one thing, Shamley was sensitive to the most frequent viewer criticism of all: "I saw your show last night and *I didn't understand the ending.*"

The truth is, a goodly number of television watchers were simply unable to grasp those droll, devastating, delightfully ironic twists. Shamley and its writers went to great pains to set up the snap-trap endings that were the Hitchcock trademark. But too often, after the trap was sprung, the mouth-breathers in the audience were still waiting for the curtain line. They were a minority, but their influence was felt. The most common command to writers was, For God's sake, make the ending *clear!*

More often than not, the endings had to be expanded on by Hitchcock himself. These were the famous "disclaimers" without which Hitchcockian irony would have been impossible. Irony is a narrative device that sometimes requires that justice *not* be served; that crime *does* pay; that villains succeed in their villainy. Enter the disclaimer. "Our friend Robert," Hitch might intone, "only *thought* he got away with murder. He failed to realize that there was a curious old lady across the street with a high-powered telescope watching his every move, in the hopes that he would do something filthy. . . ." Words to that effect. The result was, the author of an *Alfred Hitchcock Presents* would learn that his diabolically crafted plot actually hadn't succeeded at all; that according to no less an authority than Alfred Hitchcock, the plan was foiled, his antihero incarcerated, his story deflated by commonplace morality.

There was one other fear that haunted the Shamley bungalow. In the sixties (as today), television had its social critics, and denunciation of TV's sex-and-violence proclivities were loud and clear. Hard to believe, looking back at the black-and-white images of the era, when beds were rarer than broomsticks and violence rarely more than a bullet wound that didn't bleed. But Shamley, like the rest of the industry, was sensitive and thereby cautious. That sensitivity wasn't helped when several *Alfred Hitchcock Presents* episodes became an official part of police investigations.

I was involved in three of these incidents. One resulted from a story I adapted from the work of another author. It was about a husband who tied himself to a bed to give the impression of robbery; his motive was insurance. His wife helped make the situation more credible by slaying him when he was helpless. Hitchcock's disclaimer after the show didn't stop a housewife from attempting to emulate the same murder method the next day.

Very much the same circumstance occurred when we aired a story about a woman who went to a TV show and left a glass of poisoned milk behind for her husband to drink. (Her mistake was, she was given gifts for her husband on the show, and threw them away before coming home.) The New Jersey woman who took this as an inspiration for murder was only too willing to cite the Hitchcock show as her source.

Probably the most publicized instance of this kind was a crime committed in London. *Alfred Hitchcock Presents* was highly popular in England, Europe, and Asia (and still is, thanks to the fondness for anthology television abroad). One evening, a story of mine called *Not the Running Type* was watched with interest by a bank clerk who obviously saw himself as the protagonist, a bank clerk played by Paul Hartman. In the story, he embezzles several hundred thousand dollars—and promptly surrenders to the police the next morning, claiming that he simply isn't the running type. There is only one problem. He refuses to reveal the whereabouts of his loot. The detective on the case immediately concludes that he intends to trade prison time for the money. When the prisoner's sentence is over, he visits him and warns him that he will not get away with his bargain. Paul Hartman gives him the sad, canine look that was his specialty and agrees. He is still Not the Running Type. He reaches under the bed and produces the suitcase crammed with bills.

Of course, there was a twist. In the final scene, the antihero was on a world cruise, smoking a fine cigar and commenting to a fellow passenger about the benefits of compound interest.

The London clerk was excited by the simple idea, and proceeded to put the same plan in motion, embezzling a small fortune and placing his purloined pounds in various banks throughout London. There was only one hitch (no pun intended). When he showed up at the police station to surrender himself, sans money, one of the officers instantly recognized the plot of *Not the Running Type*. A check on recent deposits produced the evidence, and the case the English press called "The Alfred Hitchcock Crime" was solved.

Hitchcock's name will probably be linked with the word *crime* forever. I linked it myself, by publishing what were the first collections of "Alfred Hitchcock" stories: *Clean Crimes and Neat Murders* and *A Crime for Mothers and Others* (Avon). But I still maintain that crime was not his métier; it was storytelling. It was an enthusiasm for the most ancient form of entertainment, an art as basic as cave paintings, going all the way back to the tale-tellers who earned their saber-toothed tiger steaks by sitting around the primitive campfires and relating (exaggerated) accounts of their hunting exploits. Later, they were telling myths and fables, war sagas and love stories, waiting for the days of papyrus and printing press, of Marconi and Edison and the cathode ray tube.

Alfred Hitchcock's movies will always be his main monuments. But television is our campfire, and Hitch was one of our finest tale-tellers for all the years when he stepped into his own profile and said: "Good Evening." It was very good, Hitch.

RAY BRADBURY

And So Died Riabouchinska

THE CELLAR WAS COLD CEMENT and the dead man was cold stone and the air was filled with an invisible fall of rain, while the people gathered to look at the body as if it had been washed in on an empty shore at morning. The gravity of the earth was drawn to a focus here in this single basement room—a gravity so immense that it pulled their faces down, bent their mouths at the corners and drained their cheeks. Their hands hung weighted and their feet were planted so they could not move without seeming to walk underwater.

A voice was calling, but nobody listened.

The voice called again, and only after a long time did the people turn and look, momentarily, into the air. They were at the seashore in November and this was a gull crying over their heads in the gray color of dawn. It was a sad crying, like the birds going south for the steel winter to come. It was an ocean sounding the shore so far away that it was only a whisper of sand and wind in a seashell.

The people in the basement room shifted their gaze to a table and a golden box resting there, no more than twenty-four inches long, inscribed with the name RIABOUCHINSKA. Under the lid of this small coffin the voice at last settled with finality, and the people stared at the box, and the dead man lay on the floor, not hearing the soft cry.

"Let me out, let me out, oh, please, please, someone let me out."

And finally Mr. Fabian, the ventriloquist, bent and whispered to the golden box, "No, Ria, this is serious business. Later. Be quiet, now, that's a good girl." He shut his eyes and tried to laugh.

From under the polished lid her calm voice said, "Please don't laugh. You should be much kinder now after what's happened."

Detective Lieutenant Krovitch touched Fabian's arm. "If you don't mind, we'll save your dummy act for later. Right now there's all *this* to clean up." He glanced at the woman, who had now taken a folding chair. "Mrs. Fabian." He nodded to the young man sitting next to her. "Mr. Douglas, you're Mr. Fabian's press agent and manager?"

The young man said he was. Krovitch looked at the face of the man on the floor. "Fabian, Mrs. Fabian, Mr. Douglas—all of you say you don't know this man who was murdered here last night, never heard the name Ockham before. Yet Ockham earlier told the stage manager he knew Fabian and had to see him about something vitally important."

The voice in the box began again quietly.

Krovitch shouted. *"Damn* it, Fabian!"

Under the lid, the voice laughed. It was like a muffled bell ringing.

"Pay no attention to her, Lieutenant," said Fabian.

"Her? Or *you,* damn it! What is this? Get together, you two!"

"We'll never be together," said the quiet voice, "never again after tonight."

Krovitch put out his hand. "Give me the key, Fabian."

In the silence there was the rattle of the key in the small lock, the squeal of the miniature hinges as the lid was opened and laid back against the tabletop.

"Thank you," said Riabouchinska.

Krovitch stood motionless, just looking down and seeing Riabouchinska in her box and not quite believing what he saw.

The face was white and it was cut from marble or from the whitest wood he had ever seen. It might have been cut from snow. And the neck that held the head which was as dainty as a porcelain cup with the sun shining through the thinness of it, the neck was also white. And the hands could have been ivory and they were thin small things with tiny fingernails and whorls on the pads of the fingers, little delicate spirals and lines.

She was all white stone, with light pouring through the stone and light coming out of the dark eyes with blue tones beneath like fresh mulberries. He was reminded of milk glass and of cream poured into a crystal tumbler. The brows were arched and black and thin and the cheeks were hollowed and there was a faint pink vein in each temple and a faint blue vein barely visible above the slender bridge of the nose, between the shining dark eyes.

Her lips were half parted and it looked as if they might be slightly damp, and the nostrils were arched and modeled perfectly, as were the ears. The hair was black and it was parted in the middle and drawn back of the ears and it was real—he could see every single strand of hair. Her gown was as black as her hair and draped in such a fashion as to show her shoulders, which were carved wood as white as a stone that has lain a long time in the sun. She was very beautiful. Krovitch felt his throat move, and then he stopped and did not say anything.

Fabian took Riabouchinska from her box. "My lovely lady," he said. "Carved from the rarest imported woods. She's appeared in Paris, Rome, Istanbul. Everyone in the world loves her and thinks she's really human, some sort of incredibly delicate midget creature. They won't accept that she was once part of many forests growing far away from cities and idiotic people."

Fabian's wife, Alyce, watched her husband, not taking her eyes from his mouth. Her eyes did not blink once in all the time he was telling of the doll he held in his arms. He in turn seemed aware of no one but the doll; the cellar and its people were lost in a mist that settled everywhere.

But finally the small figure stirred and quivered. "Please, don't talk about me! You know Alyce doesn't like it."

"Alyce never has liked it."

"Shh, don't!" cried Riabouchinska. "Not here, not now." And then, swiftly, she turned to Krovitch and her tiny lips moved. "How did it all happen? Mr. Ockham, I mean, Mr. Ockham."

Fabian said, "You'd better go to sleep now, Ria."

"But I don't want to," she replied. "I've as much right to listen and talk, I'm as much a part of this murder as Alyce or—or Mr. Douglas even!"

The press agent threw down his cigarette. "Don't drag me into this, you—" And he looked at the doll as if it had suddenly become six feet tall and were breathing there before him.

"It's just that I want the truth to be told." Riabouchinska turned her head to see all of the room. "And if I'm locked in my coffin there'll be no truth, for John's a consummate liar and I must watch after him, isn't that right, John?"

"Yes," he said, his eyes shut, "I suppose it is."

"John loves me best of all the women in the world, and I love him and try to understand his wrong way of thinking."

Krovitch hit the table with his fist. "God damn, oh, God *damn* it, Fabian! If you think you can—"

"I'm helpless," said Fabian.

"But she's—"

"I know, I know what you want to say," said Fabian quietly, looking at the detective. "She's in my throat, is that it? No, no. She's not in my throat. She's somewhere else. I don't know. Here, or here." He touched his chest, his head.

"She's quick to hide. Sometimes there's nothing I can do. Sometimes she is only herself, nothing of me at all. Sometimes she tells me what to do and I must do it. She stands guard; she reprimands me; is honest where I am dishonest, good when I am wicked as all the sins that ever were. She lives a life apart. She's raised a wall in my head and lives there, ignoring me if I try to make her say improper things, cooperating if I suggest the right words and pantomime." Fabian sighed. "So if you intend going on, I'm afraid Ria must be present. Locking her up will do no good, no good at all.''

Lieutenant Krovitch sat silently for the better part of a minute, then made his decision. "All right. Let her stay. It just may be, by God, that before the night's over I'll be tired enough to ask even a ventriloquist's dummy questions.''

Krovitch unwrapped a fresh cigar, lit it, and puffed smoke. "So you don't recognize the dead man, Mr. Douglas?''

"He looks vaguely familiar. Could be an actor.''

Krovitch swore. "Let's all stop lying, what do you say? Look at Ockham's shoes, his clothing. It's obvious he needed money and came here tonight to beg, borrow, or steal some. Let me ask you this, Douglas. Are you in love with Mrs. Fabian?''

"Now, wait just a moment!'' cried Alyce Fabian.

Krovitch motioned her down. "You sit there, side by side, the two of you. I'm not exactly blind. When a press agent sits where the husband should be sitting, consoling the wife, well! The way you look at the marionette's coffin, Mrs. Fabian, holding your breath when she appears. You make fists when she talks. Hell, you're obvious.''

"If you think for one moment I'm jealous of a stick of wood!''

"Aren't you?''

"No, no, I'm not!''

Fabian moved. "You needn't tell him anything, Alyce.''

"Let her!''

They all jerked their heads and stared at the small figurine, whose mouth was now slowly shutting. Even Fabian looked at the marionette as if it had struck him a blow.

After a long while Alyce Fabian began to speak.

"I married John seven years ago because he said he loved me and because I loved him and I loved Riabouchinska. At first, anyway. But then I began to see that he really lived all of his life and paid most of his attentions to her and I was a shadow waiting in the wings every night.

"He spent fifty thousand dollars a year on her wardrobe—a

hundred thousand dollars for a dollhouse with gold and silver and platinum furniture. He tucked her in a small satin bed each night and talked to her. I thought it was all an elaborate joke at first and I was wonderfully amused. But when it finally came to me that I was indeed merely an assistant in his act, I began to feel a vague sort of hatred and distrust—not for the marionette, because after all it wasn't her doing—but I felt a terrible growing dislike and hatred for John, because it *was* his fault. He, after all, was the control, and all of his cleverness and natural sadism came out through his relationship with the wooden doll.

"And when I finally became very jealous, how silly of me! It was the greatest tribute I could have paid him and the way he had gone about perfecting the art of throwing his voice. It was all so idiotic, it was all so strange. And yet I knew that something had hold of John, just as people who drink have a hungry animal somewhere in them, starving to death.

"So I moved back and forth from anger to pity, from jealousy to understanding. There were long periods when I didn't hate him at all, and I never hated the thing that Ria was in him, for she was the best half, the good part, the honest and the lovely part of him. She was everything that he never let himself try to be."

Alyce Fabian stopped talking and the basement room was silent.

"Tell about Mr. Douglas," said a voice, whispering.

Mrs. Fabian did not look up at the marionette. With an effort she finished it out. "When the years passed and there was so little love and understanding from John, I guess it was natural I turned to—Mr. Douglas."

Krovitch nodded. "Everything begins to fall into place. Mr. Ockham was a very poor man, down on his luck, and he came to this theater tonight because he knew something about you and Mr. Douglas. Perhaps he threatened to speak to Mr. Fabian if you didn't buy him off. That would give you the best of reasons to get rid of him."

"That's even sillier than all the rest," said Alyce Fabian tiredly. "I didn't kill him."

"Mr. Douglas might have and not told you."

"Why kill a man?" said Douglas. "John knew all about us."

"I did indeed," said John Fabian, and laughed.

He stopped laughing and his hand twitched, hidden in the snowflake interior of the tiny doll, and her mouth opened and shut, opened and shut. He was trying to make her carry the laughter on after he had stopped, but there was no sound save the little empty whisper of her lips moving and gasping, while Fabian stared down at the little face and perspiration came out, shining, upon his cheeks.

The next afternoon Lieutenant Krovitch moved through the theater darkness backstage, found the iron stairs, and climbed with great thought, taking as much time as he deemed necessary on each step, up to the second-level dressing rooms. He rapped on one of the thin-paneled doors.

"Come in," said Fabian's voice from what seemed a great distance.

Krovitch entered and closed the door and stood looking at the man who was slumped before his dressing mirror. "I have something I'd like to show you," Krovitch said. His face showing no emotion whatever, he opened a manila folder and pulled out a glossy photograph, which he placed on the dressing table.

John Fabian raised his eyebrows, glanced quickly up at Krovitch, and then settled slowly back in his chair. He put his fingers to the bridge of his nose and massaged his face carefully, as if he had a headache. Krovitch turned the picture over and began to read from the typewritten data on the back. "Name, Miss Ilyana Riamonova. One hundred pounds. Blue eyes. Black hair. Oval face. Born 1914, New York City. Disappeared 1934. Believed a victim of amnesia. Of Russo-Slav parentage. Et cetera. Et cetera."

Fabian's lip twitched.

Krovitch laid the photograph down, shaking his head thoughtfully. "It was pretty silly of me to go through police files for a picture of a marionette. You should have heard the laughter at headquarters. *God*. Still, here she is—Riabouchinska. *Not* papier-mâché, *not* wood, *not* a puppet, but a woman who once lived and moved around and—disappeared.'' He looked steadily at Fabian. ''Suppose you take it from there?''

Fabian half smiled. ''There's nothing to it at all. I saw this woman's picture a long time ago, liked her looks, and copied my marionette after her.''

''Nothing to it at all.'' Krovitch took a deep breath and exhaled, wiping his face with a huge handkerchief. ''Fabian, this very morning I shuffled through a stack of *Billboard* magazines that high. In the year 1934 I found an interesting article concerning an act which played on a second-rate circuit, known as Fabian and Sweet William. Sweet William was a little boy dummy. There was a girl assistant—Ilyana Riamonova. No picture of her in the article, but I at least had a name, the name of a real person, to go on. It was simple to check police files then and dig up this picture. The resemblance, needless to say, between the live woman on one hand and the puppet on the other is nothing short of incredible. Suppose you go back and tell your story over again, Fabian.''

''She was my assistant, that's all. I simply used her as a model.''

''You're making me sweat,'' said the detective. ''Do you think I'm a fool? Do you think I don't know love when I see it? I've watched you handle the marionette; I've seen you talk to it; I've seen how you make it react to you. You're in love with the puppet naturally, because you loved the original woman very, very much. I've lived too long not to sense that. Hell, Fabian, stop fencing around.''

Fabian lifted his pale slender hands, turned them over, examined them, and let them fall.

''All right. In 1934 I was billed as Fabian and Sweet William. Sweet William was a small bulb-nosed boy dummy I carved a long time ago. I was in Los Angeles when this girl appeared at the stage door one night. She'd followed my work for years. She was desperate for a job and she hoped to be my assistant. . . .''

He remembered her in the half-light of the alley behind the theater and how startled he was at her freshness and eagerness to work with and for him and the way the cool rain touched softly down through the narrow alleyway and caught in small spangles through her hair, melting in dark warmness, and the rain beaded upon her white porcelain hand holding her coat together at her neck.

He saw her lips' motion in the dark and her voice, separated off on another sound track, it seemed, speaking to him in the autumn wind, and he remembered that without his saying yes or no or perhaps, she was suddenly on the stage with him, in the great pouring bright light, and in two months he, who had always prided himself on his cynicism and disbelief, had stepped off the rim of the world after her, plunging down a bottomless place of no limit and no light anywhere.

Arguments followed, and more than arguments—things said and done that lacked all sense and sanity and fairness. She had edged away from him at last, causing his rages and remarkable hysterias. Once he burned her entire wardrobe in a fit of jealousy. She had taken this quietly. But then one night he handed her a week's notice, accused her of monstrous disloyalty, shouted at her, seized her, slapped her again and again across the face, bullied her about and thrust her out the door, slamming it!

She disappeared that night.

When he found the next day that she was really gone and there was nowhere to find her, it was like standing in the center of a titanic explosion. All the world was smashed flat and all the echoes of the explosion came back to reverberate at midnight, at four in the morning, at dawn, and he was up early, stunned, with the sound of coffee simmering and the sound of matches being struck and cigarettes lit and himself trying to shave and looking at mirrors that were sickening in their distortion.

He clipped out all the advertisements that he took in the papers and pasted them in neat rows in a scrapbook—all the ads describing her and telling about her and asking for her back. He even put a private detective on the case. People talked. The police dropped by to question him. There was more talk.

But she was gone like a piece of white, incredibly fragile tissue paper, blown over the sky and down. A record of her was sent to the largest cities, and that was the end of it for the police. But not for Fabian. She might be dead or just running away, but wherever she was he knew that somehow and in some way he would have her back.

One night he came home, bringing his own darkness with him, and collapsed upon a chair, and before he knew it he found himself speaking to Sweet William in the totally black room.

"William, it's all over and done. I can't keep it up!"

And William cried, "Coward! Coward!" from the air above his head, out of the emptiness. "You can get her back if you want!"

Sweet William squeaked and clappered at him in the night. "Yes, you can! *Think!*" he insisted. "Think of a way. You can do it. Put me aside, lock me up. Start all over."

"Start all over?"

"Yes," whispered Sweet William, and darkness moved within darkness. "Yes. Buy wood. Buy fine new wood. Buy hard-grained wood. Buy beautiful fresh new wood. And carve. Carve slowly and carve carefully. Whittle away. Cut delicately. Make the little nostrils so. And cut her thin black eyebrows round and high, so, and make her cheeks in small hollows. Carve, carve . . ."

"No! It's foolish. I could never do it!"

"Yes, you could. Yes you could, could, could, could . . ."

The voice faded, a ripple of water in an underground stream. The stream rose up and swallowed him. His head fell forward. Sweet William sighed. And then the two of them lay like stones buried under a waterfall.

The next morning, John Fabian bought the hardest, finest-grained piece of wood that he could find and brought it home and laid it on the table, but could not touch it. He sat for hours staring at it. It was impossible to think that out of this cold chunk of material he expected his hands and his memory to re-create something warm and pliable and familiar. There was no way even faintly to approximate that quality of rain and summer and the first powderings of snow upon a clear pane of glass in the middle of a December night. No way, no way at all to catch the snowflake without having it melt swiftly in your clumsy fingers.

And yet Sweet William spoke out, sighing and whispering, after midnight, "You can do it. Oh, yes, yes, you can do it!"

And so he began. It took him an entire month to carve her hands into things as natural and beautiful as shells lying in the sun. Another month, and the skeleton, like a fossil imprint he was searching out, stamped and hidden in the wood, was revealed, all febrile and so infinitely delicate as to suggest the veins in the white flesh of an apple.

And all the while Sweet William lay mantled in dust in his box that was fast becoming a very real coffin. Sweet William croaking and wheezing some feeble sarcasm, some sour criticism, some hint, some help, but dying all the time, fading, soon to be untouched, soon to be like a sheath molted in summer and left behind to blow in the wind.

As the weeks passed and Fabian molded and scraped and polished the new wood, Sweet William lay longer and longer in stricken silence, and one day as Fabian held the puppet in his hand Sweet William seemed to look at him a moment with puzzled eyes and then there was a death rattle in his throat.

And Sweet William was gone.

Now as he worked, a fluttering, a faint motion of speech began far back in his throat, echoing and reechoing, speaking silently like a breeze among dry leaves. And then for the first time he held the doll in a certain way in his hands, and memory moved down his arms and into his fingers and from his fingers into the hollowed wood and the tiny hands flickered and the body became suddenly soft and pliable and her eyes opened and looked up at him.

And the small mouth opened the merest fraction of an inch and she was ready to speak and he knew all of the things that she must say to him; he knew the first and the second and the third things he would have her say. There was a whisper, a whisper, a whisper.

The tiny head turned this way gently, that way gently. The mouth half opened again and began to speak. And as it spoke he bent his head and he could feel the warm breath—of *course* it was there!—coming from her mouth; and when he listened very carefully, holding her to his head, his eyes shut, wasn't *it* there too, softly, *gently*—the beating of her heart?

Krovitch sat in a chair for a full minute after Fabian stopped talking. Finally he said, "I *see*. And your wife?"

"Alyce? She was my second assistant, of course. She worked very hard and, God help her, she loved me. It's hard now to know why I ever married her. It was unfair of me."

"What about the dead man—Ockham?"

"I never saw him before you showed me his body in the theater basement yesterday."

"Fabian," said the detective.

"It's the truth!"

"Fabian."

"The truth, the truth, damn it, I swear it's the truth!"

"The truth." There was a whisper like the sea coming in on the gray shore at early morning. The water was ebbing in a fine lace on the sand. The sky was cold and empty. There were no people on the shore. The sun was gone. And the whisper said again, "The truth."

Fabian sat up straight and took hold of his knees with his thin hands. His face was rigid. Krovitch found himself making the same motion he had made the day before—looking at the gray ceiling as if it were a November sky and a lonely bird going over and away, gray within the cold grayness.

"The truth." Fading. "The truth."

Krovitch lifted himself and moved as carefully as he could to the far side of the dressing room where the golden box lay open and inside the box the thing that whispered and talked and could laugh sometimes and could sometimes sing. He carried the golden box over and set it down in front of Fabian and waited for him to put his living hand within the gloved delicate hollowness, waited for the fine small mouth to quiver and the eyes to focus. He did not have to wait long.

"The first letter came a month ago."

"No."

"The first letter came a month ago."

"No, *no!*"

"The letter said, 'Riabouchinska, born 1914, died 1934. Born again in 1935.' Mr. Ockham was a juggler. He'd been on the same bill with John and Sweet William years before. He remembered that once there had been a woman, before there was a puppet."

"No, that's not true!"

"Yes," said the voice.

Snow was falling in silences and even deeper silences through the dressing room. Fabian's mouth trembled. He stared at the blank walls as if seeking some new door by which to escape. He half rose from his chair. "Please—"

"Ockham threatened to tell about us to everyone in the world."

Krovitch saw the doll quiver, saw the fluttering of the lips, saw Fabian's eyes widen and fix and his throat convulse and tighten as if to stop the whispering.

"I—I was in the room when Mr. Ockham came. I lay in my box and I listened and heard, and I *knew.*" The voice blurred, then recovered and went on. "Mr. Ockham threatened to tear me up, burn me into ashes if John didn't pay him a thousand dollars. Then suddenly there was a falling sound. A cry. Mr. Ockham's head must have struck the floor. I heard John cry out and I heard him swearing, I heard him sobbing. I heard a gasping and a choking sound."

"You heard nothing! You're deaf, you're blind! You're wood!" cried Fabian.

"But I *hear!*" she said, and stopped as if someone had put a hand to her mouth.

Fabian had leaped to his feet now and stood with the doll in his hand. The mouth clapped twice, three times, then finally made words. "The choking sound stopped. I heard John drag Mr. Ockham down the stairs under the theater to the old dressing rooms that haven't been used in years. Down, down, down, I heard them going away and away—down . . ."

Krovitch stepped back as if he were watching a motion picture that had suddenly grown monstrously tall. The figures terrified and frightened him, they were immense, they towered! They threatened to inundate him with size. Someone had turned up the sound so that it screamed.

He saw Fabian's teeth, a grimace, a whisper, a clenching. He saw the man's eyes squeeze shut.

Now the soft voice was so high and faint it trembled toward nothingness.

"I'm not made to live this way. This way. There's nothing for us now. Everyone will know, everyone will. Even when you killed him and I lay asleep last night, I dreamed. I knew, I realized. We both knew, we both realized that these would be our last days, our last hours. Because while I've lived with your weakness and I've lived with your lies, I can't live with something that kills and hurts in killing. There's no way to go on from here. How *can* I live alongside such knowledge? . . ."

Fabian held her into the sunlight which shone dimly through the small dressing room window. She looked at him and there was nothing in her eyes. His hand shook and, in shaking, made the marionette tremble, too. Her mouth closed and opened, closed and opened, closed and opened, again and again and again. Silence.

Fabian moved his fingers unbelievingly to his own mouth. A film slid across his eyes. He looked like a man lost in the street, trying to remember the number of a certain house, trying to find a certain window with a certain light. He swayed about, staring at the walls, at Krovitch, at the doll, at his free hand, turning the fingers over, touching his throat, opening his mouth. He listened.

Miles away in a cave, a single wave came in from the sea and whispered down in foam. A gull moved soundlessly, not beating its wings—a shadow.

"She's gone. She's gone. I can't find her. She's run off. I can't find her. I can't find her. I try, I try, but she's run away off far. Will you help me? Will you help me find her? Will you help me find her? Will you please help me find her?"

Riabouchinska slipped bonelessly from his limp hand, folded over and glided noiselessly down to lie upon the cold floor, her eyes closed, her mouth shut.

Fabian did not look at her as Krovitch led him out the door.

"And So Died Riabouchinska." *Alfred Hitchcock Presents*, February 12, 1956. Directed by Robert Stevenson. Teleplay by Mel Dinelli, based on Ray Bradbury's short story "And So Died Riabouchinska" (*The Saint Detective Magazine*, June-July 1953; collected in Bradbury's *The Machineries of Joy*, Simon & Schuster, 1964). With Claude Rains (Fabian), Charles Bronson (Krovitch), William Haade (Stagehand), Claire Carleton (Alice), Lowell Gilmore (Mel Douglas), Charles Cantor (Danny Slate), Harry Tyler (Bo Sewell), Iris Adrian (Maisie Sloane), Virginia Gregg (The Voice).

Ray Bradbury (1920–   ) began his writing career in lurid crime-fiction pulps like *Dime Mystery* and *Detective Tales,* selling a pile of stories of which fifteen have recently been brought together in Bradbury's paperback collection *A Memory of Murder* (Dell, 1984). Even in the early fifties, when his fantasy-horror and science fiction tales had established him as one of the finest young writers in the country, he still found time for an occasional mystery story like "And So Died Riabouchinska." The story editors for the Alfred Hitchcock TV series seem to have been fans of Bradbury in all his genres, for in its first season they aired telefilm versions of both "Riabouchinska" and "Shopping for Death," another of his crime tales of the early fifties; and then in later years they bought the rights to four more of his horrific fantasies. I can't recall a blessed thing about the "Riabouchinska" telefilm, but with a strong story, and Claude Rains and Charles Bronson in the leading roles, I find it hard to believe it was a dud.

Francis M. Nevins, Jr.

STANLEY ELLIN

The Orderly World of Mr. Appleby

MR. APPLEBY WAS A SMALL, PRIM MAN who wore rimless spectacles, parted his graying hair in the middle, and took sober pleasure in pointing out that there was no room in the properly organized life for the operations of Chance. Consequently, when he decided that the time had come to investigate the most efficient methods for disposing of his wife he knew where to look.

He found the book, a text on forensic medicine, on the shelf of a secondhand bookshop among several volumes of like topic, and since all but one were in a distressingly shabby and dog-eared state which offended him to his very core, he chose the only one in reasonably good condition. Most of the cases it presented, he discovered on closer examination, were horrid studies of the results (vividly illustrated) of madness and lust—enough to set any decent man wondering at the number of monsters inhabiting the earth. One case, however, seemed to be exactly what he was looking for, and this he made the object of his most intensive study.

It was the case of Mrs. X (the book was replete with Mrs. X's, and Mr. Y's, and Miss Z's), who died after what was presumably an accidental fall on a scatter rug in her home. However, a lawyer representing the interests of the late lamented charged her husband with murder, and at a coroner's investigation was attempting to prove his charge when the accused abruptly settled matters by dropping dead of a heart attack.

All this was of moderate interest to Mr. Appleby, whose motive, a desire to come into the immediate possession of his wife's estate, was strikingly similar to the alleged motive of Mrs. X's husband. But more important were the actual details of the case. Mrs. X had been in the act of bringing him a glass of water, said her husband, when the scatter rug, as scatter rugs will, had suddenly slipped from under her feet.

In rebuttal the indefatigable lawyer had produced a medical authority who made clear through a number of charts (all of which were handsomely reproduced in the book) that in the act of receiving the glass of water it would have been child's-play for the husband to lay one hand behind his wife's shoulder, another hand along her jaw, and with a sudden thrust produce the same drastic results as the fall on the scatter rug, without leaving any clues as to the nature of his crime.

It should be made clear now that in studying these charts and explanations relentlessly, Mr. Appleby was not acting the part of the greedy man going to any lengths to appease that greed. True, it was money he wanted, but it was money for the maintenance of what he regarded as a holy cause. And that was the Shop: *Appleby, Antiques and Curios.*

The Shop was the sun of Mr. Appleby's universe. He had bought it twenty years before with the pittance left by his father, and at best it provided him with a poor living. At worst—and it was usually at worst—it had forced him to draw on his mother's meager store of goodwill and capital. Since his mother was not one to give up a penny lightly, the Shop brought about a series of pitched battles which, however, always saw it the victor—since in the last analysis, the Shop was to Mr. Appleby what Mr. Appleby was to his mother.

This unhappy triangle was finally shattered by his mother's death, at which time Mr. Appleby discovered that she had played a far greater role in maintaining his orderly little world than he had hitherto realized. This concerned not only the money she occasionally gave him, but also his personal habits.

He ate lightly and warily. His mother had been adept at toasting and boiling his meals to perfection. His nerves were violently shaken if anything in the house was out of place, and she had been a living assurance he would be spared this. Her death, therefore, left a vast and uncomfortable gap in his life, and in studying methods to fill it he was led to contemplate marriage, and then to the act itself.

His wife was a pale, thin-lipped woman so much like his mother in appearance and gesture that sometimes on her entrance into a room he was taken aback by the resemblance. In only one respect did she fail him: she could not understand the significance of the Shop, nor his feelings about it. That was disclosed the first time he broached the subject of a small loan that would enable him to meet some business expenses.

Mrs. Appleby had been well in the process of withering on the vine when her husband-to-be had proposed to her, but to give her full due she was not won by the mere prospect of finally making a marriage. Actually, though she would have blushed at such a blunt statement of her secret thought, it was the large mournful eyes behind his rimless spectacles that turned the trick, promising, as they did, hidden depths of emotion neatly garbed in utter respectability. When she learned very soon after her wedding that the hidden depths were evidently too well hidden ever to be explored by her, she shrugged the matter off and turned to boiling and toasting his meals with good enough grace. The knowledge that the impressive *Appleby, Antiques and Curios* was a hollow shell she took in a different spirit.

She made some brisk investigations and then announced her findings to Mr. Appleby with some heat.

"Antiques and curios!" she said shrilly. "Why, that whole collection of stuff is nothing but a pile of junk. Just a bunch of worthless dust-catchers, that's all it is!"

What she did not understand was that these objects, which to the crass and commercial eye might seem worthless, were to Mr. Appleby the stuff of life itself. The Shop had grown directly from his childhood mania for collecting, assorting, labeling, and preserving anything he could lay his hands on. And the value of any item in the Shop increased proportionately with the length of time he possessed it; whether a cracked imitation of Sèvres, or clumsily faked Chippendale, or rusty saber made no difference. Each piece had won a place for itself, a permanent, immutable place, as far as Mr. Appleby was concerned; and strangely enough it was the sincere agony he suffered in giving up a piece that led to the few sales he made. The customer who was uncertain of values had only to get a glimpse of this agony to be convinced that he was getting a rare bargain. Fortunately, no customer could have imagined for a moment that it was the thought of the empty space left by the object's departure—the brief disorder which the emptiness made—and not a passion for the object itself that drew Mr. Appleby's pinched features into a mask of pain.

So, not understanding, Mrs. Appleby took an unsympathetic tack. "You'll get my mite when I'm dead and gone," she said, "and only when I'm dead and gone."

Thus unwittingly she tried herself, was found wanting, and it only remained for sentence to be executed. When the time came, Mr. Appleby applied the lessons he had gleaned from his invaluable textbook and found them accurate in every detail. It was over quickly, quietly, and outside of a splash of water on his trousers, neatly. The Medical Examiner growled something about those indescribable scatter rugs costing more lives than drunken motorists; the policeman in charge kindly offered to do whatever he could in the way of making funeral arrangements; and that was all there was to it.

It had been so easy—so undramatic, in fact—that it was not until a week later when a properly sympathetic lawyer was making him an accounting of his wife's estate that Mr. Appleby suddenly understood the whole, magnificent new world that had been opened up to him.

* * *

Discretion must sometimes outweigh sentiment, and Mr. Appleby was, if anything, a discreet man. After his wife's estate had been cleared, the Shop was moved to another location far from its original setting. It was moved again after the sudden demise of the second Mrs. Appleby, and by the time the sixth Mrs. Appleby had been disposed of, the removals were merely part of a fruitful pattern.

Because of their similarities—they were all pale, thin-featured women with pinched lips, adept at toasting and boiling, and adamant on the subjects of regularity and order—Mr. Appleby was inclined to remember his departed wives rather vaguely en masse. Only in one regard did he qualify them: the number of digits their bank accounts totaled up to. For that reason he thought of the first two Mrs. Applebys as Fours; the third as a Three (an unpleasant surprise); and the last three as Fives. The sum would have been a pretty penny by anyone else's standards, but since each succeeding portion of it had been snapped up by the insatiable *Appleby, Antiques and Curios*—in much the way a fly is snapped up by a hungry lizard—Mr. Appleby found himself soon after the burial of the sixth Mrs. Appleby in deeper and warmer financial waters than ever. So desperate were his circumstances that although he dreamed of another Five, he would have settled for a Four on the spot. It was at this opportune moment that Martha Sturgis entered his life, and after fifteen minutes' conversation with her he brushed all thoughts of Fours and Fives from his mind.

Martha Sturgis, it seemed, was a Six.

It was not only in the extent of her fortune that she broke the pattern established by the women of Mr. Appleby's previous experience. Unlike them, Martha Sturgis was a large, rather shapeless woman who in person, dress, and manner might almost be called (Mr. Appleby shuddered a little at the word) blowsy.

It was remotely possible that properly veneered, harnessed, coiffured, and appareled, she might have been made into something presentable, but from all indications Martha Sturgis was a woman who went out of her way to defy such conventions. Her hair, dyed a shocking orange-red, was piled carelessly on her head; her blobby features were recklessly powdered and painted entirely to their disadvantage; her clothes, obviously worn for comfort, were, at the same time, painfully garish; and her shoes gave evidence of long and pleasurable wear without corresponding care being given their upkeep.

Of all this and its effect on the beholder, Martha Sturgis seemed totally unaware. She strode through *Appleby, Antiques and Curios* with an energy that set movable objects dancing in their places; she smoked incessantly, lighting one cigarette from another, while Mr. Appleby fanned the air before his face and coughed suggestively; and she talked without pause, loudly and in a deep, hoarse voice that dinned strangely in a Shop so accustomed to the higher, thinner note.

In the first fourteen minutes of their acquaintance, the one quality she displayed that led Mr. Appleby to modify some of his immediate revulsion even a trifle was the care with which she priced each article. She examined, evaluated, and cross-examined in detail before moving on with obvious disapproval; and he moved along with her with mounting assurance that he could get her out of the Shop before any damage was done to the stock or his patience. And then in the fifteenth minute she spoke the Word.

"I've got half a million dollars in the bank," Martha Sturgis remarked with cheerful contempt, "but I never thought I'd get around to spending a nickel of it on this kind of stuff."

Mr. Appleby had his hand before his face preparatory to waving aside some of the tobacco smoke that eddied about him. In the time it took the hand to drop nervelessly to his side, his mind attacked an astonishing number of problems. One concerned the important finger on her left hand which was ringless; the others concerned certain mathematical problems largely dealing with short-term notes, long-term notes, and rates of interest. By the time the hand touched his side, the problems, as far as Mr. Appleby was concerned, were well on the way to solution.

And it may be noted, there was an added fillip given the matter by the very nature of Martha Sturgis's slovenly and strident being. Looking at her after she had spoken the Word, another man might perhaps have seen her through the sort of veil that a wise photographer casts over the lens of his camera in taking the picture of a prosperous but unprepossessing subject. Mr. Appleby, incapable of such self-deceit, girded himself instead with the example of the man who carried a heavy weight on his back for the pleasure it gave him in laying it down. Not only would the final act of a marriage to Martha Sturgis solve important mathematical problems, but it was an act he could play out with the gusto of a man ridding the world of an unpleasant object.

Therefore he turned his eyes, more melancholy and luminous than ever, on her and said, "It's a great pity, Mrs.—"

She told him her name, emphasizing the "Miss" before it, and Mr. Appleby smiled apologetically.

"Of course. As I was saying, it's a great pity when someone of refinement and culture—" (the "like yourself" floated delicately unsaid on the air) "—should never have known the joy in possession of fine works of art. But, as we all learn, it is never too late to begin, is it?"

Martha Sturgis looked at him sharply and then laughed a hearty bellow of laughter that stabbed his eardrums painfully. For a moment, Mr. Appleby, a man not much given to humor, wondered darkly if he had unwittingly uttered something so excruciatingly epigrammatic that it was bound to have this alarming effect.

"My dear man," said Martha Sturgis, "if it is your idea that I am here to start cluttering up my life with your monstrosities, perish the thought. What I'm here for is to buy a gift for a friend, a thoroughly infuriating and loathsome person who happens to have the nature and disposition of a bar of stainless steel. I can't think of a better way of showing my feelings toward her than by presenting her with almost anything displayed in your shop. If possible, I should also like delivery arranged so that I can be on the scene when she receives the package."

Mr. Appleby staggered under this, then rallied valiantly. "In that case," he said, and shook his head firmly, "it is out of the question. Completely out of the question."

"Nonsense," Martha Sturgis said. "I'll arrange for delivery

myself if you can't handle it. Really, you ought to understand that there's no point in doing this sort of thing unless you're on hand to watch the results."

Mr. Appleby kept tight rein on his temper. "I am not alluding to the matter of delivery," he said. "What I am trying to make clear is that I cannot possibly permit anything in my Shop to be bought in such a spirit. Not for any price you could name."

Martha Sturgis's heavy jaw dropped. "What was that you said?" she asked blankly.

It was a perilous moment, and Mr. Appleby knew it. His next words could set her off into another spasm of that awful laughter that would devastate him completely; or, worse, could send her right out of the Shop forever; or could decide the issue in his favor then and there. But it was a moment that had to be met, and, thought Mr. Appleby desperately, whatever else Martha Sturgis might be, she was a Woman.

He took a deep breath. "It is the policy of this Shop," he said quietly, "never to sell anything unless the prospective purchaser shows full appreciation for the article to be bought and can assure it the care and devotion to which it is entitled. That has always been the policy, and always will be as long as I am here. Anything other than that I would regard as desecration."

He watched Martha Sturgis with bated breath. There was a chair nearby, and she dropped into it heavily so that her skirts were drawn tight by her widespread thighs and the obscene shoes were displayed mercilessly. She lit another cigarette, regarding him meanwhile with narrowed eyes through the flame of the match, and then fanned the air a little to dispel the cloud of smoke.

"You know," she said, "this is very interesting. I'd like to hear more about it."

To the inexperienced, the problem of drawing information of the most personal nature from a total stranger would seem a perplexing one. To Mr. Appleby, whose interests had so often been dependent on such information, it was no problem at all. In very short time he had evidence that Martha Sturgis's estimate of her fortune was quite accurate; that she was apparently alone in the world without relatives or intimate friends; and—that she was not averse to the idea of marriage.

This last he drew from her during her now regular visits to the Shop where she would spread herself comfortably on a chair and talk to him endlessly. Much of her talk was about her father, to whom Mr. Appleby evidently bore a striking resemblance.

"He even dressed like you," Martha Sturgis said reflectively. "Neat as a pin, and not only about himself, either. He used to make an inspection of the house every day—march through and make sure everything was exactly where it had to be. And he kept it up right to the end. I remember an hour before he died how he went about straightening pictures on the wall."

Mr. Appleby, who had been peering with some irritation at a picture that hung slightly awry on the Shop wall, turned his attentions reluctantly from it.

"And you were with him to the end?" he asked sympathetically.

"Indeed I was."

"Well," Mr. Appleby said brightly, "one does deserve some reward for such sacrifice, doesn't one? Especially—and I hope this will not embarrass you, Miss Sturgis—when one considers that such a woman as yourself could undoubtedly have left the care of an aged father to enter matrimony almost at will. Isn't that so?"

Martha Sturgis sighed. "Maybe it is, and maybe it isn't," she said, "and I won't deny that I've had my dreams. But that's all they are, and I suppose that's all they ever will be."

"Why?" asked Mr. Appleby encouragingly.

"Because," said Martha Sturgis somberly, "I have never yet met the man who could fit those dreams. I am not a simpering schoolgirl, Mr. Appleby; I don't have to balance myself against my bank account to know why any man would devote himself to me, and frankly, his motives would be of no interest. But he must be a decent, respectable man who would spend every moment of his life worrying about me and caring for me; and he must be a man who would make the memory of my father a living thing.''

Mr. Appleby rested a hand lightly on her shoulder.

''Miss Sturgis,'' he said gravely, ''you may yet meet such a man.''

She looked at him with features that were made even more blobby and unattractive by her emotion.

''Do you mean that, Mr. Appleby?'' she asked. ''Do you really believe that?''

Faith glowed in Mr. Appleby's eyes as he smiled down at her. ''He may be closer than you dare realize,'' he said warmly.

Experience had proved to Mr. Appleby that once the ice is broken, the best thing to do is take a deep breath and plunge in. Accordingly, he let very few days elapse before he made his proposal.

''Miss Sturgis,'' he said, ''there comes a time to every lonely man when he can no longer bear his loneliness. If at such a time he is fortunate enough to meet the one woman to whom he could give unreservedly all his respect and tender feelings, he is a fortunate man indeed. Miss Sturgis—I am that man.''

''Why, Mr. Appleby!'' said Martha Sturgis, coloring a trifle. ''That's really very good of you, but . . .''

At this note of indecision his heart sank. ''Wait!'' he interposed hastily. ''If you have any doubts, Miss Sturgis, please speak them now so that I may answer them. Considering the state of my emotions, that would only be fair, wouldn't it?''

''Well, I suppose so,'' said Martha Sturgis. ''You see, Mr. Appleby, I'd rather not get married at all than take the chance of getting someone who wasn't prepared to give me exactly what I'm looking for in marriage: absolute, single-minded devotion all the rest of my days.''

''Miss Sturgis,'' said Mr. Appleby solemnly, ''I am prepared to give you no less.''

''Men say these things so easily,'' she sighed. ''But—I shall certainly think about it, Mr. Appleby.''

The dismal prospect of waiting an indefinite time for a woman of such careless habits to render a decision was not made any lighter by the sudden receipt a few days later of a note peremptorily requesting Mr. Appleby's presence at the offices of Gainsborough, Gainsborough, and Golding, attorneys-at-law. With his creditors closing in like a wolf pack, Mr. Appleby could only surmise the worst, and he was pleasantly surprised upon his arrival at Gainsborough, Gainsborough, and Golding to find that they represented, not his creditors, but Martha Sturgis herself.

The elder Gainsborough, obviously very much the guiding spirit of the firm, was a short, immensely fat man with pendulous dewlaps that almost concealed his collar, and large fishy eyes that goggled at Mr. Appleby. The younger Gainsborough was a duplicate of his brother—with jowls not quite so impressive—while Golding was an impassive young man with a hatchet face.

"This," said the elder Gainsborough, his eyes fixed glassily on Mr. Appleby, "is a delicate matter. Miss Sturgis, an esteemed client—" the younger Gainsborough nodded at this "—has mentioned entering matrimony with you, sir."

Mr. Appleby, sitting primly on his chair, was stirred by a pleased excitement. "Yes?" he said.

"And," continued the elder Gainsborough, "while Miss Sturgis is perfectly willing to concede that her fortune may be the object of attraction in any suitor's eyes—" he held up a pudgy hand to cut short Mr. Appleby's shocked protest "—she is also willing to dismiss that issue—"

"To ignore it, set it aside," said the younger Gainsborough sternly.

"—if the suitor is prepared to meet all other expectations in marriage."

"I am," said Mr. Appleby fervently.

"Mr. Appleby," said the elder Gainsborough abruptly, "have you been married before?"

Mr. Appleby thought swiftly. Denial would make any chance word about his past a deadly trap; admission, on the other hand, was a safeguard against that, and a thoroughly respectable one.

"Yes," he said.

"Divorced?"

"Good heavens, no!" said Mr. Appleby, genuinely shocked.

The Gainsboroughs looked at each other in approval. "Good," said the elder, "very good. Perhaps, Mr. Appleby, the question seemed impertinent, but in these days of moral laxity . . ."

"I should like it known in that case," said Mr. Appleby sturdily, "that I am as far from moral laxity as any human being can be. Tobacco, strong drink, and—ah—"

"Loose women," said the younger Gainsborough briskly.

"Yes," said Mr. Appleby, reddening, "are unknown to me."

The elder Gainsborough nodded. "Under any conditions," he said, "Miss Sturgis will not make any precipitate decision. She should have her answer for you within a month, however, and during that time, if you don't mind taking the advice of an old man, I suggest that you court her assiduously. She is a woman, Mr. Appleby, and I imagine that all women are much alike."

"I imagine they are," said Mr. Appleby.

"Devotion," said the younger Gainsborough. "Constancy. That's the ticket."

What he was being asked to do, Mr. Appleby reflected in one of his solitary moments, was to put aside the Shop and the orderly world it represented and to set the unappealing figure of Martha Sturgis in its place. It was a temporary measure, of course; it was one that would prove richly rewarding when Martha Sturgis had been properly wed and sent the way of the preceding Mrs. Applebys; but it was not made any easier by enforced familiarity with the woman. It was inevitable that since Mr. Appleby viewed matters not only as a prospective bridegroom but also as a prospective widower, so to speak, he found his teeth constantly set on edge by the unwitting irony which crept into so many of her tedious discussions on marriage.

"The way I see it," Martha Sturgis once remarked, "is that a man who would divorce his wife would divorce any other woman he ever married. You take a look at all these broken marriages today, and I'll bet that in practically every case you'll find a man who's always shopping around and never finding what he wants. Now, the man I marry," she said pointedly, "must be willing to settle down and stay settled."

"Of course," said Mr. Appleby.

"I have heard," Martha Sturgis told him on another, and particularly trying, occasion, "that a satisfactory marriage increases a woman's span of years. That's an excellent argument for marriage, don't you think?"

"Of course," said Mr. Appleby.

It seemed to him that during that month of trial, most of his conversation was restricted to the single phrase "of course," delivered with varying inflections; but the tactic must have been the proper one, since at the end of the month he was able to change the formula to "I do," in a wedding ceremony at which Gainsborough, Gainsborough, and Golding were the sole guests.

Immediately afterward, Mr. Appleby (to his discomfort) was borne off with his bride to a photographer's shop where innumerable pictures were made under the supervision of the dour Golding, following which, Mr. Appleby (to his delight) exchanged documents with his wife which made them each other's heirs to all properties, possessions, et cetera, whatsoever.

If Mr. Appleby had occasionally appeared rather abstracted during these festivities, it was only because his mind was neatly arranging the program of impending events. The rug (the very same one that had served so well in six previous episodes) had to be placed; and then there would come the moment when he would ask for a glass of water, when he would place one hand on her shoulder, and with the other . . . It could not be a moment that took place without due time passing; yet it could not be forestalled too long in view of the pressure exercised by the Shop's voracious creditors. Watching the pen in his wife's hand as she signed her will, he decided there would be time within a few weeks. With the will in his possession there would be no point in waiting longer than that.

Before the first of those weeks was up, however, Mr. Appleby knew that even this estimate would have to undergo drastic revision. There was no question about it: he was simply not equipped to cope with his marriage.

For one thing, her home (and now his), a brownstone cavern inherited from her mother, was a nightmare of disorder. On the principle, perhaps, that anything flung casually aside was not worth picking up since it would only be flung aside again, an amazing litter had accumulated in every room. The contents of brimming closets and drawers were recklessly exchanged, mislaid, or added to the general litter, and over all lay a thin film of dust. On Mr. Appleby's quivering nervous system all this had the effect of a fingernail dragging along an endless blackboard.

The one task to which Mrs. Appleby devoted herself, as it happened, was the one which her husband prayerfully wished she would spare herself. She doted on cookery, and during mealtimes would trudge back and forth endlessly between kitchen and dining room laden with dishes outside any of Mr. Appleby's experience.

At his first feeble protests, his wife had taken pains to explain in precise terms that she was sensitive to any criticism of her cooking, even the implied criticism of a partly emptied plate; and, thereafter, Mr. Appleby, plunging hopelessly through rare meats, rich sauces, and heavy pastries, found added to his tribulations the incessant pangs of dyspepsia. Nor were his pains eased by his wife's insistence that he prove himself a trencherman of her mettle. She would thrust plates heaped high with indigestibles under his quivering nose; and, bracing himself like a martyr facing the lions, Mr. Appleby would empty his portion into a digestive tract that cried for simple fare properly boiled or toasted.

It became one of his fondest waking dreams, that scene where he returned from his wife's burial to dine on hot tea and toast and, perhaps, a medium-boiled egg. But even that dream and its sequel—where he proceeded to set the house in order—were not sufficient to buoy him up each day when he awoke and reflected on what lay ahead of him.

Each day found his wife more insistent in her demands for his attentions. And on that day when she openly reproved him for devoting more of those attentions to the Shop than to herself, Mr.

Appleby knew the time had come to prepare for the final act. He brought home the rug that evening and carefully laid it in place between the living room and the hallway that led to the kitchen. Martha Appleby watched him without any great enthusiasm.

"That's a shabby-looking thing, all right," she said. "What is it, Appie, an antique or something?"

She had taken to calling him by that atrocious name and seemed cheerfully oblivious to the way he winced under it. He winced now.

"It is not an antique," Mr. Appleby admitted, "but I hold it dear for many reasons. It has a great deal of sentimental value to me."

Mrs. Appleby smiled fondly at him. "And you brought it for me, didn't you?"

"Yes," said Mr. Appleby, "I did."

"You're a dear," said Mrs. Appleby. "You really are."

Watching her cross the rug on slipshod feet to use the telephone, which stood on a small table the other side of the hallway, Mr. Appleby toyed with the idea that since she used the telephone at about the same time every evening, he could schedule the accident for that time. The advantages were obvious: since those calls seemed to be the only routine she observed with any fidelity, she would cross the rug at a certain time, and he would be in a position to settle matters then and there.

However, thought Mr. Appleby as he polished his spectacles, that brought up the problem of how best to approach her under such circumstances. Clearly the tried and tested methods were best, but if the telephone call and the glass of water could be synchronized . . .

"A penny for your thoughts, Appie," said Mrs. Appleby brightly. She had laid down the telephone and crossed the hallway so that she stood squarely on the rug. Mr. Appleby replaced his spectacles and peered at her through them.

"I wish," he said querulously, "you would not address me by that horrid name. You know I detest it."

"Nonsense," his wife said briefly. "I think it's cute."

"I do not."

"Well, I like it," said Mrs. Appleby with the air of one who has settled a matter once and for all. "Anyhow," she pouted, "that couldn't have been what you were thinking about before I started talking to you, could it?"

It struck Mr. Appleby that when this stout, unkempt woman pouted, she resembled nothing so much as a wax doll badly worn by time and handling. He pushed away the thought to frame some suitable answer.

"As it happens," he said, "my mind was on the disgraceful state of my clothes. Need I remind you again that there are buttons missing from practically every garment I own?"

Mrs. Appleby yawned broadly. "I'll get to it sooner or later."

"Tomorrow perhaps?"

"I doubt it," said Mrs. Appleby. She turned toward the stairs. "Come to sleep, Appie. I'm dead tired."

Mr. Appleby followed her thoughtfully. Tomorrow, he knew, he would have to get one of his suits to the tailor if he wanted to have anything fit to wear at the funeral.

He had brought home the suit and hung it neatly away; he had eaten his dinner; and he had sat in the living room listening to his wife's hoarse voice go on for what seemed interminable hours, although the clock was not yet at nine.

Now, with rising excitement, he saw her lift herself slowly from her chair and cross the room to the hallway. As she reached for the telephone Mr. Appleby cleared his throat sharply. "If you don't mind," he said, "I'd like a glass of water."

Mrs. Appleby turned to look at him. "A glass of water?"

"If you don't mind," said Mr. Appleby, and waited as she hesitated, then set down the telephone, and turned toward the kitchen. There was the sound of a glass being rinsed in the kitchen, and then Mrs. Appleby came up to him holding it out. He laid one hand appreciatively on her plump shoulder, and then lifted the other as if to brush back a strand of untidy hair at her cheek.

"Is that what happened to all the others?" said Mrs. Appleby quietly.

Mr. Appleby felt his hand freeze in midair and the chill from it run down into his marrow. "Others?" he managed to say. "What others?"

His wife smiled grimly at him, and he saw that the glass of water in her hand was perfectly steady. "Six others," she said. "That is, six by my count. Why? Were there any more?"

"No," he said, then caught wildly at himself. "I don't understand what you're talking about!"

"Dear Appie. Surely you couldn't forget six wives just like that. Unless, of course, I've come to mean so much to you that you can't bear to think of the others. That would be a lovely thing to happen, wouldn't it?"

"I was married before," Mr. Appleby said loudly. "I made that quite clear myself. But this talk about six wives!"

"Of course you were married before, Appie. And it was quite easy to find out to whom—and it was just as easy to find out about the one before that—and all the others. Or even about your mother, or where you went to school, or where you were born. You see, Appie, Mr. Gainsborough is really a very clever man."

"Then it was Gainsborough who put you up to this!"

"Not at all, you foolish little man," his wife said contemptuously. "All the time you were making your plans I was unmaking them. From the moment I laid eyes on you I knew you for what you are. Does that surprise you?"

Mr. Appleby struggled with the emotions of a man who had picked up a twig to find a viper in his hand. "How could you know?" he gasped.

"Because you were the image of my father. Because in everything—the way you dress, your insufferable neatness, your priggish arrogance, the little moral lectures you dote on—you are what he was. And all my life I hated him for what he was, and what it did to my mother. He married her for her money, made her every day a nightmare, and then killed her for what was left of her fortune."

"Killed her?" said Mr. Appleby, stupefied.

"Oh, come," his wife said sharply. "Do you think you're the only man who was ever capable of that? Yes, he killed her—murdered her, if you prefer—by asking for a glass of water and then breaking her neck when she offered it to him. A method strangely similar to yours, isn't it?"

Mr. Appleby found the incredible answer rising to his mind, but refused to accept it. "What happened to him?" he demanded. "Tell me, what happened! Was he caught?"

"No, he was never caught. There were no witnesses to what he did, but Mr. Gainsborough had been my mother's lawyer, a dear friend of hers. He had suspicions and demanded a hearing. He brought a doctor to the hearing who made it plain how my father could have killed her and made it look as if she had slipped on a rug, but before there was any decision my father died of a heart attack."

"That was the case—the case I read!" Mr. Appleby groaned, and then was silent under his wife's sardonic regard.

"When he was gone," she went on inexorably, "I swore I would someday find a man exactly like that, and I would make that man live the life my father should have lived. I would know his every habit and every taste, and none of them should go satisfied. I would know he married me for my money, and he would never get a penny of it until I was dead and gone. And that would be a long, long time, because he would spend his life taking care that I should live out my life to the last possible breath."

Mr. Appleby pulled his wits together, and saw that despite her emotion, she had remained in the same position. "How can you make him do that?" he asked softly, and moved an inch closer.

"It does sound strange, doesn't it, Appie?" she observed. "But hardly as strange as the fact that your six wives died by slipping on a rug—very much like this one—while bringing you a glass of water—very much like this one. So strange that Mr. Gainsborough was led to remark that too many coincidences will certainly hang a man. Especially if there is reason to bring them to light in a trial for murder."

Mr. Appleby suddenly found the constriction of his collar unbearable. "That doesn't answer my question," he said craftily. "How can you make sure that I would devote my life to prolonging yours?"

"A man whose wife is in a position to have him hanged should be able to see that clearly."

"No," said Mr. Appleby in a stifled voice, "I only see that such a man is forced to rid himself of his wife as quickly as possible."

"Ah, but that's where the arrangements come in."

"Arrangements? What arrangements?" demanded Mr. Appleby.

"I'd like very much to explain them," his wife said. "In fact, I see the time has come when it's imperative to do so. But I do find it uncomfortable standing here like this."

"Never mind that," said Mr. Appleby impatiently, and his wife shrugged.

"Well, then," she said coolly, "Mr. Gainsborough now has all the documents about your marriages—the way the previous deaths took place, the way you always happened to get the bequests at just the right moment to pay your shop's debts.

"Besides this, he has a letter from me, explaining that in the event of my death an investigation be made immediately and all necessary action be taken. Mr. Gainsborough is really very efficient. The fingerprints and photographs . . ."

"Fingerprints and photographs!" cried Mr. Appleby.

"Of course. After my father's death it was found that he had made all preparations for a quick trip abroad. Mr. Gainsborough has assured me that in case you had such ideas in mind you should get rid of them. No matter where you are, he said, it will be quite easy to bring you back again."

"What do you want of me?" asked Mr. Appleby numbly. "Surely you don't expect me to stay now, and—"

"Oh, yes, I do. And since we've come to this point, I may as well tell you I expect you to give up your useless shop once and for all, and make it a point to be at home with me the entire day."

"Give up the Shop!" he exclaimed.

"You must remember, Appie, that in my letter asking for a full investigation at my death, I did not specify death by any particular means. I look forward to a long and pleasant life with you always at my side, and perhaps—mind you, I only say perhaps—someday I shall turn over that letter and all the evidence to you. You can see how much it is to your interest, therefore, to watch over me very carefully."

The telephone rang with abrupt violence, and Mrs. Appleby nodded toward it. "Almost as carefully," she said softly, "as Mr. Gainsborough. Unless I call him every evening at nine to report I am well and happy, it seems he will jump to the most shocking conclusions."

"Wait," said Mr. Appleby. He lifted the telephone, and there was no mistaking the voice that spoke.

"Hello," said the elder Gainsborough. "Hello, Mrs. Appleby?"

Mr. Appleby essayed a cunning move. "No," he said, "I'm afraid she can't speak to you now. What is it?"

The voice in his ear took on an unmistakable cold menace. "This is Gainsborough, Mr. Appleby, and I wish to speak to your wife immediately. I will give you ten seconds to have her at this telephone, Mr. Appleby. Do you understand?"

Mr. Appleby turned dully toward his wife and held out the telephone. "It's for you," he said, and then saw with a start of terror that as she turned to set down the glass of water, the rug skidded slightly under her feet. Her arms flailed the air as she fought for balance; the glass smashed at his feet, drenching his neat trousers; and her face twisted into a silent scream. Then her body struck the floor and lay inertly in the position with which he was so familiar.

Watching her, he was barely conscious of the voice emerging tinnily from the telephone in his hand.

"The ten seconds are up, Mr. Appleby," it said shrilly. "Do you understand? *Your time is up!*"

"The Orderly World of Mr. Appleby." *Alfred Hitchcock Presents*, April 15, 1956. Directed by James Neilson. Teleplay by Victor Wolfson and Robert C. Dennis, based on Stanley Ellin's short story "The Orderly World of Mr. Appleby" *(Ellery Queen's Mystery Magazine*, May 1950; collected in Ellin's *Mystery Stories*, Simon & Schuster, 1956). With Robert H. Harris (Mr. Appleby), Louise Larabee (Lena), Meg Mundy (Martha Sturgis), Michael Ansara (Dizar), Gage Clarke (Gainsboro), Helen Spring (Mrs. Grant), Edna Holland (Mrs. Murchie), Mollie Glassing (Ella).

I blushingly admit that I have no recollection at all of this TV performance; but my wife says we did see it and that like most of the Hitchcock treatments of my stories, it was well done. I can only plead that that was twenty-eight years ago, and I've reached the point where events of last week dim fast in what's left of my mind.

Stanley Ellin

CORNELL WOOLRICH

Momentum

PAINE HUNG AROUND OUTSIDE the house waiting for old Ben Burroughs' caller to go, because he wanted to see him alone. You can't very well ask anyone for a loan of $250 in the presence of someone else, especially when you have a pretty strong hunch you're going to be turned down flat and told where to get off, into the bargain.

But he had a stronger reason for not wanting witnesses to his interview with the old skinflint. The large handkerchief in his back pocket, folded triangularly, had a special purpose, and that little instrument in another pocket—wasn't it to be used in prying open a window?

While he lurked in the shrubbery, watching the lighted window and Burroughs' seated form inside it, he kept rehearsing the plea he'd composed, as though he were still going to use it.

"Mr. Burroughs, I know it's late, and I know you'd rather not be reminded that I exist, but desperation can't wait, and I'm desperate." That sounded good. "Mr. Burroughs, I worked for your concern faithfully for ten long years, and the last six months of its existence, to help keep it going. I voluntarily worked at half-wages, on your given word that my defaulted pay would be made up as soon as things got better. Instead of that, you went into phony bankruptcy to cancel your obligations.''

Then a little soft soap to take the sting out of it. ''I haven't come near you all these years, and I haven't come to make trouble now. If I thought you really didn't have the money, I still wouldn't. But it's common knowledge by now that the bankruptcy was feigned; it's obvious by the way you continue to live that you salvaged your own investment; and I've lately heard rumors of your backing a dummy corporation under another name to take up where you left off. Mr. Burroughs, the exact amount of the six months' promissory half-wages due me is two hundred and fifty dollars.''

Just the right amount of dignity and self-respect, Pauline had commented at this point; not wishy-washy or maudlin, just quiet and effective.

And then for a bang-up finish, and every word of it true. ''Mr. Burroughs, I have to have help tonight; it can't wait another twenty-four hours. There's a hole the size of a fifty-cent piece in the sole of each of my shoes, I have a wedge of cardboard in the bottom of each one. We haven't had light or gas in a week now. There's a bailiff coming tomorrow morning to put out the little that's left of our furniture and seal the door.

''If I was alone in this, I'd still fight it through, without going to anyone. But, Mr. Burroughs, I have a wife at home to support. You may not remember her, a pretty little dark-haired girl who once worked as a stenographer in your office for a month or two. You surely wouldn't know her now, she's aged twenty years in the past two.''

That was about all. That was about all anyone could have said. And yet Paine knew he was licked before he even uttered a word of it.

He couldn't see the old man's visitor. The caller was out of range of the window. Burroughs was seated in a line with it, profile toward Paine. Paine could see his mean, thin-lipped mouth moving. Once or twice he raised his hand in a desultory gesture. Then he seemed to be listening and finally he nodded slowly. He held his forefinger up and shook it, as if impressing some point on his auditor. After that he rose and moved deeper into the room, but without getting out of line with the window.

He stood against the far wall, hand out to a tapestry hanging there. Paine craned his neck, strained his eyes. There must be a wall safe behind there the old codger was about to open.

If he only had a pair of binoculars handy.

Paine saw the old miser pause, turn his head, and make some request of the other person. A hand abruptly grasped the looped shade cord and drew the shade to the bottom.

Paine gritted his teeth. The old fossil wasn't taking any chances, was he? You'd think he was a mind reader, knew there was someone out there. But a chink remained, showing a line of light at the bottom. Paine sidled out of his hiding place and slipped up to the window. He put his eyes to it, focused on Burroughs' dialing hand, to the exclusion of everything else.

A three-quarters turn to the left, about to where the numeral 8 would be on the face of the clock. Then back to about where 3 would be. Then back the other way, this time to 10. Simple enough. He must remember that—8-3-10.

Burroughs was opening it now and bringing out a cash box. He set it down on the table and opened it. Paine's eyes hardened and his mouth twisted sullenly. Look at all that money! The old fossil's gnarled hand dipped into it, brought out a sheaf of bills, counted them. He put back a few, counted the remainder a second time, and set them on the tabletop while he returned the cash box, closed the safe, straightened out the tapestry.

A blurred figure moved partly into the way at this point, too close to the shade gap to come clearly into focus, but without obliterating the little stack of bills on the table. Burroughs' clawlike hand picked them up, held them out. A second hand, smoother, reached for them. The two hands shook.

Paine prudently retreated to his former lookout point. He knew where the safe was now, that was all that mattered. He wasn't a moment too soon. The shade shot up an instant later, this time with Burroughs' hand guiding its cord. The other person had withdrawn offside again. Burroughs moved after him out of range, and the room abruptly darkened. A moment later a light flickered on in the porch ceiling.

Paine quickly shifted to the side of the house, in the moment's grace given him, in order to make sure his presence wasn't detected.

The door opened. Burroughs' voice croaked a curt "Night," to which the departing visitor made no answer. The interview had evidently not been an altogether cordial one. The door closed again, with quite a little force. A quick step crossed the porch, went along the cement walk to the street, away from where Paine stood pressed flat against the side of the house. He didn't bother trying to see who it was. It was too dark for that, and his primary purpose was to keep his own presence concealed.

When the anonymous tread had safely died away in the distance, Paine moved to where he could command the front of the house. Burroughs was alone in it now, he knew; he was too niggardly even to employ a full-time servant. A dim light showed for a moment or two through the fanlight over the door, coming from the back of the hall. Now was the time to ring the doorbell, if he expected to make his plea to the old duffer before he retired.

He knew that, and yet something seemed to be keeping him from stepping up onto the porch and ringing the doorbell. He knew what it was, too, but he wouldn't admit it to himself.

"He'll only say no, point-blank, and slam the door in my face" was the excuse he gave himself as he crouched back in the shrubbery, waiting. "And then once he's seen me out here, I'll be the first one he'll suspect afterwards when—"

The fanlight had gone dark now and Burroughs was on his way upstairs. A bedroom window on the floor above lighted up. There was still time; if he rang even now, Burroughs would come downstairs again and answer the door. But Paine didn't make the move, stayed there patiently waiting.

The bedroom window blacked out at last, and the house was now dark and lifeless. Paine stayed there, still fighting with himself. Not a battle, really, because that had been lost long ago; but still giving himself excuses for what he knew he was about to do. Excuses for not going off about his business and remaining what he had been until now—an honest man.

How could he face his wife if he came back empty-handed tonight? Tomorrow their furniture would be piled on the sidewalk. Night after night he had promised to tackle Burroughs, and each time he'd put it off, walked past the house without summoning up nerve enough to go through with it. Why? For one thing, he didn't have the courage to stomach the sharp-tongued, sneering refusal that he was sure he'd get. But the more important thing had been the realization that once he made his plea, he automatically canceled this other, unlawful way of getting the money. Burroughs had probably forgotten his existence after all these years, but if he reminded him of it by interviewing him ahead of time—

He tightened his belt decisively. Well, he wasn't coming home to her empty-handed tonight, but he still wasn't going to tackle Burroughs for it either. She'd never need to find out just how he'd got it.

He straightened and looked all around him. No one in sight. The house was isolated. Most of the streets around it were only laid out and paved by courtesy: they bordered vacant lots. He moved in cautiously but determinedly toward the window of that room where he had seen the safe.

Cowardice can result in the taking of more risks than the most reckless courage. He was afraid of little things—afraid of going home and facing his wife empty-handed, afraid of asking an ill-tempered old reprobate for money because he knew he would be reviled and driven away—and so he was about to break into a house, become a burglar for the first time in his life.

It opened so easily. It was almost an invitation to unlawful entry. He stood up on the sill, and the cover of a paper book of matches, thrust into the intersection between the two window halves, pushed the tongue of the latch out of the way.

He dropped down to the ground, applied the little instrument he had brought to the lower frame, and it slid effortlessly up. A minute later he was in the room, had closed the window so it wouldn't look suspicious from the outside. He wondered why he'd always thought until now that it took skill and patience to break into a house. There was nothing to it.

He took out the folded handkerchief and tied it around the lower part of his face. For a minute he wasn't going to bother with it, and later he was sorry he had, in one way. And then again, it probably would have happened anyway, even without it. It wouldn't keep him from being seen, only from being identified.

He knew enough not to light the room lights, but he had nothing so scientific as a pocket torch with him to take their place. He had to rely on ordinary matches, which meant he could only use one hand for the safe dial, after he had cleared the tapestry out of the way.

It was a toy thing, a gimcrack. He hadn't even the exact combination, just the approximate position—8-3-10. It wouldn't work the first time, so he varied it slightly, and then it clicked free.

He opened it, brought out the cash box, set it on the table. It was as though the act of setting it down threw a master electric switch. The room was suddenly drenched with light, and Burroughs stood in the open doorway, bathrobe around his wizened frame, left hand out to the wall switch, right hand holding a gun trained on Paine.

Paine's knees knocked together, his windpipe constricted, and he died a little—the way only an amateur caught red-handed at his first attempt can, a professional never. His thumb stung unexpectedly, and he mechanically whipped out the live match he was holding.

"Just got down in time, didn't I?" the old man said with spiteful satisfaction. "It mayn't be much of a safe, but it sets off a buzzer up by my bed every time it swings open—see?"

He should have moved straight across to the phone, right there in the room with Paine, and called for help, but he had a vindictive streak in him; he couldn't resist standing and rubbing it in.

"Ye know what ye're going to get for this, don't ye?" he went on, licking his indrawn lips. "And I'll see that ye get it, too, every last month of it that's coming to ye." He took a step forward. "Now get away from that. Get all the way back over there and don't ye make a move until I—"

A sudden dawning suspicion entered his glittering little eyes. "Wait a minute. Haven't I seen you somewhere before? There's something familiar about you." He moved closer. "Take off that mask," he ordered. "Let me see who the devil you are!"

Paine became panic-stricken at the thought of revealing his face. He didn't stop to think that as long as Burroughs had him at gunpoint anyway, and he couldn't get away, the old man was bound to find out who he was sooner or later.

He shook his head in unreasoning terror.

"No!" he panted hoarsely, billowing out the handkerchief over his mouth. He even tried to back away, but there was a chair or something in the way, and he couldn't.

That brought the old man in closer. "Then by golly I'll take it off for ye!" he snapped. He reached out for the lower triangular point of it. His right hand slanted out of line with Paine's body as he did so, was no longer exactly covering it with the gun. But the variation was nothing to take a chance on.

Cowardice. Cowardice that spurs you to a rashness the stoutest courage would quail from. Paine didn't stop to think of the gun. He suddenly hooked onto both the old man's arms, spread-eagled them. It was such a harebrained chance to take that Burroughs wasn't expecting it, and accordingly it worked. The gun clicked futilely, pointed up toward the ceiling; it must have jammed, or else the first chamber was empty and Burroughs hadn't known it.

Paine kept warding that arm off at a wide angle. But his chief concern was the empty hand clawing toward the handkerchief. That he swiveled far downward the other way, out of reach. He twisted the scrawny skin around the old man's skinny right wrist until pain made the hand flop over open and drop the gun. It fell between them to the floor, and Paine scuffed it a foot or two out of reach with the side of his foot.

Then he locked that same foot behind one of Burroughs' and pushed him over it. The old man went sprawling backward on the floor, and the short, unequal struggle was over. Yet even as he went, he was victorious. His downflung left arm, as Paine released it to send him over, swept up in an arc, clawed, and took the handkerchief with it.

He sprawled there now, cradled on the point of one elbow, breathing malign recognition that was like a knife through Paine's heart. "You're Dick Paine, you dirty crook! I know ye now! You're Dick Paine, my old employee! You're going to pay for this—"

That was all he had time to say. That was his own death warrant. Paine was acting under such neuromuscular compulsion brought on by the instinct of self-preservation that he wasn't even conscious of stooping to retrieve the fallen gun. The next thing he knew it was in his hand, pointed toward the accusing mouth that was all he was afraid of.

He jerked the trigger. For the second time it clicked—either jammed or unloaded at that chamber. He was to have that on his conscience afterward, that click—like a last chance given him to keep from doing what he was about to do. That made it something different; that took away the shadowy little excuse he would have had until now; that changed it from an impulsive act committed in the heat of combat to a deed of cold-blooded, deliberate murder, with plenty of time to think twice before it was committed. And conscience makes cowards of us all. And he was a coward to begin with.

Burroughs even had time to sputter the opening syllables of a desperate plea for mercy, a promise of immunity. True, he probably wouldn't have kept it.

"Don't! Paine—Dick, don't! I won't say anything. I won't tell 'em you were here—"

But Burroughs knew who he was. Paine tugged at the trigger, and the third chamber held death in it. This time the gun crashed, and Burroughs' whole face was veiled in a huff of smoke. By the time it had thinned he was already dead, head on the floor, a tenuous thread of red streaking from the corner of his mouth, as though he had no more than split his lip.

Paine was the amateur even to the bitter end. In the death hush that followed, his first half-audible remark was: "Mr. Burroughs, I didn't mean to—"

Then he just stared in white-faced consternation. "Now I've done it! I've killed a man—and they kill you for that! Now I'm in for it!"

He looked at the gun, appalled, as though it alone, and not he, were to blame for what had happened. He picked up the handkerchief, dazedly rubbed at the weapon, then desisted again. It seemed to him safer to take it with him, even though it was Burroughs' own. He had an amateur's mystic dread of fingerprints. He was sure he wouldn't be able to clean it thoroughly enough to remove all traces of his own handling; even in the very act of trying to clean it, he might leave others. He sheathed it in the inner pocket of his coat.

He looked this way and that. He'd better get out of here; he'd better get out of here. Already the drums of flight were beginning to beat in him, and he knew they'd never be silent again.

The cash box was still standing there on the table where he'd left it, and he went to it, flung the lid up. He didn't want this money anymore; it had curdled for him, it had become bloody money. But he had to have some, at least, to make it easier to keep from getting caught. He didn't stop to count how much there was in it; there must have been at least a thousand, by the looks of it. Maybe even fifteen or eighteen hundred.

He wouldn't take a cent more than was coming to him. He'd only take the two hundred and fifty he'd come here to get. To his frightened mind that seemed to make his crime less heinous, if he contented himself with taking just what was rightfully his. That seemed to keep it from being outright murder and robbery, enabled him to maintain the fiction that it had been just a collection of a debt accompanied by a frightful and unforeseen accident. And one's conscience, after all, is the most dreaded policeman of the lot.

And furthermore, he realized as he hastily counted it out, thrust the sum into his back trouser pocket, buttoned the pocket down, he couldn't tell his wife that he'd been here—or she'd know what he'd done. He'd have to make her think that he'd got the money somewhere else. That shouldn't be hard. He'd put off coming here to see Burroughs night after night; he'd shown her plainly that he hadn't relished the idea of approaching his former boss; she'd been the one who had kept egging him on.

Only tonight she'd said, "I don't think you'll ever carry it out. I've about given up hope."

So what more natural than to let her think that in the end he hadn't? He'd think up some other explanation to account for the presence of the money; he'd have to. If not right tonight, then tomorrow. It would come to him after the shock of this had worn off a little and he could think more calmly.

Had he left anything around that would betray him, that they could trace to him? He'd better put the cash box back; there was just a chance that they wouldn't know exactly how much the old skinflint had had on hand. They often didn't, with his type. He wiped it off carefully with the handkerchief he'd had around his face, twisted the dial closed on it, dabbed at that. He didn't go near the window again; he put out the light and made his way out by the front door of the house.

He opened it with the handkerchief and closed it after him again, and after an exhaustive survey of the desolate street, came down off the porch, moved quickly along the front walk, turned left along the gray tape of sidewalk that threaded the gloom toward the distant trolley line that he wasn't going to board at this particular stop, at this particular hour.

He looked up once or twice at the star-flecked sky as he trudged along. It was over. That was all there was to it. Just a jealously guarded secret now. A memory that he daren't share with anyone else, not even Pauline. But deep within him he knew better. It wasn't over, it was just beginning. That had been just the curtain raiser, back there. Murder, like a snowball rolling down a slope, gathers momentum as it goes.

He had to have a drink. He had to try to drown the damn thing out of him. He couldn't go home dry with it on his mind. They stayed open until four, didn't they, places like that? He wasn't much of a drinker, he wasn't familiar with details like that. Yes, there was one over there, on the other side of the street. And this was far enough away, more than two-thirds of the way from Burroughs' to his own place.

It was empty. That might be better; then again it might not. He could be too easily remembered. Well, too late now, he was already at the bar. "A straight whiskey." The barman didn't even have time to turn away before he spoke again. "Another one."

He shouldn't have done that; that looked suspicious, to gulp it that quick.

"Turn that radio off," he said hurriedly. He shouldn't have said that, that sounded suspicious. The barman had looked at him when he did. And the silence was worse, if anything. Unbearable. Those throbbing drums of danger. "Never mind, turn it on again."

"Make up your mind, mister," the barman said in mild reproof.

He seemed to be doing all the wrong things. He shouldn't have come in here at all, to begin with. Well, he'd get out, before he put his foot in it any worse. "How much?" He took out the half-dollar and the quarter that was all he had.

"Eighty cents."

His stomach dropped an inch. Not *that* money! He didn't want to have to bring that out, it would show too plainly on his face. "Most places they charge thirty-five a drink."

"Not this brand. You didn't specify." But the barman was on guard now, scenting a deadbeat. He was leaning over the counter, right square in front of him, in a position to take in every move he made with his hands.

He shouldn't have ordered that second drink. Just for a nickel he was going to have to take that whole wad out right under this man's eyes. And maybe he wouldn't remember that tomorrow, after the jumpy way Paine had acted in here!

"Where's the washroom?"

"That door right back there behind the cigarette machine." But the barman was now plainly suspicious; Paine could tell that by the way he kept looking at him.

Paine closed it after him, sealed it with his shoulder blades, unbuttoned his back pocket, riffled through the money, looking for the smallest possible denomination. A ten was the smallest, and there was only one of them; that would have to do. He cursed himself for getting into such a spot.

The door suddenly gave a heave behind him. Not a violent one, but he wasn't expecting it. It threw him forward off balance. The imperfectly grasped outspread fan of money in his hand went scattering all over the floor. The barman's head showed through the aperture. He started to say: "I don't like the way you're acting. Come on now, get out of my pla—" Then he saw the money.

Burroughs' gun had been an awkward bulk for his inside coat pocket all along. The grip was too big, it overspanned the lining. His abrupt lurch forward had shifted it. It felt as if it was about to fall out of its own weight. He clutched at it to keep it in.

The barman saw the gesture, closed in on him with a grunted "I thought so!" that might have meant nothing or everything.

He was no Burroughs to handle, he was an ox of a man. He pinned Paine back against the wall and held him there more or less helpless. Even so, if he'd only shut up, it probably wouldn't have happened. But he made a tunnel of his mouth and bayed: "Pol-eece! Holdup! Help!"

Paine lost the little presence of mind he had left, became a blurred pinwheel of hand motion, impossible to control or forestall. Something exploded against the barman's midriff, as though he'd had a firecracker tucked in under his belt.

He coughed his way down to the floor and out of the world.

Another one. Two now. Two in less than an hour. Paine didn't think the words, they seemed to glow out at him, emblazoned on the grimy washroom walls in characters of fire, like in that Biblical story.

He took a step across the prone, white-aproned form as stiffly as though he were high up on stilts. He looked out through the door crack. No one in the bar. And it probably hadn't been heard outside in the street; it had had two doors to go through.

He put the damned thing away, the thing that seemed to be spreading death around just by being in his possession. If he hadn't brought it with him from Burroughs' house, this man would have been alive now. But if he hadn't brought it with him, he would have been apprehended for the first murder by now. Why blame the weapon, why not just blame fate?

That money, all over the floor. He squatted, went for it bill by bill, counting it as he went. Twenty, forty, sixty, eighty. Some of them were on one side of the corpse, some on the other; he had to cross over, not once but several times, in the course of his grisly paper chase. One was even pinned partly under him, and when he'd wangled it out, there was a swirl of blood on the edge. He grimaced, thrust it out, blotted it off. Some of it stayed on, of course.

He had it all now, or thought he did. He couldn't stay in here another minute, he felt as if he were choking. He got it all into his pocket any old way, buttoned it down. Then he eased out, this time looking behind him at what he'd done, not before him. That was how he missed seeing the drunk, until it was too late and the drunk had already seen him.

The drunk was pretty drunk, but maybe not drunk enough to take a chance on. He must have weaved in quietly, while Paine was absorbed in retrieving the money. He was bending over reading the list of selections on the coin phonograph. He raised his head before Paine could get back in again, and to keep him from seeing what lay on the floor in there Paine quickly closed the door behind him.

"Say, itsh about time," the drunk complained. "How about a little servish here?"

Paine tried to shadow his face as much as he could with the brim of his hat. "I'm not in charge here," he mumbled. "I'm just a customer myself—"

The drunk was going to be sticky. He barnacled onto Paine's lapels as he tried to sidle by. "Don't gimme that. You just hung up your coat in there, you think you're quitting for the night. Well, you ain't quitting until I've had my drink—''

Paine tried to shake him off without being too violent about it and bringing on another hand-to-hand set-to. He hung on like grim death. Or rather, he hung on *to* grim death—without knowing it.

Paine fought down the flux of panic, the ultimate result of which he'd already seen twice now. Any minute someone might come in from the street. Someone sober. ''All right,'' he breathed heavily, ''hurry up, what'll it be?''

''Thass more like it, now you're being reg'lar guy.'' The drunk released him and he went around behind the bar. ''Never anything but good ole Four Roses for mine truly—''

Paine snatched down a bottle at random from the shelf, handed it over bodily. ''Here, help yourself. You'll have to take it outside with you, I'm—we're closing up for the night now.'' He found a switch, threw it. It only made part of the lights go out. There was no time to bother with the rest. He hustled the bottle-nursing drunk out ahead of him, pulled the door to after the two of them so that it would appear to be locked even if it wasn't.

The drunk started to make loud plaint, looping around on the sidewalk. ''You're a fine guy, not even a glass to drink it out of!''

Paine gave him a slight push in one direction, wheeled, and made off in the other.

The thing was, how drunk was he? Would he remember Paine, would he know him if he saw him again? He hurried on, spurred to a run by the night-filling hails and imprecations resounding behind him. He couldn't do it again. Three lives in an hour. He couldn't!

The night was fading when he turned into the little courtyard that was his own. He staggered up the stairs, but not from the two drinks he'd had, from the two deaths.

He stood outside his own door at last—3-B. It seemed such a funny thing to do after killing people—fumble around in your pockets for your latchkey and fit it in, just like other nights. He'd been an honest man when he'd left here, and now he'd come back a murderer. A double one.

He hoped she was asleep. He couldn't face her right now, couldn't talk to her even if he tried. He was all in emotionally. She'd find out right away just by looking at his face, by looking in his eyes.

He eased the front door closed, tiptoed to the bedroom, looked in. She was lying there asleep. Poor thing, poor helpless thing, married to a murderer.

He went back, undressed in the outer room. Then he stayed in there. Not even stretched out on top of the sofa, but crouched beside it on the floor, head and arms pillowed against its seat. The drums of terror kept pounding. They kept saying, "What am I gonna do now?"

The sun seemed to shoot up in the sky, it got to the top so fast. He opened his eyes and it was all the way up. He went to the door and brought in the paper. It wasn't in the morning papers yet, they were made up too soon after midnight.

He turned around, and Pauline had come out, was picking up his things. "All over the floor, never saw a man like you—"

He said, "Don't—" and stabbed his hand toward her, but it was already too late. He'd jammed the bills in so haphazardly the second time, in the bar, that they made a noticeable bulge there in his back pocket. She opened it and took them out, and some of them dribbled onto the floor.

She just stared. "Dick!" She was incredulous, overjoyed. "Not Burroughs? Don't tell me you finally—"

"No!" The name went through him like a red-hot skewer. "I didn't go anywhere near him. He had nothing to do with it!"

She nodded corroboratively. "I thought not, because—"

He wouldn't let her finish. He stepped close to her, took her by both shoulders. "Don't mention his name to me again. I don't want to hear his name again. I got it from someone else."

"Who?"

He knew he'd have to answer her, or she'd suspect something.

He swallowed, groped blindly for a name. "Charlie Chalmers," he blurted out.

"But he refused you only last week!"

"Well, he changed his mind." He turned on her tormentedly. "Don't ask me any more questions, Pauline. I can't stand it! I haven't slept all night. There it is, that's all that matters." He took his trousers from her, went into the bathroom to dress. He'd hidden Burroughs' gun the night before in the built-in laundry hamper in there; he wished he'd hidden the money with it. He put the gun back in the pocket where he'd carried it last night. If she touched him there—

He combed his hair. The drums were a little quieter now, but he knew they'd come back again; this was just the lull before the storm.

He came out again, and she was putting cups on the table. She looked worried now. She sensed that something was wrong. She was afraid to ask him, he could see, maybe afraid of what she'd find out. He couldn't sit here eating just as though this was any other day. Any minute someone might come here after him.

He passed by the window. Suddenly he stiffened, gripped the curtain. "What's that man doing down there?" She came up behind him. "Standing there talking to the janitor—"

"Why, Dick, what harm is there in that? A dozen people a day stop and chat with—"

He edged back a step behind the frame. "He's looking up at our windows! Did you see that? They both turned and looked up this way! Get back!" His arm swept her around behind him.

"Why should we? We haven't done anything."

"They're coming in the entrance to this wing! They're on their way up here—"

"Dick, why are you acting this way, what's happened?"

"Go in the bedroom and wait there." He was a coward, yes. But there are varieties. At least he wasn't a coward that hid behind a woman's skirts. He prodded her in there ahead of him. Then he gripped her shoulder a minute. "Don't ask any questions. If you love me, stay in here until they go away again."

He closed the door on her frightened face. He cracked the gun. Two left in it. "I can get them both," he thought, "if I'm careful. I've got to."

It was going to happen again.

The jangle of the doorbell battery steeled him. He moved with deadly slowness toward the door, feet flat and firm upon the floor. He picked up the newspaper from the table on his way by, rolled it into a funnel, thrust his hand and the gun down into it. The pressure of his arm against his side was sufficient to keep it furled. It was as though he had just been reading and had carelessly tucked the paper under his arm. It hid the gun effectively as long as he kept it slanting down.

He freed the latch and shifted slowly back with the door, bisected by its edge, the unarmed half of him all that showed. The janitor came into view first, as the gap widened. He was on the outside. The man next to him had a derby hat riding the back of his head, a bristly mustache, was rotating a cigar between his teeth. He looked like—one of those who come after you.

The janitor said with scarcely veiled insolence, "Paine, I've got a man here looking for a flat. I'm going to show him yours, seeing as how it'll be available from today on. Any objections?"

Paine swayed there limply against the door like a garment bag hanging on a hook, as they brushed by. "No," he whispered deflatedly. "No, go right ahead."

He held the door open to make sure their descent continued all the way down to the bottom. As soon as he'd closed it, Pauline caught him anxiously by the arm. "Why wouldn't you let me tell them we're able to pay the arrears now and are staying? Why did you squeeze my arm like that?"

"Because we're not staying, and I don't want them to know we've got the money. I don't want anyone to know. We're getting out of here."

"Dick, what is it? Have you done something you shouldn't?"

"Don't ask me. Listen, if you love me, don't ask any questions. I'm—in a little trouble. I've got to get out of here. Never mind why. If you don't want to come with me, I'll go alone."

"Anywhere you go, I'll go." Her eyes misted. "But can't it be straightened out?"

Two men dead beyond recall. He gave a bitter smile. "No, it can't."

"Is it bad?"

He shut his eyes, took a minute to answer. "It's bad, Pauline. That's all you need to know. That's all I want you to know. I've got to get out of here as fast as I can. From one minute to the next it may be too late. Let's get started now. They'll be here to dispossess us sometime today anyway; that'll be a good excuse. We won't wait, we'll leave now."

She went in to get ready. She took so long doing it he nearly went crazy. She didn't seem to realize how urgent it was. She wasted as much time deciding what to take and what to leave behind as though they were going on a weekend jaunt to the country. He kept going to the bedroom door, urging, "Pauline, hurry! Faster, Pauline!"

She cried a great deal. She was an obedient wife; she didn't ask him any more questions about what the trouble was. She just cried about it without knowing what it was.

He was down on hands and knees beside the window, in the position of a man looking for a collar button under a dresser, when she finally came out with the small bag she'd packed. He turned a stricken face to her. "Too late—I can't leave with you. Someone's already watching the place."

She inclined herself to his level, edged up beside him.

"Look straight over to the other side of the street. See him? He hasn't moved for the past ten minutes. People don't just stand like that for no reason—"

"He may be waiting for someone."

"He is," he murmured somberly. "Me."

"But you can't be sure."

"No, but if I put it to the test by showing myself, it'll be too late by the time I find out. You go by yourself ahead of me."

"No, if you stay, let me stay with you—"

"I'm not staying, I can't! I'll follow you and meet you somewhere. But it'll be easier for us to leave one at a time than both together. I can slip over the roof or go out the basement way. He won't stop you, they're not looking for you. You go now and wait for me. No, I have a better idea. Here's what you do. You get two tickets and get on the train at the downtown terminal without waiting for me—" He was separating some of the money, thrusting it into her reluctant hand while he spoke. "Now listen closely. Two tickets to Montreal—"

An added flicker of dismay showed in her eyes. "We're leaving the country?"

When you've committed murder, you have no country anymore. "We have to, Pauline. Now there's an eight o'clock limited for there every night. It leaves the downtown terminal at eight sharp. It stops for five minutes at the station uptown at twenty after. That's where I'll get on. Make sure you're on it or we'll miss each other. Keep a seat for me next to you in the day coach—"

She clung to him despairingly. "No, no. I'm afraid you won't come. Something'll happen. You'll miss it. If I leave you now I may never see you again. I'll find myself making the trip up there alone, without you—"

He tried to reassure her, pressing her hands between his. "Pauline, I give you my word of honor—" That was no good, he was a murderer now. "Pauline, I swear to you—"

"Here—on this. Take a solemn oath on this, otherwise I won't go." She took out a small carnelian cross she carried in her handbag, attached to a little gold chain—one of the few things they hadn't pawned. She palmed it, pressed the flat of his right hand over it. They looked into each other's eyes with sacramental intensity.

His voice trembled. "I swear nothing will keep me from that train; I'll join you on it no matter what happens, no matter who tries to stop me. Rain or shine, *dead or alive*, I'll meet you aboard it at eight-twenty tonight!"

She put it away, their lips brushed briefly but fervently.

"Hurry up now," he urged. "He's still there. Don't look at him on your way past. If he should stop you and ask who you are, give another name—"

He went to the outside door with her, watched her start down the stairs. The last thing she whispered up was: "Dick, be careful for my sake. Don't let anything happen to you between now and tonight."

He went back to the window, crouched down, cheekbones to sill. She came out under him in a minute or two. She knew enough not to look up at their windows, although the impulse must have been strong. The man was still standing over there. He didn't seem to notice her. He even looked off in another direction.

She passed from view behind the building line; their windows were set in on the court that indented it. Paine wondered if he'd ever see her again. Sure, he would; he had to. He realized that it would be better for her if he didn't. It wasn't fair to enmesh her in his own doom. But he'd sworn an oath, and he meant to keep it.

Two, three minutes ticked by. The cat-and-mouse play continued. He crouched motionless by the window, the other man stood motionless across the street. She must be all the way down at the corner by now. She'd take the bus there, to go downtown. She might have to wait a few minutes for one to come along, she might still be in sight. But if the man was going to go after her, accost her, he would have started by now. He wouldn't keep standing there.

Then, as Paine watched, he did start. He looked down that way, threw away something he'd been smoking, began to move purposefully in that direction. There was no mistaking that he was looking *at* or *after* someone, by the intent way he held his head. He passed from sight.

Paine began to breathe hot and fast. "I'll kill him. If he touches her, tries to stop her, I'll kill him right out in the open street in broad daylight." It was still fear, cowardice, that was at work, although it was almost unrecognizable as such by now.

He felt for the gun, left his hand on it, inside the breast of his coat, straightened to his feet, ran out of the flat and down the stairs. He cut across the little set-in paved courtyard at a sprint, flashed out past the sheltering building line, turned down in the direction they had both taken.

Then as the panorama before him registered, he staggered to an abrupt stop, stood taking it in. It offered three component but separate points of interest. He only noticed two at first. One was the bus down at the corner. The front third of it protruded, door open. He caught a glimpse of Pauline's back as she was in the act of stepping in, unaccompanied and unmolested.

The door closed automatically, and it swept across the vista and disappeared at the other side. On the other side of the street but nearer at hand, the man who had been keeping the long vigil had stopped a second time, was gesticulating angrily to a woman laden with parcels whom he had joined. Both voices were so raised they reached Paine without any trouble.

"A solid half-hour I've been standing there and no one home to let me in!"

"Well, is it my fault you went off without your key? Next time take it with you!"

Nearer at hand still, on Paine's own side of the street, a lounging figure detached itself from the building wall and impinged on his line of vision. The man had been only yards away the whole time, but Paine's eyes had been trained on the distance; he'd failed to notice him until now.

His face suddenly loomed out at Paine. His eyes bored into Paine's with unmistakable intent. He didn't look like one of those that come to get you. He acted like it. He thumbed his vest pocket for something, some credential or identification. He said in a soft, slurring voice that held an inflexible command in it, "Just a minute there, buddy. Your name's Paine, ain't it? I want to see you—"

Paine didn't have to give his muscular coordination any signal; it acted for him automatically. He felt his legs carry him back into the shelter of the courtyard in a sort of slithering jump. He was in at the foot of the public stairs before the other man had even rounded the building line. He was in behind his own door before the remorselessly slow but plainly audible tread had started up them.

The man seemed to be coming up after him alone. Didn't he know Paine had a gun? He'd find out. He was up on the landing now. He seemed to know which floor to stop at, which door to come to a halt before. Probably the janitor had told him. Then why hadn't he come sooner? Maybe he'd been waiting for someone to join him, and Paine had upset the plan by showing himself so soon.

Paine realized he'd trapped himself by returning here. He should have gone on up to the roof and over. But the natural instinct of the hunted, whether four-legged or two, is to find a hole, get in out of the open. It was too late now: he was right out there on the other side of the door. Paine tried to keep his harried breathing silent.

To his own ears it grated like sand sifted through a sieve.

He didn't ring the bell and he didn't knock; he tried the knob, in a half-furtive, half-badgering way. That swirl of panic began to churn in Paine again. He couldn't let him get in; he couldn't let him get away, either. He'd only go and bring others back with him.

Paine pointed the muzzle of the gun to the crack of the door, midway between the two hinges. With his other hand he reached out for the catch that controlled the latch, released it.

Now if he wanted to die, he should open this door.

The man had kept on trying the knob. Now the door slipped in past the frame. The crack at the other side widened in accompaniment as it swung around. Paine ran the gun bore up it even with the side of his head.

The crash was thunderous. He fell into the flat, with only his feet and ankles outside.

Paine came out from behind the door, dragged him the rest of the way in, closed it. He stopped; his hands probed here and there. He found a gun, a heftier, more businesslike one than his. He took that. He found a billfold heavy with cash. He took that, too. He fished for the badge.

There wasn't any in the vest pocket he'd seen him reach toward downstairs. There was only a block of cheaply printed cards. *Star Finance Company. Loans. Up to any amount without security.*

So he hadn't been one, after all; he'd evidently been some kind of a loan shark, drawn by the scent of Paine's difficulties.

Three times now in less than twenty-four hours.

Instinctively he knew he was doomed now, if he hadn't before. There wasn't any more of the consternation he had felt the first two times. He kept buying off time with bullets, that was all it was now. And the rate of interest kept going higher, the time limit kept shortening. There wasn't even any time to feel sorry.

Doors had begun opening outside in the hall, voices were calling back and forth. "What was that—a shot?"

"It sounded like in 3-B."

He'd have to get out now, right away, or he'd be trapped in here again. And this time for good. He shifted the body out of the line of vision from outside, buttoned up his jacket, took a deep breath; then he opened the door, stepped out, closed it after him. Each of the other doors was open with someone peering out from it. They hadn't ganged up yet in the middle of the hall. Most of them were women, anyway. One or two edged timidly back when they saw him emerge.

"It wasn't anything," he said. "I dropped a big clay jug in there just now."

He knew they didn't believe him.

He started down the stairs. At the third step he looked over the side, saw the cop coming up. Somebody had already phoned or sent out word. He reversed, flashed around his own landing, and on up from there.

The cop's voice said, "Stop where you are!" He was coming on fast now. But Paine was going just as fast.

The cop's voice said, "Get inside, all of you! I'm going to shoot!"

Doors began slapping shut like firecrackers. Paine switched over abruptly to the rail and shot first.

The cop jolted, but he grabbed the rail and stayed up. He didn't die as easy as the others. He fired four times before he lost his gun. He missed three times and hit Paine the fourth time.

It went in his chest on the right side, and knocked him across the width of the staircase. It flamed with pain, and then it didn't hurt so much. He found he could get up again. Maybe because he had to. He went back and looked down. The cop had folded over the railing and gone sliding down it as far as the next turn, the way a kid does on a banister. Only sidewise, on his stomach. Then he dropped off onto the landing, rolled over and lay still, looking up at Paine without seeing him.

Four.

Paine went on up to the roof, but not fast, not easily anymore. The steps were like an escalator going the other way, trying to carry him down with them. He went across to the roof of the next flat, and down through that, and came out on the street behind his own. The two buildings were twins, set back-to-back. The prowl car was already screeching to a stop, out of sight back there at his own doorway. He could hear it over the roofs, on this side.

He was wet across the hip. Then he was wet as far down as the knee. And he hadn't been hit in those places, so he must be bleeding a lot. He saw a taxi and he waved to it, and it backed up and got him. It hurt getting in. He couldn't answer for a minute when the driver asked him where to. His sock felt sticky under his shoe now, from the blood. He wished he could stop it until eight-twenty. He had to meet Pauline on the train, and that was a long time to stay alive.

The driver had taken him off the street and around the corner without waiting for him to be more explicit. He asked where to, a second time.

Paine said, "What time is it?"

"Quarter to six, cap."

Life was awfully short—and awfully sweet. He said, "Take me to the park and drive me around in it." That was the safest thing to do, that was the only place they wouldn't look for you.

He thought, "I've always wanted to drive around in the park.

Not go anywhere, just drive around in it slow. I never had the money to do it before.''

He had it now. More money than he had time left to spend it.

The bullet must still be in him. His back didn't hurt, so it hadn't come out. Something must have stopped it. The bleeding had let up. He could feel it drying on him. The pain kept trying to pull him over double, though.

The driver noticed it, said: ''Are you hurt?''

''No, I've got kind of a cramp, that's all.''

''Want me to take you to a drugstore?''

Paine smiled weakly. ''No, I guess I'll let it ride.''

Sundown in the park. So peaceful, so prosaic. Long shadows across the winding paths. A belated nursemaid or two pushing a perambulator homeward. A loiterer or two lingering on the benches in the dusk. A little lake, with a rowboat on it—a sailor on shore leave rowing his sweetheart around. A lemonade and popcorn man trundling his wagon home for the day.

Stars were coming out. At times the trees were outlined black against the copper western sky. At times the whole thing blurred and he felt as if he were being carried around in a maelstrom. Each time he fought through and cleared his senses again. He had to make that train.

''Let me know when it gets to be eight o'clock.''

''Sure, cap. It's only quarter to seven now.''

A groan was torn from Paine as they hit a lumpy spot in the driveway. He tried to keep it low, but the driver must have heard it.

''Still hurts you, huh?'' he inquired sympathetically. ''You oughta get it fixed up.'' He began to talk about his own indigestion. ''Take me, for instance. I'm okay until I eat tamales and root beer. Any time that I eat tamales and root beer—''

He shut up abruptly. He was staring fixedly into the rear-sight mirror. Paine warily clutched his lapels together over his darkened shirtfront. He knew it was too late to do any good.

The driver didn't say anything for a long time. He was thinking it over, and he was a slow thinker. Then finally he suggested off-handedly, "Care to listen to the radio?"

Paine knew what he was out for. He thought, "He wants to see if he can get anything on me over it."

"May as well," the driver urged. "It's thrown in with the fare, won't cost you nothing extra."

"Go ahead," Paine consented. He wanted to see if he could hear anything himself.

It made the pain a little easier to bear, as music always does. "I used to dance, too," Paine thought, listening to the tune, "before I started killing people."

It didn't come over for a long time.

"A citywide alarm is out for Richard Paine. Paine, who was about to be dispossessed from his flat, shot and killed a finance company employee. Then when Officer Harold Carey answered the alarm, he met the same fate. However, before giving up his life in the performance of his duty, the patrolman succeeded in seriously wounding the desperado. A trail of blood left by the fugitive on the stairs leading up to the roof over which he made good his escape seems to confirm this. He's still at large but probably won't be for long. Watch out for this man, he's dangerous."

"Not if you leave him alone, let him get to that train," Paine thought ruefully. He eyed the suddenly rigid silhouette in front of him. "I'll have to do something about him—now—I guess."

It had come through at a bad time for the driver. Some of the main driveways through the park were heavily trafficked and pretty well lighted. He could have got help from another car. But it happened to come through while they were on a dark, lonely byway with not another machine in sight. Around the next turn the bypass rejoined one of the heavy-traffic arteries. You could hear the hum of traffic from where they were.

"Pull over here," Paine ordered. He'd had the gun out. He was only going to clip him with it, stun him, and tie him up until after eight-twenty.

You could tell by the way the driver pulled his breath in short that he'd been wise to Paine ever since the news flash, had only been waiting until they got near one of the exits or got a red light. He braked. Then suddenly he bolted out, tried to duck into the underbrush.

Paine had to get him and get him fast, or he'd get word to the park division. They'd cork up the entrances on him. He knew he couldn't get out and go after him. He pointed low, tried to hit him in the foot or leg, just bring him down.

The driver had tripped over something, gone flat, a moment ahead of the trigger fall. The bullet must have ploughed into his back instead. He was inert when Paine got out to him, but still alive. Eyes open, as though his nerve centers had been paralyzed.

He could hardly stand up himself, but he managed to drag him over to the cab and somehow got him in. He took the cap and put it on his own head.

He could drive—or at least he'd been able to before he was dying. He got under the wheel and took the machine slowly on its way. The sound of the shot must have been lost out in the open, or else mistaken for a backfire; the stream of traffic was rolling obliviously by when he slipped into it unnoticed. He left it again at the earliest opportunity, turned off at the next dark, empty lane that offered itself.

He stopped once more, made his way to the back door, to see how the cabman was. He wanted to help him in some way if he could. Maybe leave him in front of a hospital.

It was too late. The driver's eyes were closed. He was already dead by this time.

Five.

It didn't have any meaning anymore. After all, to the dying, death is nothing. "I'll see you again in an hour or so," he said.

He got the driver's coat off him and shrouded him with it, to keep the pale gleam of his face from peering up through the gloom of the cab's interior, in case anyone got too close to the window. He was unequal to the task of getting him out again and leaving him behind in the park. The lights of some passing car might have picked him up too soon. And it seemed more fitting to let him rest in his own cab, anyway.

It was ten to eight now. He'd better start for the station. He might be held up by lights on the way, and the train only stopped a few minutes at the uptown station.

He had to rejoin the main stream of traffic to get out of the park. He hugged the outside of the driveway and trundled along. He went off the road several times. Not because he couldn't drive, but because his senses fogged. He pulled himself and the cab out of it each time. "Train, eight-twenty," he waved before his mind like a red lantern. But like a spendthrift, he was using up years of his life in minutes, and pretty soon he was going to run short.

Once an alarm car passed him, shrieking by, taking a shortcut through the park from one side of the city to the other. He wondered if they were after him. He didn't wonder very hard. Nothing mattered much anymore. Only eight-twenty—train—

He kept folding up slowly over the wheel, and each time it touched his chest, the machine would swerve crazily as though it felt the pain, too. Twice, three times, his fenders were grazed, and he heard faint voices swearing at him from another world, the world he was leaving behind. He wondered if they'd call him names like that if they knew he was dying.

Another thing: he couldn't maintain a steady flow of pressure on the accelerator. The pressure would die out each time, as when current is failing, and the machine would begin drifting to a stop. This happened just as he was leaving the park, crossing the big circular exit plaza. It was controlled by lights, and he stalled on a green out in the middle. There was a cop in control on a platform. The cop shot the whistle out of his own mouth blowing it so hard at him. He nearly flung himself off the platform waving him on.

Paine just sat there, helpless.

The cop was coming over to him, raging like a lion. Paine wasn't afraid because of what the back of his cab held: he was long past that kind of fear. But if this cop did anything to keep him from that eight-twenty train—

He reached down finally, gripped his own leg by the ankle,

lifted it an inch or two clear of the floor, let it fall back again, and the cab started. It was ludicrous. But then some of the aspects of death often are.

The cop let him go, only because to have detained him longer would have created a worse traffic snarl than there was already.

He was nearly there now. Just a straight run crosstown, then a short one north. It was good he remembered this, because he couldn't see the street signs anymore. Sometimes the buildings seemed to lean over above him as though they were about to topple down on him. Sometimes he seemed to be climbing a steep hill, where he knew there wasn't any. But he knew that was just because he was swaying around in the driver's seat.

The same thing happened again a few blocks farther on, directly in front of a large, swank apartment house, just as the doorman came flying out blowing a whistle. He'd caught hold of Paine's rear door and swung it wide before the latter could stop him, even though the cab was still rolling. Two women in evening dress came hurrying out of the entrance behind him, one in advance of the other.

"No—taken," Paine kept trying to say. He was too weak to make his voice heard, or else they ignored it. And he couldn't push his foot down for a moment.

The foremost one shrieked, "Hurry, Mother. Donald'll never forgive me. I promised him seven-thirty—"

She got one foot on the cab doorstep. Then she just stood there transfixed. She must have seen what was inside; it was better lighted here than in the park.

Paine tore the cab away from her, open door and all; left her standing there petrified, out in the middle of the street in her long white satin gown, staring after him. She was too stunned even to scream.

And then he got there at last. He got a momentary respite, too. Things cleared a little. Like the lights going up in a theater when the show is over, before the house darkens for the night.

The uptown station was built in under a viaduct that carried the overhead tracks across the city streets. He couldn't stop in front of it; no parking was allowed. And there were long lines of cabs on both sides of the no-parking zone. He turned the corner into the little dead-end alley that separated the viaduct from the adjoining buildings. There was a side entrance to the station looking out on it.

Four minutes. It was due in another four minutes. It had already left downtown, was on its way, hurtling somewhere between the two points. He thought, "I better get started. I may have a hard time making it." He wondered if he could stand up at all.

He just wanted to stay where he was and let eternity wash over him.

Two minutes. It was coming in overhead, he could hear it rumbling and ticking along the steel viaduct, then sighing to a long-drawn-out stop.

That sidewalk looked awfully wide, from the cab door to the station entrance. He brought up the last dregs of vitality in him, broke away from the cab, started out, zigzagging and going down lower at the knees every minute. The station door helped pull him up straight again. He got into the waiting room, and it was so big he knew he'd never be able to cross it. One minute left. So near and yet so far.

The starter was calling it already. "Montreal express—eight-twenty!—Pittsfield, Burlington, Rouse's Point, Montreyall! Bo-o-ard!"

There were rows of lengthwise benches at hand, and they helped him bridge the otherwise insuperable length of the waiting room. He dropped into the outside seat in the first row, pulled himself together a little, scrambled five seats over, toppled into that; repeated the process until he was within reach of the ticket barrier. But time was going, the train was going, life was going fast.

Forty-five seconds left. The last dilatory passengers had already gone up. There were two ways of getting up, a long flight of stairs and an escalator.

He wavered toward the escalator, made it. He wouldn't have

been able to get by the ticket taker but for his hackman's cap—an eventuality he and Pauline hadn't foreseen.

"Just meeting a party," he mumbled almost unintelligibly, and the slow treadmill started to carry him up.

A whistle blew upstairs on the track platform. Axles and wheelbases gave a preliminary creak of motion.

It was all he could do to keep his feet even on the escalator. There wasn't anyone in back of him, and if he once went over he was going to go plunging all the way down to the bottom of the long chute. He dug his nails into the ascending hand-belts at both sides, hung on like grim life.

There was a hubbub starting up outside on the street somewhere. He could hear a cop's whistle blowing frenziedly.

A voice shouted: "Which way'd he go?"

Another answered: "I seen him go in the station."

They'd at last found what was in the cab.

A moment after the descending waiting-room ceiling had cut off his view, he heard a spate of running feet come surging in down there from all directions. But he had no time to think of that now. He was out on the open platform upstairs at last. Cars were skimming silkily by. A vestibule door was coming, with a conductor just lifting himself into it. Paine went toward it, body low, one arm straight out as in a fascist salute.

He gave a wordless cry. The conductor turned, saw him. There was a tug, and he was suddenly sprawled inside on the vestibule floor. The conductor gave him a scathing look, pulled the folding steps in after him, slammed the door.

Too late, a cop, a couple of redcaps, a couple of taxi drivers, came spilling out of the escalator shed. He could hear them yelling a car-length back. The trainmen back there wouldn't open the doors. Suddenly the long, lighted platform snuffed out and the station was gone.

They probably didn't think they'd lost him, but they had. Sure, they'd phone ahead; they'd stop the train to have him taken off at Harmon, where it changed from electricity to coal power. But they wouldn't get him. He wouldn't be on it. Just his body.

Each man knows when he's going to die; he knew he wouldn't even live for five minutes.

He went staggering down a long, brightly lighted aisle. He could hardly see their faces anymore. But she'd know him; it'd be all right. The aisle ended, and he had to cross another vestibule. He fell down on his knees, for lack of seat backs to support himself by.

He squirmed up again somehow, got into the next car.

Another long, lighted aisle, miles of it.

He was nearly at the end; he could see another vestibule coming. Or maybe that was the door to eternity. Suddenly, from the last seat of all, a hand darted out and claimed him, and there was Pauline's face looking anxiously up at him. He twisted like a wrung-out dishcloth and dropped into the empty outside seat beside her.

"You were going to pass right by," she whispered.

"I couldn't see you clearly, the lights are flickering so."

She looked up at them in surprise, as though for her they were steady.

"I kept my word," he breathed. "I made the train. But oh, I'm tired—and now I'm going to sleep." He started to slip over sidewise toward her. His head dropped onto her lap.

She had been holding her handbag on it, and his fall displaced it. It dropped to the floor, opened, and everything in it spilled out around her feet.

His glazing eyes opened for one last time and centered feebly on the little packet of bills, with a rubber band around them, that had rolled out with everything else.

"Pauline, all that money—where'd you get that much? I only gave you enough to buy the train tickets—"

"Burroughs gave it to me. It's the two hundred and fifty we were talking about for so long. I knew in the end you'd never go near him and ask for it, so I went to him myself—last night right after you left the house. He handed it over willingly, without a word. I tried to tell you that this morning, but you wouldn't let me mention his name. . . ."

"Momentum." *Alfred Hitchcock Presents,* June 24, 1956. Directed by Robert Stevens. Teleplay by Francis Cockrell, based on Cornell Woolrich's story "Murder Always Gathers Momentum" (*Detective Fiction Weekly,* December 14, 1940; collected as "Momentum" in Woolrich's *Somebody on the Phone,* Lippincott, 1950, as by William Irish). With Skip Homeier (Dick Paine), Joanne Woodward (Beth Paine), Ken Christy (A. T. Burroughs), Henry Hunter (Man from Finance Company), Mike Ragan (Cab Driver), Billy Newell (Charlie), Frank Kreig (Janitor).

Cornell Woolrich (1903–1968) was the greatest suspense writer that ever lived, and his 1942 story "Rear Window" brought him to the attention of the greatest suspense director that ever lived. When *Alfred Hitchcock Presents* went on the air in 1955, a year after the release of Hitchcock's classic *Rear Window* feature, it was natural that the series story editors should look for more Woolrich material. Three of his stories were purchased and adapted into thirty-minute telefilms for the series. Unfortunately, none were directed by Hitchcock himself and none worked well on the small screen. Woolrich's "Momentum" was an excellent downbeat thriller, but director Robert Stevens and scriptwriter Francis Cockrell didn't even try to capture the bleak Depression ambience and *noir* sensibility of the story. In the telefilm, for example, it's not economic desperation but the needling of his money-mad wife that drives Paine to slide down the path to doom. In a bright 1950s setting, the story just doesn't work.

Francis M. Nevins, Jr.

RICHARD DEMING

The Better Bargain

THE WOMAN WAS A GOLDEN BLONDE with a body which turned every male head in the park. She was tall, probably five feet seven, with long, full-calved legs and a waist so slim it emphasized the fullness of her hips and the abundance of her erect bosom.

She wore a light summer frock which covered her without really concealing any of her assets, no stockings, and a blue hair ribbon instead of a hat. Her only visible jewelry was a tiny gold wristwatch, because she had removed and dropped into her bag her wedding band and a four-carat diamond engagement ring.

Nevertheless she managed to look expensive. The frock, though simple, was a Parisian original, and her open-toed pumps and matching bag were hand-worked alligator hide.

The man was no taller than the blond woman, slim, with sharply defined features and a lithe manner of moving. He was conservatively dressed in a hand-tailored tan gabardine suit, light tan shoes and a Panama hat. He, too, looked expensive in a quiet sort of way.

They met in front of the bear pits, casually, without greeting, merely drifting together and strolling side by side toward the exit from the park's zoo.

He asked, "How much time have you today?"

"Till five," she said. "Three hours. Let's make the most of it. Let's not stop for a drink or anything first."

"On a day like this we ought to spend it at the beach," he said in a mildly teasing voice.

She looked at him quickly, blushed. The man laughed and her blush deepened.

"Why do you like to make me feel I'm a hussy?"

"Do I?" he asked, immediately concerned. "I was only teasing. I think of you as a princess."

They had reached the exit, and he led her to a small coupe parked a few yards beyond. A decal on the lower right-hand corner of the windshield announced that the coupe was the property of the Conway Car Rental Service.

As they drove away, a thin, nondescript-looking man who had wandered toward the zoo exit a few moments after they did, climbed into a sedan standing not far from where the coupe had been parked and followed at a discreet distance.

The man and woman drove straight to the Bide-A-Wile Motel on Route 60, no more than three miles from the park where they had met. The man registered as "Thomas Jones and wife" giving their address merely as "Texas" and they entered one of the cabins.

The thin, nondescript man following them parked his sedan fifty yards down the road in a position where he could keep his eye on the cabin.

At a quarter of five the man and woman reappeared and the man drove her to a cabstand at the corner of Fourth and Walton.

As she started to get out of the coupe, he said, "Am I ever going to know who you are, Princess?"

She stopped with the door half open, turned, and frowned at him. "Let's not start that again, darling. You'll spoil everything."

"I'm human," he said in a patient voice. "I have a natural curiosity. You walk into my arms out of the blue like some goddess from a Greek myth who has decided to take an earthly lover. We have a few hours, and then you fly back to Mount Olympus. Is it going on this way forever?''

Her frown turned into a smile. "Now it's Greek mythology. I love it when you talk like that. Have you read something on every subject in the world?''

"Stop changing the subject, my dear," he said. "I'm very curious. Why can't I know who you are?''

She touched fingers to his lips. "Remember our agreement? I don't ask questions and neither do you. Have I pried into your affairs? Even so much as asked your business?''

"At least I told you my name," he said dryly.

"I didn't ask. To quote Shakespeare, as you so often do, what's in a name?''

"But why?" he asked. "What possible reason could you have for all this mystery? Do you realize we've been lovers for over two months and I don't know a single thing about you? Maybe I could accept it if you'd at least give me a reason.''

She was silent for a moment, then asked quietly, *"Would* you accept it if I gave you a reason? Would you drop the subject and never mention it again?''

He said cautiously, "If it was a valid enough reason.''

"It's valid from my point of view. I don't intend to tell you unless you agree to my terms in advance.''

He thought for a time, finally decided. "What can I lose? I may as well stop asking questions anyway, because you never answer any. Give me your reason and I'll drop the subject.''

She took a deep breath, let it out slowly and said, "If I told you my name, you'd know who I was.''

"Really?" he asked. "If you told me your name, I'd know who you were. Amazing. Truly amazing. I'd never have guessed that.''

"I mean you'd recognize the name.''

He looked at her. "You mean you're somebody famous?''

"No, of course not. But the name is well known. The last name, that is. You've probably never heard of me, but if I told you my name, you'd know who my . . . father is.''

The man frowned. "So?"

"If you ever learn that, it will be all over."

"Why?"

"Because it will. That's all I'm going to tell you. Now stop asking questions before you pry too much out of me and end everything right now."

He looked a little upset. "I haven't pried too much yet, have I?"

"Not if you drop it right there."

Pushing the door the rest of the way open, she climbed out of the car. "See you Friday. Same time, same place?"

"All right," he said. "I'll be there."

The woman climbed into the first of two idle taxis parked at the stand and said, "Forty-two twenty-seven Forsyth."

She glanced back through the rear window, saw that the rented coupe was still parked at the curb, and watched it until the taxi turned a corner and cut off the view. Then she opened her bag, took out her wedding band and diamond ring, and replaced them on her finger.

Should she have told him even as much as she had, she wondered as she leaned back in the seat? She had almost said that he would know who her husband was—only at the last second changing it to father. If he did ever learn, it *would* end things. Not because she would have to leave him, as she had deliberately implied, but because he would drop her like a hot rivet.

Was it fair putting him in such danger without his even knowing it, she wondered? Then she decided that, fair or not, she couldn't stand the thought of losing him. And she would if he ever learned her husband's name.

He would realize, just as she did, that if the King ever discovered her infidelity, both of them would almost certainly die. . . .

Louis (King Louis) Indelicato, gang lord and political boss of Saint Cecilia, stood over six feet tall and weighed nearly three hundred pounds. A good deal of his weight was muscle, for he had massive shoulders, a huge chest, and thick legs as solid as tree trunks. But enough was fat to give him a bulging stomach and an embryo double chin.

After waving the thin, nondescript man to one of the plush visitor's chairs in his private office, he selected a cigar from his desk humidor, struck fire to it without offering one to the thin man, and said, "Shoot, Cutter."

Cutter said, "At about two yesterday afternoon she met a man in front of the bear pits at Bryant Park's zoo, Mr. Indelicato. Guy about thirty, not bad looking. Average size, well dressed. Looks like some kind of junior executive. They drove straight to the Bide-A-Wile Motel on Route Sixty and stayed there from a quarter after two until a quarter of five. Then he dropped her in front of the cabstand at Fourth and Walton."

King Louis asked unemotionally, "Who's the guy?"

"I couldn't find out yesterday," the thin man said apologetically. "I'll get a make on him next time they meet."

"Didn't you follow him after he dropped her?"

"Naturally," Cutter said. "But I lost him at a fast-changing stop light. I did the best I could after I lost him. He was driving a rented coupe from Conway's Car Rental Service, and I checked with them to see who had rented it. I had marked down the license number, see. But they were a little huffy about giving out information, and I didn't want to press it because I was afraid they might call him up and tip him off that somebody'd been checking. I went back to the motel and talked the proprietor into letting me take a gander at their registration card, too. But that didn't get me any farther. They'd registered as Thomas Jones and wife from Texas, and the name's probably as phony as the address. I won't lose him next time."

"There won't be any next time," Indelicato said. Pulling a wallet from his pocket, he extracted two one-hundred-dollar bills and tossed them on the desk. "There's your fee for three days, plus a fifty-dollar tip. You can drop the case."

A little dubiously, Cutter picked up the money. "Aren't you satisfied with me, Mr. Indelicato? After all, I've only had three days, and this is the first time your wife—"

"You did fine," King Louis interrupted. "I just don't need you anymore. I'll take over personally from here. On your way out, tell that dumb Swede sitting on his butt in the outer office that I want him."

"Sure, Mr. Indelicato," the thin man said, rising.

"One more thing, Cutter. I suppose you maintain some kind of records?"

"Yes, sir. I haven't typed this one up yet, though. Haven't even set up a folder on it."

"Then don't," King Louis said.

"Don't?"

"Not even so much as a book entry that I was ever your client. And don't try to cross me on it. One of these days when you've stopped expecting it, I'll have some of my boys drop by to check your files. I'd hate to find out you didn't know how to follow instructions."

"They won't find anything," the thin man said sincerely. "If you don't want a record made, there won't be one, naturally."

"Good." The King dismissed him with a wave.

The "dumb Swede" Indelicato had referred to was a large, flat-faced blond man with the build of a professional wrestler. When he came into the office he said, "Something, boss?"

"Something, Simp. Pass the word along that I want Harry Silver to get in touch with me."

Simp whistled. "Him, boss? Somebody get out of line?"

"Just do what you're told and skip the questions," the big man snapped.

"Sure, boss. Sure. I'll get the word right out."

Harry Silver moved languidly into the office, seated himself, and touched flame to a gold-tipped cigarette.

"What's on your mind, King?" he asked.

The racket boss studied the lean face of the free-lance killer a few moments before replying. Even with all the power behind him, he was never quite comfortable in the presence of Harry Silver.

Finally he said, "Got a job for you, Harry."

Silver elevated eyebrows as red as his hair. "Don't your own boys carry guns anymore?"

"This is a special job. I wouldn't trust any of the morons who work for me."

The slim professional killer shrugged. "It must be special if you're willing to lay out my fee. I don't work often, and when I do, I come high."

"I know it. This is worth ten grand to me."

Harry Silver failed to look impressed. Letting twin spirals of smoke seep from his nostrils, he said indifferently, "I fix my fee according to the job. It may be less than that, maybe more. I'll tell you after I hear the setup."

"More than ten grand?" Indelicato said, frowning.

"If I think it's worth it. We don't haggle about the price. Give me the pitch and I'll tell you my fee. It'll be a take-it-or-leave-it proposition, because I don't bargain. If you leave it, that's okay. I guess I don't have to tell you that you won't have to worry about a spill from me later."

The King wasn't used to not being in absolute control of situations. He frowned slightly, then reflected that when you were dealing with the top man in his field, you could expect a certain degree of independence.

"Happen to know my wife, Marion?" he asked.

The professional killer shook his head. "Never had the pleasure of meeting her."

"She's twenty-five years old," King Louis said. "Twenty years younger than me. We've been married three years, and I've given her everything. Even made her my sole heir, though she isn't aware of that. I don't believe in putting temptation in people's ways. I don't know whether she was in love with me when we married or not, but she entered the contract with her eyes wide open. She knew what my business was, and she knew how I am. I don't accept half portions. With me it's all or nothing. She knew she could have anything in the world except one thing."

The red eyebrows raised inquiringly.

"She knew I'd never stand still for another man," the gang leader said quietly.

Silver drew deeply on his cigarette and exhaled through his nose. He didn't say anything.

"I've been suspecting another man for about a month," the King went on. "From little things. Her elaborate explanations about where she'd been and what she'd been doing when I asked a casual question about how she'd spent the day. Her kind of breathless look when . . ." He paused and waved an impatient hand. "Hell, it doesn't matter why I suspected. Five days ago I hired a shamus named Amos Cutter to check on her. Know him?"

Harry Silver shook his head.

"A skinny little guy. Looks like nothing, but he's a sharp operator. And a clam. I've used him before for stuff. Yesterday he reported to me that my suspicions were right. My wife definitely has a lover. I jerked Cutter off the case before he could learn the man's identity, because I didn't particularly want him to know it. As I said, he's a clam, but the less he knows about my business the better I like it. All I really wanted him for was to find out for sure Marion was cheating. You can track down who the man is as easily as he could."

"I suppose," Silver said. "If she meets him again."

"She'll meet him again," King Louis said. "And lead you right to him. My house is at forty-two twenty-seven Forsyth, and I want you to start watching it daytimes. She has to meet him in the daytime because she's home with me at night. You won't have any trouble spotting my wife. She's not a bad-looking blonde with a pretty fair shape. And in addition to her wedding ring she wears a four-carat diamond engagement ring I gave her. It stands out like a headlamp. This is her picture."

Reaching into a desk drawer, Indelicato brought out an eight-by-ten cardboard folder and passed it across to the red-haired man. Leaning forward, Silver punched out his gold-tipped cigarette. He did not immediately open the folder.

"Suppose this man turns out not to be a lover after all?" Silver asked. "Maybe your wife's playing horses on the sly, and he's just a bookie."

"He's her lover," Indelicato said definitely. "Cutter gave me enough to convince me there couldn't be any mistake about that. Anyway, I'd expect you to make sure you had the right man before doing anything. If I wanted somebody to make a mistake like bumping my wife's bookmaker, I'd send one of my own morons."

Silver gave him a wintry smile. "You won't have to worry about mistakes. I don't make them. Let me get this straight now. As soon as I'm satisfied I have the right man, you want him put away?"

"Both of them," King Louis said in a tight voice. "Preferably while they're right in the act."

The red eyebrows went up. "Your wife too?"

"I told you I don't accept half portions," the racket boss said. "Both of them. And I want them to know why before you do it. I want them to know it's with my compliments."

"You want it with a knife or a gun?"

King Louis blinked. "That's up to you. What difference does it make? Except won't it be a little tough tackling both at the same time with a knife?"

The professional killer smiled. "I can do tricks with a knife you never dreamed of. It won't be tough. But I don't much like rubbing women. The fee for this is going to be out of sight."

"Name it."

"Twenty thousand dollars."

King Louis blinked again, but he barely hesitated before saying, "A deal. Half now and half when the job's done. How's that?"

"All when the job's done. I don't need a retainer."

When the gang boss looked surprised, Silver said in a suddenly cold voice, "You won't renege. Not even you will renege on me, King."

After studying the man for a moment, Indelicato admitted, "No, I guess I won't, Harry."

Silver wasn't listening to him, however. He had finally opened the cardboard folder and was studying the attractive face in the picture broodingly. He looked at it a long time before closing the folder again.

"One more thing," he said then. "The cops have a habit of picking me up for routine questioning every time somebody gets killed. And with your wife one of the corpses, you're going to be in for routine suspicion too. Naturally I'll have an alibi rigged, and I assume you will too. But it won't look good if anyone knows about a contact between us."

"Nobody but Simp knows you've been here."

"Then we're all set," Silver said.

Rising languorously, he tossed the photograph onto the desk and walked to the door. With a bare wave of good-bye he opened it, went out, and pulled it shut behind him.

King Louis had hardly placed the picture of his wife back into the desk drawer when the door reopened and Harry Silver came back into the room. The gang boss looked at him in surprise as the redhaired man crossed to the desk, carefully removed the gold-tipped cigarette butt from the ashtray where he had crushed it out, and dropped it into his coat pocket.

"You reduced to sniping butts?" the King asked.

Without smiling, the professional killer said, "You're not very good at description, King. Your description of your wife was about as accurate as describing a Michelangelo madonna as a picture, or Brahms' Lullaby as a song."

The gang boss frowned up at him. "What are you talking about? You know I can't follow you when you shoot off into your damned book-learning."

"I'll make it simple," Silver said. "You described your wife as a not bad-looking blonde with a pretty fair shape. Hell, man, don't you know she's a raving beauty?"

Indelicato let his mouth drop open. "What . . . what in the hell *is* this?"

"I figured out a better bargain," the killer said unemotionally.

"You shouldn't have told me Marion is your sole heir. Instead of just twenty thousand bucks, I'm going to marry a rich widow."

The big man's eyes narrowed and his right foot surreptitiously felt for the concealed button beneath his desk.

"You needn't bother ringing," Silver said. "Simp's still out there, but he can't hear your buzz. His head just came about a quarter of the way loose from his neck."

He made a movement which was almost lazy; there was a sharp click; and suddenly a seven-inch blade gleamed in his hand.

"What . . . what in the hell's the matter with you, Harry?" King Louis asked in a croaking voice.

"Nothing's the matter with me," Silver said. "I just happened to recognize your wife's picture."

As he stared with fascination at the glittering knife blade, it penetrated King Louis's numb mind that he wasn't the only one poor at description.

Amos Cutter had completely neglected to mention that his wife's lover had red hair.

"A Better Bargain." *Alfred Hitchcock Presents*, December 9, 1956. Directed by Herschel Daugherty. Teleplay by Bernard C. Schoenfeld, based on Richard Deming's story "The Better Bargain" *(Manhunt*, April 1956). With Robert Middleton (Louis Koster), Kathleen Hughes (Marian), Henry Silva (Harry Silver), Don Hanmer (Mr. Cutter), Jack Lampert (Baldy).

If you watched *Alfred Hitchcock Presents* regularly, the twist in the tail of "A Better Bargain" must have leapt out at you, and I suspect that it was written with precisely that market in mind. Richard Deming (1915–1983) was a prolific and workmanlike utility writer, turning out with equal facility movie and TV tie-in novels, sports biographies, books on the American legal system for young adults, and well over a hundred short stories of crime and suspense, mainly for *Manhunt* and *Alfred Hitchcock's Mystery Magazine.* I don't recall seeing the telefilm version, but I can't help wondering how, in a visual medium, director Herschel Daugherty and scripter Bernard C. Schoenfeld kept from giving away the climactic twist prematurely. As the cast list shows, the King Louis character was de-ethnicized for TV.

Francis M. Nevins, Jr.

THOMAS BURKE

The Hands of
Mr. Ottermole

MURDER (SAID OLD QUONG)—oblige me by passing my pipe—murder is one of the simplest things in the world to do. Killing a man is a much simpler matter than killing a duck. Not always so safe, perhaps, but simpler. But to certain gifted people it is both simple and entirely safe. Many minds of finer complexion than my own have discolored themselves in seeking to name the identity of the author of those wholesale murders which took place last year. Who that man or woman really was, I know no more than you do, but I have a theory of the person it could have been; and if you are not pressed for time I will elaborate that theory into a little tale.''

As I had the rest of that evening and the whole of the next day for dalliance in my ivory tower, I desired that he would tell me the story; and, having reckoned up his cash register and closed the ivory gate, he told me—between then and the dawn—his story of the Mallon End murders. Paraphrased and condensed, it came out something like this.

At six o'clock of a January evening Mr. Whybrow was walking home through the cobweb alleys of London's East End. He had left the golden clamor of the great High Street to which the tram had brought him from the river and his daily work, and was now in the chessboard of byways that is called Mallon End. None of the rush and gleam of the High Street trickled into these byways. A few paces south—a flood tide of life, foaming and beating. Here—only slow shuffling figures and muffled pulses. He was in the sink of London, the last refuge of European vagrants.

As though in tune with the street's spirit, he too walked slowly, with head down. It seemed that he was pondering some pressing trouble, but he was not. He had no trouble. He was walking slowly because he had been on his feet all day; and he was bent in abstraction because he was wondering whether the Missis would have herrings for his tea, or haddock; and he was trying to decide which would be the more tasty on a night like this. A wretched night it was, of damp and mist, and the mist wandered into his throat and his eyes, and the damp had settled on pavement and roadway, and where the sparse lamplight fell it sent up a greasy sparkle that chilled one to look at. By contrast it made his speculations more agreeable, and made him ready for that tea—whether herring or haddock. His eye turned from the glum bricks that made his horizon, and went forward half a mile. He saw a gas-lit kitchen, a flamy fire, and a spread tea table. There was toast in the hearth and a singing kettle on the side and a piquant effusion of herrings, or maybe of haddock, or perhaps sausages. The vision gave his aching feet a throb of energy. He shook imperceptible damp from his shoulders, and hastened toward its reality.

But Mr. Whybrow wasn't going to get any tea that evening—or any other evening. Mr. Whybrow was going to die. Somewhere within a hundred yards of him, another man was walking: a man much like Mr. Whybrow and much like any other man, but without the only quality that enables mankind to live peaceably together and not as madmen in a jungle. A man with a dead heart eating into itself and bringing forth the foul organisms that arise from death and corruption. And that thing in man's shape, on a whim or a settled idea—one cannot know—had said within himself that Mr. Whybrow should never taste another herring. Not that Mr. Whybrow had injured him. Not that he had any dislike of Mr. Whybrow. Indeed, he knew nothing of him save as a familiar figure about the streets. But, moved by a force that had taken possession of his empty cells, he had picked on Mr. Whybrow with that blind choice that makes us pick one restaurant table that has nothing to mark it from four or five other tables, or one apple from a dish of half-a-dozen equal apples; or that drives nature to send a cyclone upon one corner of this planet and destroy five hundred lives in that corner, and leave another five hundred in the same corner unharmed. So this man had picked on Mr. Whybrow as he might have picked on you or me, had we been within his daily observation; and even now he was creeping through the blue-toned streets, nursing his large white hands, moving ever closer to Mr. Whybrow's tea table, and so closer to Mr. Whybrow himself.

He wasn't, this man, a bad man. Indeed, he had many of the social and amiable qualities, and passed as a respectable man, as most successful criminals do. But the thought had come into his moldering mind that he would like to murder somebody, and as he held no fear of God or man, he was going to do it, and would then go home to *his* tea. I don't say that flippantly, but as a statement of fact. Strange as it may seem to the humane, murderers must and do sit down to meals after a murder. There is no reason why they shouldn't, and many reasons why they should. For one thing, they need to keep their physical and mental vitality at full beat for the business of covering their crime. For another, the strain of their effort makes them hungry, and satisfaction at the accomplishment of a desired thing brings a feeling of relaxation toward human pleasures. It is accepted among non-murderers that the murderer is always overcome by fear for his safety and horror at his act; but this type is rare. His own safety is, of course, his immediate concern, but vanity is a marked quality of most murderers, and that, together with the thrill of conquest, makes him confident that he can secure it; and when he has restored his strength with food, he goes about securing it as a young hostess goes about the arranging of her first big dinner—a little anxious, but no more. Criminologists and detectives tell us that *every* murderer, however intelligent or cunning, always makes one slip in his tactics—one little slip that brings the affair home to him. But that is only half-true. It is true only of the murderers who are caught. Scores of murderers are not caught: therefore, scores of murderers do not make any mistake at all. This man didn't.

As for horror or remorse, prison chaplains, doctors, and lawyers have told us that of murderers they have interviewed under condemnation and the shadow of death, only one here and there has expressed any contrition for his act or shown any sign of mental misery. Most of them display only exasperation at having been caught when so many have gone undiscovered, or indignation at being condemned for a perfectly reasonable act. However normal and humane they may have been before the murder, they are utterly without conscience after it. For what is conscience? Simply a polite nickname for superstition, which is a polite nickname for fear. Those who associate remorse with murder are, no doubt, basing their ideas on the world-legend of the remorse of Cain, or are projecting their own frail minds into the mind of the murderer, and getting false reactions. Peaceable folk cannot hope to make contact with this mind, for they are not merely different in mental type from the murderer; they are different in their personal chemistry and construction. Some men can and do kill—not one man, but two or three—and go calmly about their daily affairs. Other men could not, under the most agonizing provocation, bring themselves even to wound. It is men of this sort who imagine the murderer in torments of remorse and fear of the law, whereas he is actually sitting down to his tea.

The man with the large white hands was as ready for his tea as Mr. Whybrow was, but he had something to do before he went to it. When he had done that something, and made no mistake about it, he would be even more ready for it, and would go to it as comfortably as he went to it the day before, when his hands were stainless.

Walk on, then, Mr. Whybrow, walk on; and as you walk, look your last upon the familiar features of your nightly journey. Follow your jack-o'-lantern tea table. Look well upon its warmth and color and kindness; feed your eyes with it and tease your nose with its gentle domestic odors, for you will never sit down to it. Within ten minutes' pacing of you, a pursuing phantom has spoken in his heart, and you are doomed. There you go—you and phantom—two nebulous dabs of mortality moving through green air along pavements of powder-blue, the one to kill, the other to be killed. Walk on. Don't annoy your burning feet by hurrying, for the more slowly you walk, the longer you will breathe the green air of this January dusk, and see the dreamy lamplight and the little shops, and hear the agreeable commerce of the London crowd and the haunting pathos of the street organ. These things are dear to you, Mr. Whybrow. You don't know it now, but in fifteen minutes you will have two seconds in which to realize how inexpressibly dear they are.

Walk on, then, across this crazy chessboard. You are in Lagos Street now, among the tents of the wanderers of Eastern Europe. A minute or so, and you are in Loyal Lane, among the lodging houses that shelter the useless and the beaten of London's camp followers. The lane holds the smell of them, and its soft darkness seems heavy with the wail of the futile. But you are not sensitive to impalpable things, and you plod through it, unseeing, as you do every evening, and come to Blean Street, and plod through that. From basement to sky rise the tenements of an alien colony. Their windows slot the ebony of their walls with lemon. Behind those windows, strange life is moving, dressed with forms that are not of London or of England, yet, in essence, the same agreeable life that you have been living, and tonight will live no more. From high above you comes a voice crooning *The Song of Katta*. Through a window you see a family keeping a religious rite. Through another you see a woman pouring out tea for her husband. You see a man mending a pair of boots; a mother bathing her baby. You have seen all these things before, and never noticed them. You do not notice them now, but if you knew that you were never going to see them again, you would notice them. You never *will* see them again, not because your life has run its natural course, but because a man whom you have often passed in the street has at his own solitary pleasure decided to usurp the awful authority of nature, and destroy you. So perhaps it's as well that you don't notice them, for your part in them is ended. No more for you these pretty moments of our earthly travail: only one moment of terror, and then a plunging darkness.

Closer to you this shadow of massacre moves, and now he is twenty yards behind you. You can hear his footfall, but you do not turn your head. You are familiar with footfalls. You are in London, in the easy security of your daily territory, and footfalls behind you, your instinct tells you, are no more than a message of human company.

But can't you hear something in those footfalls—something that goes with a widdershins beat? Something that says: *Look out, look out. Beware, beware.* Can't you hear the very syllables of *murd-er-er, murd-er-er?* No; there is nothing in footfalls. They are neutral. The foot of villainy falls with the same quiet note as the foot of honesty. But those footfalls, Mr. Whybrow, are bearing on to you a pair of hands, and there *is* something in hands. Behind you that pair of hands is even now stretching its muscles in preparation for your end. Every minute of your days, you have been seeing human hands. Have you ever realized the sheer horror of hands—those appendages that are a symbol for our moments of trust and affection and salutation? Have you thought of the sickening potentialities that lie within the scope of that five-tentacled member? No, you never have; for all the human hands that you have seen have been stretched to you in kindness or fellowship. Yet, though the eyes can hate and the lips can sting, it is only that dangling member that can gather the accumulated essence of evil and electrify it into currents of destruction. Satan may enter into man by many doors, but in the hands alone can he find the servants of his will.

Another minute, Mr. Whybrow, and you will know all about the horror of human hands.

You are nearly home now. You have turned into your street—Caspar Street—and you are in the center of the chessboard. You can see the front window of your little four-roomed house. The street is dark, and its three lamps give only a smut of light that is more confusing than darkness. It is dark—empty, too. Nobody about; no lights in the front parlors of the houses, for the families are at tea in their kitchens; and only a random glow in a few upper rooms occupied by lodgers. Nobody about but you and your following companion, and you don't notice him. You see him so often that he is never seen. Even if you turned your head and saw him, you would only say "Good evening" to him, and walk on. A suggestion that he was a possible murderer would not even make you laugh. It would be too silly.

And now you are at your gate. And now you have found your door key. And now you are in, and hanging up your hat and coat. The Missis has just called a greeting from the kitchen, whose smell is an echo of that greeting (herrings!), and you have answered it, when the door shakes under a sharp knock.

Go away, Mr. Whybrow. Go away from that door. Don't touch it. Get right away from it. Get out of the house. Run with the Missis to the back garden, and over the fence. Or call the neighbors. But don't touch that door. Don't, Mr. Whybrow, don't open . . .

Mr. Whybrow opened the door.

That was the beginning of what became known as London's Strangling Horrors. Horrors they were called because they were something more than murders: they were motiveless, and there was an air of black magic about them. Each murder was committed at a time when the street where the bodies were found was empty of any perceptible or possible murderer. There would be an empty alley. There would be a policeman at its end. He would turn his back on the empty alley for less than a minute. Then he would look round and run into the night with news of another strangling. And in any direction he looked, nobody to be seen and no report to be had of anybody being seen. Or he would be on duty in a long-quiet street, and suddenly be called to a house of dead people whom a few seconds earlier he had seen alive. And, again, whichever way he looked nobody to be seen; and although police whistles put an immediate cordon around the area and searched all houses, no possible murderer to be found.

The first news of the murder of Mr. and Mrs. Whybrow was brought by the station sergeant. He had been walking through Caspar Street on his way to the station for duty, when he noticed the open door of No. 98. Glancing in, he saw by the gaslight of the passage a motionless body on the floor. After a second look he blew his whistle; and when the constables answered him, he took one to join him in a search of the house, and sent others to watch all neighboring streets and make inquiries at adjoining houses. But neither in the house nor in the streets was anything found to indicate the murderer. Neighbors on either side, and opposite, were questioned, but they had seen nobody about, and had heard nothing. One had heard Mr. Whybrow come home—the scrape of his latchkey in the door was so regular an evening sound, he said, that you could set your watch by it for half-past six—but he had heard nothing more than the sound of the opening door until the sergeant's whistle. Nobody had been seen to enter the house or leave it, by front or back, and the necks of the dead people carried no fingerprints or other traces. A nephew was called in to go over the house, but he could find nothing missing; and anyway his uncle possessed nothing worth stealing. The little money in the house was untouched, and there were no signs of any disturbance of the property, or even of struggle. No signs of anything but brutal and wanton murder.

Mr. Whybrow was known to neighbors and workmates as a quiet, likable, home-loving man; such a man as could not have any enemies. But, then, murdered men seldom have. A relentless enemy who hates a man to the point of wanting to hurt him seldom wants to murder him, since to do that puts him beyond suffering. So the police were left with an impossible situation: no clue to the murderer and no motive for the murders, only that they had been done.

The first news of the affair sent a tremor through London generally, and an electric thrill through all Mallon End. Here was a murder of two inoffensive people, not for gain and not for revenge; and the murderer, to whom, apparently, killing was a casual impulse, was at large. He had left no traces, and provided he had no companions, there seemed no reason why he should not remain at large. Any clearheaded man who stands alone and has no fear of God or man, can, if he chooses, hold a city, even a nation, in subjection; but your everyday criminal is seldom clearheaded and dislikes being lonely. He needs, if not the support of confederates, at least somebody to talk to; his vanity needs the satisfaction of perceiving at first hand the effect of his work. For this he will frequent bars and coffee shops and other public places. Then, sooner or later, in a glow of comradeship, he will utter the one word too much; and the nark, who is everywhere, has an easy job.

But though the doss-houses and saloons and other places were "combed" and set with watches, and it was made known by whispers that good money and protection were assured to those with information, nothing attaching to the Whybrow case could be found. The murderer clearly had no friends and kept no company. Known men of this type were called up and questioned, but each was able to give a good account of himself; and in a few days the police were at a dead end. Against the constant public gibe that the thing had been done almost under their noses, they became restive, and for four days each man of the force was working his daily beat under a strain. On the fifth day they became still more restive.

It was the season of annual teas and entertainments for the children of the Sunday Schools; and on an evening of fog, when London was a world of groping phantoms, a small girl, in the bravery of best Sunday frock and shoes, shining face and new-washed hair, set out from Logan Passage for St. Michael's Parish Hall. She never got there. She was not actually dead until half-past six, but she was as good as dead from the moment she left her mother's door. Somebody like a man, pacing the street from which the passage led, saw her come out; and from that moment she was dead. Through the fog somebody's large white hands reached after her, and in fifteen minutes they were about her.

At half-past six a whistle screamed trouble, and those answering it found the body of little Nellie Vrinoff in a warehouse entry in Minnow Street. The sergeant was first among them, and he posted his men to useful points, ordering them here and there in the tart tones of repressed rage, and berating the officer whose beat the street was. "I saw you, Magson, at the end of the lane. What were you up to there? You were there ten minutes before you turned." Magson began an explanation about keeping an eye on a suspicious-looking character at that end, but the sergeant cut him short: "Suspicious characters be damned. You don't want to look for suspicious characters. You want to look for *murderers*. Messing about . . . and then this happens right where you ought to be. Now think what they'll say."

With the speed of ill news came the crowd, pale and perturbed; and on the story that the unknown monster had appeared again, and this time to a child, their faces streaked the fog with spots of hate and horror. But then came the ambulance and more police, and swiftly they broke up the crowd; and as it broke, the sergeant's thought was thickened into words, and from all sides came low murmurs of "Right under their noses." Later inquiries showed that four people of the district, above suspicion, had passed that entry at intervals of seconds before the murder, and seen nothing and heard nothing. None of them had passed the child alive or seen her dead. None of them had seen anybody in the street except themselves. Again the police were left with no motive and with no clue.

And now the district, as you will remember, was given over, not to panic, for the London public never yields to that, but to apprehension and dismay. If these things were happening in their familiar streets, then anything might happen. Wherever people met—in the streets, the markets, and the shops—they debated the one topic. Women took to bolting their windows and doors at the first fall of dusk. They kept their children closely under their eye. They did their shopping before dark, and watched anxiously— while pretending they weren't watching—for the return of their husbands from work. Under the cockney's semi-humorous resignation to disaster, they hid an hourly foreboding. By the whim of one man with a pair of hands, the structure and tenor of their daily life were shaken, as they always can be shaken by any man contemptuous of humanity and fearless of its laws. They began to realize that the pillars that supported the peaceable society in which they lived were mere straws that anybody could snap; that laws were powerful only so long as they were obeyed; that the police were potent only so long as they were feared. By the power of his hands this one man had made a whole community do something new: he had made it think, and left it gasping at the obvious.

And then, while it was yet gasping under his first two strokes, he made his third. Conscious of the horror that his hands had created, and hungry as an actor who has once tasted the thrill of the multitude, he made fresh advertisement of his presence; and on Wednesday morning, three days after the murder of the child, the papers carried to the breakfast tables of England the story of a still more shocking outrage.

At 9:32 on Tuesday night a constable was on duty in Jarnigan Road, and at that time spoke to a fellow officer named Petersen at the top of Clemming Street. He had seen this officer walk down that street. He could swear that the street was empty at that time, except for a lame bootblack whom he knew by sight, and who passed him and entered a tenement on the side opposite that on which his fellow officer was walking. He had the habit, as all constables had just then, of looking constantly behind him and around him, whichever way he was walking, and he was certain that the street was empty. He passed his sergeant at 9:33, saluted him, and answered his inquiry for anything seen. He reported that he had seen nothing, and passed on. His beat ended at a short distance from Clemming Street, and having paced it, he turned and came again at 9:34 to the top of the street. He had scarcely reached it before he heard the hoarse voice of the sergeant: "Gregory! You there? Quick. Here's another. My God, it's Petersen! Garroted. Quick, call 'em up!"

That was the third of the Strangling Horrors, of which there were to be a fourth and a fifth; and the five horrors were to pass into the unknown and unknowable. That is, unknown as far as authority and the public were concerned. The identity of the murderer *was* known, but to two men only. One was the murderer himself; the other was a young journalist.

This young man, who was covering the affairs for his paper, the *Daily Torch,* was no smarter than the other zealous newspapermen who were hanging about these byways in the hope of a sudden story. But he was patient, and he hung a little closer to the case than the other fellows, and by continually staring at it he at last raised the figure of the murderer like a genie from the stones on which he had stood to do his murders.

After the first few days the men had given up any attempt at exclusive stories, for there were none to be had. They met regularly at the police station, and what little information there was they shared. The officials were agreeable to them, but no more. The sergeant discussed with them the details of each murder; suggested possible explanations of the man's methods; recalled from the past those cases that had some similarity; and on the matter of motive reminded them of the motiveless Neil Cream and the wanton John Williams, and hinted that work was being done which would soon bring the business to an end; but about that work he would not say a word. The Inspector, too, was gracefully garrulous on the thesis of Murder, but whenever one of the party edged the talk toward what was being done in this immediate matter, he glided past it. Whatever the officials knew, they were not giving it to newspapermen. The business had fallen heavily upon them, and only by a capture made by their own efforts could they rehabilitate themselves in official and public esteem. Scotland Yard, of course, was at work, and had all the station's material; but the station's hope was that they themselves would have the honor of settling the affair; and however useful the cooperation of the press might be in other cases, they did not want to risk a defeat by a premature disclosure of their theories and plans.

So the sergeant talked at large, and propounded one interesting theory after another, all of which the newspapermen had thought of themselves.

The young man soon gave up these morning lectures on the philosophy of crime, and took to wandering about the streets and making bright stories out of the effect of the murders on the normal life of the people. A melancholy job made more melancholy by the district. The littered roadways, the crestfallen houses, the bleared windows—all held the acid misery that evokes no sympathy: the misery of the frustrated poet. The misery was the creation of the aliens, who were living in this makeshift fashion because they had no settled homes, and would neither take the trouble to make a home where they *could* settle, nor get on with their wandering.

There was little to be picked up. All he saw and heard were indignant faces, and wild conjectures of the murderer's identity and of the secret of his trick of appearing and disappearing unseen. Since a policeman himself had fallen a victim, denunciations of the force had ceased, and the unknown was now invested with a cloak of legend. Men eyed other men as though thinking: It might be *him*. It might be *him*. They were no longer looking for a man who had the air of a Madame Tussaud murderer; they were looking for a man, or perhaps some harridan woman, who had done these particular murders. Their thoughts ran mainly on the foreign set. Such ruffianism could scarcely belong to England, nor could the bewildering cleverness of the thing. So they turned to Rumanian gypsies and Turkish carpet-sellers. There, clearly, would be found the "warm" spot. These Eastern fellows—they knew all sorts of tricks, and they had no real religion—nothing to hold them within bounds. Sailors returning from those parts had told tales of conjurors who made themselves invisible; and there were tales of Egyptian and Arab potions that were used for abysmally queer purposes. Perhaps it *was* possible to them; you never knew. They were so slick and cunning, and they had such gliding movements; no Englishman could melt away as they could. Almost certainly the murderer would be found to be one of that sort—with some dark trick of his own—and just because they were sure that he *was* a magician, they felt that it was useless to look for him. He was a power, able to hold them in subjection and to hold himself untouchable. Superstition, which so easily cracks the frail shell of reason, had got into them. He could do anything he chose; he would never be discovered. These two points they settled, and they went about the streets in a mood of resentful fatalism.

They talked of their ideas to the journalist in half-tones, looking right and left, as though *HE* might overhear them and visit them. And though all the district was thinking of him and ready to pounce upon him, yet, so strongly had he worked upon them, that if any man in the street—say, a small man of commonplace features and form—had cried *"I* am the Monster!"* would their stifled fury have broken into flood and have borne him down and engulfed him? Or would they not suddenly have seen something unearthly in that everyday face and figure, something unearthly in his everyday boots, something unearthly about his hat, something that marked him as one whom none of their weapons could alarm or pierce? And would they not momentarily have fallen back from this devil, as the devil fell back from the cross made by the sword of Faust, and so have given him time to escape? I do not know; but so fixed was their belief in his invincibility that it is at least likely that they would have made this hesitation, had such an occasion arisen. But it never did. Today this commonplace fellow, his murder lust glutted, is still seen and observed among them as he was seen and observed all the time; but because nobody then dreamt, or now dreams, that he was what he was, they observed him then, and observe him now, as people observe a lamppost.

Almost was their belief in his invincibility justified; for, five days after the murder of the policeman Petersen, when the experience and inspiration of the whole detective force of London were turned toward his identification and capture, he made his fourth and fifth strokes.

At nine o'clock that evening, the young newspaperman, who hung about every night until his paper was away, was strolling along Richards Lane. Richards Lane is a narrow street, partly a stall-market, and partly residential. The young man was in the residential section, which carries on one side small working-class cottages, and on the other the wall of a railway goods-yard. The great wall hung a blanket of shadow over the lane, and the shadow and the cadaverous outline of the now deserted market stalls gave it the appearance of a living lane that had been turned to frost in the moment between breath and death. The very lamps, that elsewhere were nimbuses of gold, had here the rigidity of gems. The journalist, feeling this message of frozen eternity, was telling himself that he was tired of the whole thing, when in one stroke the frost was broken. In the moment between one pace and another, silence and darkness were racked by a high scream and through the scream a voice: "Help! help! *He's here!*"

Before he could think what movement to make, the lane came to life. As though its invisible populace had been waiting on that cry, the door of every cottage was flung open, and from them and from the alleys poured shadowy figures bent in question-mark form. For a second or so they stood as rigid as the lamps; then a police whistle gave them direction, and the flock of shadows sloped up the street. The journalist followed them, and others followed him. From the main street and from surrounding streets they came, some risen from unfinished suppers, some disturbed in their ease of slippers and shirtsleeves, some stumbling on infirm limbs, and some upright and armed with pokers or the tools of their trade. Here and there above the wavering cloud of heads moved the bold helmets of policemen. In one dim mass they surged upon a cottage whose doorway was marked by the sergeant and two constables; and voices of those behind urged them on with "Get in! Find him! Run round the back! Over the wall!" And those in front cried, "Keep back! Keep back!"

And now the fury of a mob held in thrall by unknown peril broke loose. He was here—on the spot. Surely this time he *could not* escape. All minds were bent upon the cottage; all energies thrust toward its doors and windows and roof; all thought was turned upon one unknown man and his extermination. So that no one man saw any other man. No man saw the narrow, packed lane and the mass of struggling shadows, and all forgot to look among themselves for the monster who never lingered upon his victims. All forgot, indeed, that they, by their mass crusade of vengeance, were affording him the perfect hiding place. They saw only the house, and they heard only the rending of woodwork and the smash of glass at back and front, and the police giving orders or crying with the chase; and they pressed on.

But they found no murderer. All they found was news of murder and a glimpse of the ambulance, and for their fury there was no other object than the police themselves, who fought against this hampering of their work.

The journalist managed to struggle through to the cottage door, and to get the story from the constable stationed there. The cottage was the home of a pensioned sailor and his wife and daughter. They had been at supper, and at first it appeared that some noxious gas had smitten all three in mid-action. The daughter lay dead on the hearth rug, with a piece of bread and butter in her hand. The father had fallen sideways from his chair, leaving on his plate a filled spoon of rice pudding. The mother lay half under the table, her lap filled with the pieces of a broken cup and splashes of cocoa. But in three seconds the idea of gas was dismissed. One glance at their necks showed that this was the Strangler again; and the police stood and looked at the room and momentarily shared the fatalism of the public. They were helpless.

This was his fourth visit, making seven murders in all. He was to do, as you know, one more—and to do it that night; and then he was to pass into history as the unknown London horror, and return to the decent life that he had always led, remembering little of what he had done and worried not at all by the memory. Why did he stop? Impossible to say. Why did he begin? Impossible again. It just happened like that; and if he thinks at all of those days and nights, I surmise that he thinks of them as we think of foolish or dirty little sins that we committed in childhood. We say that they were not really sins because we were not then consciously ourselves: we had not come to realization; and we look back at that foolish little creature that we once were and forgive him because he didn't know. So, I think, with this man.

There are plenty like him. Eugene Aram, after the murder of Daniel Clarke, lived a quiet, contented life for fourteen years, unhaunted by his crime and unshaken in his self-esteem. Dr. Crippen murdered his wife, and then lived pleasantly with his mistress in the house under whose floor he had buried the wife. Constance Kent, found Not Guilty of the murder of her young brother, led a peaceful life for five years before she confessed. George Joseph Smith and William Palmer lived amiably among their fellows untroubled by fear or by remorse for their poisonings and drownings. Charles Peace, at the time he made his one unfortunate essay, had settled down into a respectable citizen with an interest in antiques. It happened that, after a lapse of time, these men were discovered; but more murderers than we guess are living decent lives today, and will die in decency, undiscovered and unsuspected. As this man will.

But he had a narrow escape, and it was perhaps this narrow escape that brought him to a stop. The escape was due to an error of judgment on the part of the journalist.

As soon as he had the full story of the affair, which took some time, he spent fifteen minutes on the telephone, sending the story through, and at the end of the fifteen minutes, when the stimulus of the business had left him, he felt physically tired and mentally disheveled. He was not yet free to go home; the paper would not go away for another hour; so he turned into a bar for a drink and some sandwiches.

It was then, when he had dismissed the whole business from his mind and was looking about the bar and admiring the landlord's taste in watch chains and his air of domination, and was thinking that the landlord of a well-conducted tavern had a more comfortable life than a newspaperman, that his mind received from nowhere a spark of light. He was not thinking about the Strangling Horrors; his mind was on his sandwich. As a public-house sandwich, it was a curiosity. The bread had been thinly cut, it was buttered, and the ham was not two months stale; it was ham as it should be. His mind turned to the inventor of this refreshment, the Earl of Sandwich, and then to George the Fourth, and then to the

Georges, and to the legend of that George who was worried to know how the apple got into the apple dumpling. He wondered whether George would have been equally puzzled to know how the ham got into the ham sandwich, and how long it would have been before it occurred to him that the ham could not have got there unless somebody had put it there. He got up to order another sandwich, and in that moment a little active corner of his mind settled the affair. If there was ham in his sandwich, somebody must have put it there. If seven people had been murdered, somebody must have been there to murder them. There was no aeroplane or automobile that would go into a man's pocket; therefore, that somebody must have escaped either by running away or standing still; and again therefore—

He was visualizing the front-page story that his paper would carry if his theory was correct, and if—a matter of conjecture—his editor had the necessary nerve to make a bold stroke, when a cry of "Time, gentlemen, please! All out!" reminded him of the hour. He got up and went out into a world of mist, broken by the ragged discs of roadside puddles and the streaming lightning of motor buses. He was certain that he had *the* story, but even if it was proved, he was doubtful whether the policy of his paper would permit him to print it. It had one great fault. It was truth, but it was impossible truth. It rocked the foundations of everything that newspaper readers believed and that newspaper editors helped them to believe. They might believe that Turkish carpet-sellers had the gift of making themselves invisible. They would not believe this.

As it happened, they were not asked to, for the story was never written. As his paper had by now gone away, and as he was nourished by his refreshment and stimulated by his theory, he thought he might put in an extra half hour by testing that theory. So he began to look about for the man he had in mind—a man with white hair and large white hands; otherwise an everyday figure whom nobody would look twice at. He wanted to spring his idea on this man without warning, and he was going to place himself within reach of a man armored in legends of dreadfulness and grue. This might appear to be an act of supreme courage—that one man, with no hope of immediate outside support, should place himself at the mercy of one who was holding a whole parish in terror. But it wasn't. He didn't think about the risk. He didn't think about his duty to his employers or loyalty to his paper. He was moved simply by an instinct to follow a story to its end.

He walked slowly from the tavern and crossed into Fingal Street, making for Deever Market, where he had hope of finding his man. But his journey was shortened. At the corner of Lotus Street he saw him—or a man who looked like him. This street was poorly lit, and he could see little of the man: but he *could* see white hands. For some twenty paces he stalked him; then drew level with him; and at a point where the arch of a railway crossed the street, he saw that this was his man. He approached him with the current conversational phrase of the district: "Well, seen anything of the murderer?" The man stopped to look sharply at him; then, satisfied that the journalist was not the murderer, said:

"Eh? No, nor's anybody else, curse it. Doubt if they ever will."

"I don't know. I've been thinking about them, and I've got an idea."

"So?"

"Yes. Came to me all of a sudden. Quarter of an hour ago. And I'd felt that we'd all been blind. It's been staring us in the face."

The man turned again to look at him, and the look and the movement held suspicion of this man who seemed to know so much. "Oh? Has it? Well, if you're so sure, why not give us the benefit of it?"

"I'm going to." They walked level, and were nearly at the end of the little street where it meets Deever Market when the journalist turned casually to the man. He put a finger on his arm. "Yes, it seems to me quite simple now. But there's still one point I don't understand. One little thing I'd like to clear up. I mean the motive. Now, as man to man, tell me, Sergeant Ottermole, just *why* did you kill all those inoffensive people?"

The sergeant stopped, and the journalist stopped. There was

just enough light from the sky, which held the reflected light of the continent of London, to give him a sight of the sergeant's face, and the sergeant's face was turned to him with a wide smile of such urbanity and charm that the journalist's eyes were frozen as they met it. The smile stayed for some seconds. Then said the sergeant, "Well, to tell you the truth, Mister Newspaperman, I don't know. I really don't know. In fact, I've been worried about it myself. But I've got an idea—just like you. Everybody knows that we can't control the workings of our minds. Don't they? Ideas come into our minds without asking. But everybody's supposed to be able to control his body. Why? Eh? We get our minds from lord-knows-where—from people who were dead hundreds of years before we were born. Mayn't we get our bodies in the same way? Our faces—our legs—our heads—they aren't completely ours. We don't make 'em. They come to us. And couldn't ideas come into our bodies like ideas come into our minds? Eh? Can't ideas live in nerve and muscle as well as in brain? Couldn't it be that parts of our bodies aren't really us, and couldn't ideas come into those parts all of a sudden, like ideas come into . . . into"—he shot his arms out, showing the great white-gloved hands and hairy wrists; shot them out so swiftly to the journalist's throat that his eyes never saw them—"into *my hands!*"

"The Hands of Mr. Ottermole." *Alfred Hitchcock Presents*, May 5, 1957. Directed by Robert Stevens. Teleplay by Francis Cockrell, from Thomas Burke's story "The Hands of Mr. Ottermole" (collected in Burke's *The Pleasantries of Old Quong,* London: Constable, 1931, U.S. title *A Tea-Shop in Limehouse,* Boston: Little, Brown, 1931). With Theodore Bikel (Sergeant), Rhys Williams (Summers), A. E. Gould-Porter (Whybrow), Barry Harvey (Whybrow's Nephew).

Thomas Burke (1886–1945) was one of the best-known English short story writers of the nineteen teens and twenties, specializing in lurid tales of London's Chinatown and the East End docks where he had grown up. (One of his Chinatown stories was the basis of D. W. Griffith's silent film classic *Broken Blossoms.*) Today, however, he's remembered almost exclusively for "The Hands of Mr. Ottermole," which panels of mystery writers have chosen again and again over the past fifty years as perhaps the finest crime story ever written. It was a natural for *Alfred Hitchcock Presents,* and director Robert Stevens, who was at his best with gothic horror material of this sort, invested the telefilm with a dank East-End-of-London ambience comparable to Hitchcock's own silent classic, *The Lodger*.

Francis M. Nevins, Jr.

FREDRIC BROWN

The Dangerous People

MR. BELLEFONTAINE SHIVERED A LITTLE, standing there on the edge of the platform of the little railroad station. The weather was cool enough, but it wasn't the cold that made him shiver. It was that distant siren sounding off again. A far, faint wail in the night—the wail of a tortured fiend.

He'd heard it first half an hour before, while he'd been getting a haircut in the little one-man barbershop on the main street of this little one-horse town. And the barber had told him what it was.

"But that's five miles away," he told himself. It didn't relieve his mind, though. A strong, desperate man could travel five miles in less than an hour, and anyway, maybe he'd escaped some time before they'd missed him. He must have; if they'd seen him go, they could probably have caught him.

Maybe, even, he'd escaped this afternoon, and had been free for hours. What time was it now? Not much after seven, and his train didn't get here until almost eight. Got dark early these days.

Mr. Bellefontaine had walked a bit too rapidly from the barbershop to the station, more rapidly than a man who has asthma should. The steps up to the station platform had taken what little wind remained in him and he had put down his briefcase to rest a moment before he crossed the platform to the station.

He was still breathing hard, but thought he could make the rest of the distance now and get in out of the darkness. He picked up the briefcase and was almost startled by its unaccustomed weight, until he remembered the revolver that was in it.

Odd for him, of all people, to be carrying a revolver—even one unloaded and wrapped in paper, with the box of cartridges for it wrapped separately and in the other compartment of the case. But Mr. Murgatroyd, the client he had come out here to see on legal business, had asked him as a personal favor to take the gun back to Milwaukee with him and give it to his, Mr. Murgatroyd's brother, to whom Mr. Murgatroyd had promised it.

"Awfully difficult thing to ship," Murgatroyd had said. "Wouldn't know how to send it, parcel post or freight or what. Might even be illegal to mail one; I don't know."

"Couldn't be," Bellefontaine had told his client, "because they sell the things by mail. Maybe, though, they have to go express."

"Well," Murgatroyd had said, "you're going straight through to Milwaukee anyway, so it won't be any trouble, and you won't have to take it to him or anything. Just call him up and he'll come around to your office and get it. Fact, I already wrote him I'd ask you to take it."

So there hadn't been any out, without offending a client; and Mr. Bellefontaine had brought the pistol along, little as he had cared to have such a thing in his possession.

"Damn this asthma," he thought as he opened the door of the little railroad station and stepped inside, "and damn a small-town drugstore that doesn't have any ephedrine for it in stock. Next time, I'll bring a few capsules with me—" He blinked to get his eyes used to the light, and looked around.

There was only one man in the station besides himself, a tall, thin man, shabbily dressed and with bloodshot eyes. He'd been sitting with his head in his hands when Mr. Bellefontaine came in, but now he looked up and said, "Hullo."

"Hello," said Mr. Bellefontaine, tersely. "Getting—uh—colder out."

The clock in the wall over the ticket window said seven-ten. Forty-five minutes to wait. Through the ticket window he could see into the inner room of the station where the gray-haired station agent was pecking something on an ancient typewriter at a table against the far wall. Mr. Bellefontaine didn't go to the ticket window; he already had his return ticket.

The tall man sat on one side of a potbellied little coal stove near the wall at the far side of the waiting room. There was a comfortable-looking rocking chair on the other side of the stove, but Mr. Bellefontaine didn't want to cross the room and sit there just yet.

He was still breathing hard from the effect of the brisk walk on his asthma, and he wanted to get all his wind back first. He'd probably have to talk as soon as he sat down there, and if he had to talk in short, jerky sentences, he'd have to explain about his annoying infirmity.

So, as an excuse for standing there awhile, he turned around to stare out through the glass pane of the door, as though he were watching something outside.

He saw, though, his own reflection in the pane. A chubby little man, very pink-faced and going bald, although that didn't show with his hat on. But his shell-rimmed glasses gave him a very serious look—which fitted him well, for Mr. Bellefontaine took himself very seriously. He was forty now, and by the time he was fifty he was going to be a very important corporation lawyer.

The siren wailed again.

Mr. Bellefontaine shivered slightly at the sound, and then went over and sat in the rocker by the coal stove. His briefcase thunked heavily on the floor as he put it down.

"Taking the seven-fifty-five?" the tall man asked.

Mr. Bellefontaine nodded. "Through to Milwaukee."

"I get off at Madison," said the tall man. "We got a couple of hundred miles to go together; might as well get acquainted. My name's Jones. Bookkeeper for the Saxe Paint Company."

Mr. Bellefontaine introduced himself, then added, "Saxe Paint? I thought it was in Chicago."

"Branch office in Madison."

"Oh," said Mr. Bellefontaine. It was his turn to say something, but he couldn't think of anything to say. In the silence, the
siren wailed again. It sounded louder this time, and he shivered.

"That thing gives me the willies," he said.

The tall man picked up the poker and opened the door of the
stove. "Cold in here," he said, taking a poke at the fire. "Say,
what *is* that siren?"

"Asylum for the Criminally Insane," he said. "An escape."
Unconsciously, he dropped his voice. "Probably a homicidal maniac. That's the kind they have in that place."

"Oh," said the tall man, rather blankly. He poked harder at the
fire, then slammed the stove door shut and sat back down in his
chair, still holding the poker.

It was, Mr. Bellefontaine noticed, a very heavy poker for so
small a stove. His long legs spread apart, the tall man swung it
meditatively up and down between his knees. He watched the
swinging poker instead of Mr. Bellefontaine's face. Suddenly he
asked, "Is there a description out? Know what the maniac looks
like?"

"Uh—no," said Mr. Bellefontaine. His eyes were suddenly
caught by the arc of that heavy poker.

What if—he thought. He caught himself abruptly. No, that was
silly. Or was it? There was something—

Suddenly he knew what it was. He'd thought the tall man was
rather poorly dressed; now Mr. Bellefontaine realized, looking at
him, that it wasn't that at all. The clothes were of good—at least
average—quality. Only they didn't *fit* him.

That suit had been made for a man of average height, and so
had the topcoat. The cuffs of the trousers were turned down, although they'd been pressed to stay up and still showed the fold of
the pressing. That was why they hung so peculiarly about the ankles. They were still an inch or so too short; so were the sleeves of
the topcoat and the suit coat.

Mr. Bellefontaine sat very still and pretended not to look, but
out of the corner of his eye, he continued his examination furtively. The tall man's shirt was undoubtedly too big around at the

collar. It had been made for a man with a much thicker neck. Jones's scrawny neck stuck up through it with wide clearance on all sides.

And his eyes, wild and bloodshot—

He would head for a railroad, thought Mr. Bellefontaine. *Some little station like this, a good distance from the asylum. On the way he'd burgle a house to get clothes in exchange for his uniform. Or maybe he'd even kill a man he met to get those clothes. And the clothes, of course, wouldn't fit him.*

Mr. Bellefontaine sat very still, and could feel his face become cool as it drained of color. Of course, he could be wrong, but— *Jones,* he thought. *The very name a man would be likely to give if he hadn't thought about what name to use until time to introduce himself. Saxe Paint Company, a big, widely advertised outfit, just the sort he'd think of first.*

And he slipped there, on the Madison part, but covered up by saying it was a branch office.

And he didn't seem to have any suitcase. Only the clothes he had on, and they weren't his own. Stolen clothes, and maybe he'd killed to get them! Killed a man only an hour or less ago. A short stocky man with a thick neck—

Slowly the poker swung up and down in that hypnotizing arc. Slowly the bloodshot eyes of the tall man swung up from it to Mr. Bellefontaine's face. He said, "Do you think—" Then his voice changed. "What's wrong? What's the matter?"

Mr. Bellefontaine gulped, then managed to say, "N-nothing."

The bloodshot eyes kept on looking at him for a long minute and then slowly dropped to the swinging poker. The tall man didn't go on with whatever he'd started to ask.

He knows, thought Mr. Bellefontaine dully. *I gave myself away. He knows that I know who he is. If I try to walk out of here now, he'll know I'm going for the police. He can get me with that poker long before I reach the door.*

He wouldn't even need the poker. He could strangle me. But no, he'll use the poker. The way he swings it and looks at it, he's thinking of it as a weapon.

But will he kill me anyway, even if I don't make a move? He might; he's mad. Madmen don't need reasons.

The inside of his mouth was very dry. His lips seemed stuck together, and Mr. Bellefontaine had to run his tongue between them before he could open his mouth to speak. He had to say something—something casual, to try to reassure the madman. Carefully he worked out each word, so he wouldn't stumble or stutter.

He said, "Getting c-colder out." Only when he'd said it, did he remember that he'd said the same thing once before. Well, people often repeat themselves.

The tall man looked at him, then looked down again. "Yeah," he said. No inflection, nothing to show what he was thinking.

Suddenly, then, Mr. Bellefontaine remembered the revolver. If only it were loaded and in his pocket, instead of being unloaded, wrapped up, and in the briefcase. How could he possibly—?

His eyes, darting about in frantic search, saw the door marked "Men." Could he make it? Would the killer stop him if he walked toward the door?

There were beads of perspiration on his forehead as he stood up slowly and picked up the briefcase. A shred of courage came back and he managed to make his voice almost calm as he said, "You'll excuse me a minute?" and walked around behind the stove and behind the chair the madman was occupying toward the door of the washroom.

Out of the corner of his eye he saw that the tall man turned to watch him. But he wasn't getting up!

Mr. Bellefontaine closed the door of the washroom quickly, and looked for a key in the lock. There wasn't one; nor was there a bolt. His hands trembled as he jerked the zipper on the briefcase.

His eyes roamed about, but saw nothing helpful. No window he could get out of—just a tiny one up high in the wall, well out of reach. No way he could barricade the door. There was a flimsy bolt on the door of the toilet booth, but a man could shove that door open with one hand.

No, no safety here. All he could do was load the revolver and have it in his pocket ready when he went out again. And he couldn't stay too long. He must hurry . . . hurry. . . .

Mr. Jones stared curiously a moment at the closed door of the washroom, then shrugged his shoulders and went back to doodling with the poker.

What a goof *that* guy was. Definitely off his rocker, that was obvious. He'd hoped he'd have someone to talk to on the train, but if *that* was the best company available, he'd take vanilla. Well, he'd try to sleep on the train.

He could sure use sleep, after last night. You wouldn't expect a wild party like that, way out here in the sticks. But Madge, his sister, had been in the mood to celebrate and so had Hank, his brother-in-law. The liquor had been bad, but plentiful. It had been an anniversary party, all right. What saps those neighbors of theirs, the Wilkinses, had made of themselves.

But, Mr. Jones thought wryly, no more of a sap than he had made of himself, staggering out into the barnyard for some fresh air and falling flat on his face in gooey mud. Lord, would his suit look the same again when it came back to him? Here he was having to wear some of Hank's clothes till he got back to Madison.

It would be a long time before he drank *that* much again. Fun at the time, but Lord how you felt the next day, even the next evening. Good thing he hadn't had to go to work today, with his eyes looking the way they did. The gang at the office would razz hell out of him.

Tomorrow—oh, damn Saxe paint and all bookkeeping! He'd quit tomorrow if Old Man Rogers, the branch manager, hadn't told him that in a few more months he'd be able to put him on the road. Selling wouldn't be so bad. And he *did* know paint, so it would be worth sticking to the books a couple of months more.

The door of the washroom opened and the funny-looking little guy came out. Mr. Jones turned around to look, and—yes, he still had that crazy look on his face. A sort of tightened-up, stiff look, as if his face were a mask glued on him.

He walked oddly, too, coming back—carried that briefcase in

his left hand this time and had his right hand stuck deep in his top-coat pocket.

What the devil had he taken the briefcase with him for, anyway? Surely he hadn't thought someone would run off with it in the few minutes he'd been in there. Unless, of course, he had something valuable in it, jewelry or something. Nope, too heavy for jewelry, the way it had thudded against the floor the first time he'd put it down. More like hardware samples, only hardware salesmen didn't carry their samples in brown leather brief-cases.

He watched curiously as the little man sat down in the chair again without taking his hand out of his topcoat pocket, and again put the briefcase down on the floor. Only this time it didn't *thunk*. It looked and sounded lighter, as if it contained nothing, or only a few papers. As though there were nothing to weight it down, it fell over, and the little guy picked it up again and leaned it against the side of the rocker to keep it from falling. It *was* empty, or at least something heavy had been taken out of it.

Still idly curious, Mr. Jones looked up from the mysterious briefcase to the tense white face above it.

Was the guy crazy? *Really* crazy?

Faintly, in the silence, came the wail of the siren. And at the sound, the little man started; his face went slack with fear, and then froze again.

Mr. Jones's scalp prickled. Pretending not to have noticed, he looked down again quickly at the poker in his hand. His knuckles tightened about the handle of it as he realized that it was his only weapon against a homicidal maniac.

Lord, why hadn't he guessed it sooner?

He came in here panting and out of breath; he'd been running. He turned around and watched through the glass of the door to see if he'd been followed.

Then he'd acted rational for a while. Madmen did; they had periods when you couldn't tell them at all from normal people.

A homicidal maniac, he thought. *Does he intend to kill me; is that why he's acting that way? Getting crazier by the minute, working himself up to a kill?*

But he's a little guy. I ought to be able to handle him, although maniacs are supposed to be terribly strong. But I know how to handle my dukes a little. Unless he's got a gun!

Suddenly, and beyond all doubt, Mr. Jones knew what had been in the briefcase; he knew why the madman had gone to the washroom—to transfer that gun from the case to the right-hand pocket of the topcoat, where his hand right now was gripped around it, his finger on the trigger.

Still pretending to look down at the poker, Mr. Jones glanced sidelong out of the corners of his eyes at the bulge in the topcoat pocket. A gun, all right. It was a much bigger bulge than just a hand would make, and besides, he could see the outline of the barrel of it making a raised little ridge toward the end of the pocket. A revolver, probably, with a five- or six-inch barrel.

If he were an escaped maniac, he tried to tell himself, *he wouldn't have told me what that siren was. But then, I asked him what it was. He might have thought I knew already, and suspected him because of the breathless way he made his entrance. So he had to tell me the truth, in case I already knew. And that screwy name he gave—Bellefontaine—a name out of a book. Real people seldom have names like that.*

But those were just arguments; the gun was a fact. You can't argue around a gun aimed at you by a homicidal maniac.

Why was he waiting?

From a long way off came the sound of a train whistle. Mr. Jones managed, without turning his head, to cast a sidelong glance at the clock. Fifteen minutes too soon for the passenger train, the seven-fifty-five. Must be a freight train going through, probably in the opposite direction.

Yes, he could hear it coming now, and it sounded like a freight. It wasn't slowing down. He heard a door close in the other room of the station and guessed what it was. The station agent was going out on the platform. Yes, there were footsteps on the platform, and then the rumble of the coming train drowned them out.

When the engine was directly opposite the station, right outside the window— Of course, *that* was what he was waiting for. That rush of deafening, roaring sound that would drown out the sound of the shot!

Mr. Jones tensed, tightened his grip on the poker until his knuckles went dead white, and shifted his weight forward. He could make it in one step, raising the poker as he did so. If the muzzle of that pistol, outlined through the cloth of the madman's topcoat, started to lift—

Roar of the coming train, louder, nearer—a crescendo rushing roar of obliterating sound—louder, *louder*—

And as Mr. Jones leaned forward the muzzle of the gun *was* lifting.

The man in the blue uniform with the brass buttons closed the door carefully behind him and turned to the two men sitting on either side of the stove. They looked funny, sitting there in such awkward, strained attitudes, as if they were scared stiff.

Should he? No, it would be too dangerous. He had the uniform now, and it would be so easy to get on the train and make his getaway, far from the search zone. But it would be so damned easy to kill those fellows, with the gun holstered at his belt—a gun that the uniform gave him the right to wear openly and without fear.

He said, "Evening, gentlemen," and one of them mumbled something back; the other didn't answer at all. The tall one, who was playing with the poker, asked, "Have they caught the— maniac?" and he glanced out of the corners of his eyes at the little plump fellow, almost as though he was trying to signal something.

He laughed. "No, they haven't caught him yet," he said. "I don't think they will."

It was so funny, so excruciatingly funny. He said, "They'll have real trouble getting him now. He killed a policeman at

Waynesville and stole his gun and uniform. And they don't even know it yet!''

He laughed again, and was still chuckling when he reached for the gun in his holster.

But the gun wasn't even out of the leather before a blasting, unexpected shot that seemed to come from inside the little man's pocket whizzed by his ear, and the tall man with the poker was already halfway across the room toward him. He didn't even have the gun raised before a second shot from the little man's pistol hit him in the upper arm and the poker was already smashing down at his head. He tried to duck, and succeeded only in avoiding the full force of the tall man's blow. . . .

The freight train was whistling far off when he came to. Someone was excitedly using the telephone in the station agent's side of the station building.

He was tied hand and foot. He struggled, briefly, and then relaxed and sighed, looking up at the two men standing over him. He thought back.

Why, they'd been ready and looking for trouble when he walked in! The little one must already have had his hand on that pistol, and the big one had been swinging the poker, ready. People usually have to build up to making a sudden attack, but these guys had gone off like a charge of dynamite.

Lord, if there were people as dangerous as *that* running around loose, he'd be safer back in the asylum where they'd take care of him. Why, they'd almost killed him. They must be *crazy!*

"The Dangerous People." *Alfred Hitchcock Presents*, June 23, 1957. Directed by Robert Stevens. Teleplay by Francis Cockrell, based on Fredric Brown's short story "No Sanctuary" (*Dime Mystery*, March 1945; collected as "The Dangerous People" in Brown's *Mostly Murder*, Dutton, 1953). With Albert Salmi (Mr. Jones), Robert H. Harris (Mr. Bellefontaine), Ken Clark (Policeman).

Fredric Brown (1906–1972) is better known as a science fiction writer, but from the late 1930s until the early sixties, when illness made him stop writing, he also turned out dozens of crime and suspense stories for the pulp magazines, plus more than twenty mystery novels. His best suspense tales combine bizarre humor with a *noir* mood close to that of Cornell Woolrich, and several were adapted (some by Brown himself) for *Alfred Hitchcock Presents*. Director Robert Stevens' penchant for horror-cum-suspense material was made to order for Brown's which-of-them-is-the-madman story line, and I remember the episode vividly enough so that I'd dearly love to see it again.

Francis M. Nevins, Jr.

CLARK HOWARD

Enough Rope for Two

THE GREYHOUND BUS pulled into the Los Angeles main terminal at noon. Joe Kedzie got off and walked out into the sunlight of a city he had not seen in ten years. Instinctively, he headed for Main Street. He walked slowly, recalling how the stores and clothes and cars had all changed. No more double-breasted suits. Very few black cars—mostly red and yellow and pink and chartreuse now. The stores were all modern, larger, with a lot of glass. And the skirts—a little longer maybe, but tight in the right places. He pushed the thought of women from his mind. There would be time for them later. After he had his hundred grand.

At Main, he turned the corner and began to pass the cheap bars and honky-tonks he had known so well. He remembered the shooting gallery, the penny arcade, the strip joints, the cafe where the pushers made—and probably still make—their headquarters. This part of the world will never change, he thought. If I was sent up for another ten years, it would still be the same when I got back again.

Between a bar and a Chinese hand laundry was the entrance to the Main Line Hotel. Kedzie opened the door and walked up the six steps to the lobby. A young, pimply-faced man was behind the desk. He held a racing form and studied it sleepily. Kedzie stood at the desk until it became apparent that the youth was ignoring him; he then reached across the counter and yanked the racing form out of his hand. The clerk jumped up, his face flushing.

"What's the idea!" he demanded.

".Just want a little service," said Kedzie calmly, laying the paper on the desk. "Does Madge Griffin still live here?"

The desk clerk tried to act tough. "Who wants to know?"

"Don't play games with me, punk," said Kedzie harshly, "or I'll break your arm! Does Madge Griffin live here or doesn't she?"

"She lives here," said the clerk, scared now. "Room two-twelve."

Kedzie nodded. He left the desk and walked across the lobby and up a flight of stairs. Two-twelve was the last room at the end of the dingy hallway. He stood before the door and lighted a cigarette, then rapped softly. Madge's voice came through the door.

"Who is it?"

"Errol Flynn. Open up."

He heard her walk across the room; then the door opened. She stood framed in the doorway, her eyes widening, plainly startled.

"Joe!"

"Hello, Madge."

She moved aside, as he moved forward, to let him enter. The room was small, not as crummy as he had expected, but still crummy enough. He walked to a chair and sat down. She watched him curiously for a moment, then closed the door and leaned back against it.

"How've you been, Madge?" he asked in his matter-of-fact tone, as if he had seen her a month ago instead of ten years ago.

"I've been getting along, Joe. How have you been?"

He grunted, but did not answer. He looked her over, taking his time. Ten years older, but she still had it, and just enough of it wherever it belonged. He decided that she was just a little heavier in the hips than when she had been his girl. Still—and this thought amused him—she wasn't then, and still wasn't now, the kind you would want if you had a hundred grand.

"How'd you know where to find me, Joe?" she asked suddenly.

"Just a guess. I figured you'd come back here. It's just about your speed."

"What's that supposed to mean?" she demanded, her eyes flashing angrily.

"Forget it, baby," he said easily, and to change the subject added, "Have you got a drink?"

She walked over to the closet and took a nearly full bottle of gin from the shelf. "There's nothing to mix it with," she said. "Want it straight?"

He shook his head. "It would probably knock me out. Forget it."

She put the bottle back on the shelf. Kedzie crushed out his cigarette and lighted a fresh one. It figures, he thought. A bottle of gin in the closet. Madge never could stand the stuff. But gin was always Maxie's drink. He's not far away. Just wait and be patient. He'll show up.

Madge walked over to the bed and sat down. They began to talk, idly, pleasantly. Two people have a lot to talk about after ten years. Kedzie waited for her to mention Maxie, but she did not. That convinced him that she knew where he was. And the minute she left the room and got to a telephone, Maxie would know that he, Kedzie, was back in town.

They talked until five o'clock. Finally she asked, "What are you going to do now, Joe?"

He decided to play it straight. "What do you mean?"

"I mean, have you got a place to stay tonight?"

"No, not yet. I'm so used to having my bunk waiting for me, I guess I forgot that I have to take care of those things myself now." The bait had been dropped. He waited for her to snap at it. After a moment's hesitation, she did.

"Why don't you let me get you a room here, Joe? Then you won't have to bother looking for a place."

"Well, I don't know, Madge. I don't—"

"Look, I'll tell you what—I'll go down to the desk and get you a room, and then go down the street to Jasi's and get a pizza and some cold beer. You can lay down and rest while I'm gone; then when I get back, we can eat right here in the room. You look tired, Joe. Why don't you take off your coat and lay down for a while?''

''Well, I am pretty tired. First bus ride in ten years, you know.''

''You just rest, Joe.'' She picked up her purse quickly. ''I'll only be a couple minutes.''

When she was gone, he took off his coat and stretched out on the bed. It won't be long now, he thought. Five minutes from now she'll be in a phone booth. Maxie should be here by eight o'clock.

Madge returned an hour later with the food. Kedzie pulled a small writing desk up to the bed and put the pizza on it. He sat down on the side of the bed and began to eat. Madge opened two cans of beer and brought them to the table. She drew up a chair opposite him and sat down.

Kedzie ate sparingly and left half the beer in the can. He was not accustomed to highly seasoned food, much less alcohol. Later, when he had his money, he would eat only of the best.

It was nearly seven when they finished eating. Kedzie lighted a cigarette and walked over to the open window and the lights of Main Street.

Madge walked over and stood beside him. ''What are you thinking about, Joe?'' she asked.

''Just the lights, down there—how many times I dreamed about them while I was in the Joint.''

''Was it really bad, Joe—all those years?'' Her voice was gentle, sincere. It was a tone that Joe Kedzie did not accept coming from her.

''No,'' he said sarcastically, ''it was a hell of a lot of fun. I wanted to stay, but they wouldn't let me. Said you had to leave when your time was up.''

Once again he saw the anger flash in her eyes. He didn't care. She had served her purpose as far as he was concerned, for she had told Maxie where to find him.

"You always were like that, Joe!" she said hotly. "Always crawling into your shell, always keeping everything to yourself, never trusting anybody. You haven't changed a bit in ten years!"

He looked at her coldly, feeling the urge to slam his fist into her face. He wanted to tell her he hadn't grown stupid in ten years, that he wasn't so blind he hadn't figured out she and Maxie had caused him to fall after the payroll job. He wanted to scream out to her that he had thought about that possibility even before the job. He wanted to let her know the reason they hadn't pulled off their little double cross completely was because he had figured out another hiding place for the money beforehand, had put it in a place only he knew about.

Kedzie was at the point of cursing her, when a knock sounded at the door. A moment's hesitation, apprehension, and Madge walked over to the door, and opened it.

For the second time that day, Joe Kedzie looked upon a face he had not seen in ten years. Maxie had not changed much. He still looked like what he was—a sharpie. You can spot a guy like him anywhere, thought Kedzie. Handsome, always smiling, shifty-eyed, overdressed. The kind that's always on the make for a fast buck.

"Hello, Joe-boy," said Maxie, with a false air of friendliness.

"Hello, Maxie." You son of a bitch, thought Kedzie, you took ten years away from me!

Maxie stepped in and closed the door. He walked casually to the bed and sat down. Madge moved to a chair in the corner, away from both men. Kedzie dropped his cigarette out the window and sat back against the sill.

"Heard you were out, Joe-boy," said Maxie. "Thought I better look you up before you left town."

"What makes you think I'm leaving town?" asked Kedzie calmly.

Maxie flashed the wide smile that was his trademark. He leaned back on his elbows. "Just thought you might be heading back toward El Paso. Thought maybe you might have left something around there someplace.''

"The only thing I left in El Paso was a day of glory for the local cops.''

"Nothing else?''

"Nothing that you've got any interest in, buddy.''

Maxie sat up quickly. His jaw tightened and both hands closed into fists. "Look, Joe,'' he said harshly, "I've waited for that dough as long as you have! I've got a right to my share!''

Kedzie remained calm. He casually lighted another cigarette. "The only difference is, Maxie,'' he said easily, "is that you waited outside while I waited inside.''

"That's the breaks, Joe.'' Maxie stood up. His face was serious, challenging. "The money's still only half yours.''

Kedzie looked down at the floor. There was a hundred thousand dollars riding on this play. There was no sense in risking it all with Maxie at this late date. He thought of the tail that had followed him from prison, that had expected to be taken right to the dough; the trouble he'd had throwing the tail clear off the track. After all that, it made sense to play it easy for a while longer.

"I'll lay it on the line for you, Maxie,'' he said. "I figure I'm entitled to that dough more than you. I figure I've earned it by taking the rap for the job. So I don't intend to split that package with you or anybody else.''

Anger showed plainly on Maxie's face. Got to make it good, thought Kedzie. If this doesn't work I'll have to kill him right now, right here. He continued talking.

"The only thing that's holding me back is that I need a stake to get to the dough. I need some cash—a couple of hundred at least— and a car. I want some clothes, so I can get out of this burlap I'm wearing.''

Maxie's anger had clearly changed from anger to curiosity. It's working, thought Kedzie.

"I'll make a deal with you,'' Kedzie went on. "You get me a car, a couple of hundred bucks, and some decent clothes, and I'll cut you in for a quarter of the dough. You'll get twenty-five grand, no strings attached. How about it?''

Maxie looked thoughtfully at Kedzie, thinking that it wouldn't be easy to force Kedzie to tell him where the money was hidden.

"I'll go along with that, Joe-boy," he said, and added quickly, "—but only on one condition.''

"Name it,'' said Kedzie.

"I stay with you every minute from here on out, and we go for the money together.''

"How about the car,'' asked Kedzie, "and the other things?''

"I'll fix it so Madge can get everything you want. You and me will stay right here in this room until we're ready to go for the money.''

"It's a deal,'' said Kedzie. "And if you can get what I need to-night, we'll leave in the morning.''

"The sooner the better.'' Maxie grinned eagerly. "Madge can go out and rent a car tonight. On the way back she can stop at my place and pick up clothes for you.''

"How about the two hundred?''

Maxie smiled. "I've got three bills in my pocket right now. A long shot came in at Hollywood Park today. So we're all set, Joe-boy. Two days from now we can be in El Paso.''

It was Joe Kedzie's turn to smile. "We're not going to El Paso, partner,'' he said slyly. "Surprised?''

Maxie's grin vanished, and suspicion shadowed his face. "What do you mean?'' he asked quickly.

"The dough isn't in El Paso. It's in New Mexico—right out in the middle of nowhere.''

Suddenly Maxie began to laugh, somewhat hysterically. He laughed long and loud. He was thinking of all the hours and days he had spent asking questions in El Paso, trying to follow every move Joe Kedzie had made, trying to trace where Kedzie had hidden the money.

Joe Kedzie also began to laugh, but he was not thinking about the past, only the future.

* * *

At ten minutes before eight the next morning, Joe Kedzie and Maxie walked out of the Main Line Hotel onto Main Street. Kedzie had shed the rough gray suit the prison had discharged him in, and now wore slacks and a short-sleeve sport shirt. On his arm he held one of Maxie's sport coats. Maxie, following him, carried a small tan suitcase with their extra clothes.

They walked down the block to a green Ford sedan Madge had rented for them. Maxie unlocked the car and tossed the suitcase on the backseat.

"You drive," said Kedzie. "I don't have a license." Maxie nodded and slid behind the wheel. He turned the ignition on and started the motor. Before he could shift into gear, Kedzie spoke again. "How about the two hundred, Maxie?"

Maxie looked at him oddly. "I've got it," he said flatly.

"Give it to me," said Kedzie.

Maxie shook his head in anger and disgust, but he drew a wallet from his inside coat pocket and counted out two hundred dollars in tens and twenties. He tossed the bills, with a display of anger, on the seat between them. Kedzie gathered them up, folded them neatly in half, and put them in his shirt pocket.

They drove out to Sunset Boulevard, then swung onto the Ramona Freeway. Kedzie sat back and relaxed, feeling fresh and invigorated on his first free morning in ten years. He ignored Maxie completely and interested himself in looking out the window at the stores and the cars and the girls.

The car sped along, through Monterey Park, Covina, past Pomona, and on into San Bernardino. By eleven o'clock they had reached Indio. They stopped for gas and Kedzie got out and picked up a road map. They left Indio on Route 99, heading south.

At one o'clock they pulled into El Centro. Maxie stopped at the first highway restaurant outside town and they went in and ordered lunch. Kedzie borrowed a pencil from the waitress and spread the road map out on the table. He began to figure their mileage. When he was finished, he said, "It's a little over three hundred to Tucson. If we drive straight through, we should make it by nine tonight."

"How far do we have to go past Tucson?" asked Maxie irritably.

"Not far," said Kedzie.

"I asked how far," said Maxie.

"Getting anxious, Maxie?" Joe Kedzie asked, smiling.

Maxie cursed as he got up from the table. He went over to a pinball machine and dropped a coin into it. Kedzie watched him, thinking, If you'd spent the last ten years where I did, rat, you'd have more patience.

They pulled into Tucson, tired and dirty, at nine-fifteen that night. All along the highway they saw NO VACANCY signs lighting their path. Finally, five miles past the eastern city limits, they found a motel room.

Maxie registered at the office, and they dropped the suitcase off at the room. Then they drove back into Tucson for something to eat. It was nearly midnight when they returned to the motel and went to bed.

By eight o'clock the next morning, they were on the road again. Kedzie decided he'd take a chance and drive; he was tired of just sitting. Fifty miles southeast of Tucson, they turned off onto Route 666 and headed north. The highway made a wide, sweeping arc around the Dos Cabezas mountain range, then swung south again. Shortly before eleven o'clock they crossed the state line into New Mexico. The first road sign they saw said: LORDSBURG 20 MILES.

"We're about there," said Kedzie casually. "It's about an hour's drive after we pass Lordsburg." Maxie grunted. "We'll have to stop in Lordsburg," continued Kedzie. "There's some things I have to buy."

Maxie glanced at him suspiciously. "Like what, for instance?" he asked irritably.

"Like a long piece of rope, for instance."

"What the hell do we need a rope for?" demanded Maxie.

"You want the money, don't you? Well, we'll need a rope to

get it. The package is at the bottom of a forty-foot well that must've gone dry a long time ago.''

Maxie's mouth dropped open. ''Well, I'll be damned!''

''We'll need some other things, too—a flashlight, maybe a small shovel in case we have to do some digging. I guess a couple of feet of sand could have blown down that well in all this time.''

In Lordsburg they stopped at the first large General Store they came to. Inside, Kedzie asked the clerk for sixty feet of strong rope. The clerk led him into the storeroom and showed him several large bolts of rope. Kedzie picked out the sturdiest he could find, and the clerk began to measure off sixty feet. Kedzie walked back out into the store and picked up a small hand shovel from a display rack. He handed it to Maxie. When the clerk brought the heavy roll of rope out, Kedzie took this, too, and handed it to Maxie.

''Put this stuff in the car,'' he said easily. ''I'll get a flashlight and be right out.''

Maxie turned and carried the things out of the store. After Kedzie had picked out a flashlight and batteries, he walked across the room to a glass showcase. He appeared casual as he looked over the merchandise. When the clerk approached him, he said, ''Let's see one of those target pistols.''

The clerk opened the case and took out a medium-size, black automatic pistol. ''This is the Sports Standard,'' he said, going into his sales pitch. ''One of the best made. Only weighs half a pound. Shoots twenty-two-caliber shorts or longs. A real accurate piece for targets or small game.''

''How much for this one?'' asked Kedzie.

''That's the six-and-three-quarter barrel. It'll run you forty-four-fifty plus tax.''

''Okay,'' said Kedzie quickly, glancing toward the front door. ''Give me a box of shells, too, and then figure up the whole bill.''

Outside, Maxie closed the door of the car and walked back to the store to see what was keeping Kedzie. When he looked through the window, he saw Kedzie forcing bullets into a magazine. A new target pistol lay on the counter before him. Maxie's face turned white and his hands began to tremble. He watched Kedzie shove the loaded magazine into the grip of the weapon and tuck the gun in his belt, and under his shirt.

Maxie turned and walked back to the car, feeling sick. He opened the door and slid under the wheel. He looked at the dashboard. Kedzie had done all the driving that morning; he had the car keys. He knows, thought Maxie helplessly. He knows I fingered him after the payroll job and now he's going to kill me for it. He never meant to give me a split of the dough. The whole deal was a trick to get me out here so he could kill me!

Suddenly a thought occurred to Maxie, a possible way out.

He turned in the seat and looked back at the rope and shovel lying on the floorboard. Quickly he reached back and opened the suitcase. He fumbled through the soiled clothing and drew out his shaving kit. His hands shook as he unzipped the case.

When Kedzie got back to the car, he found Maxie sitting calmly behind the wheel. He got in and handed Maxie the car keys. "Take Route 80," he said, "south out of town and keep going until I tell you where to turn."

The highway ran in an almost straight line past Lordsburg. It was a thin gray streak surrounded on either side by dry, flat land. The brilliant sun overhead moved up to a point directly in the center of the sky as the noon hour approached. It cast its heat down onto the sands of the Hidalgo country and made all living creatures look for shade. By twelve o'clock the temperature had risen to a hundred and one.

Inside the car, Joe Kedzie sat sideways with one hand inside his shirt and against the cold metal of the gun. Maxie kept his eyes straight ahead, squinting against the sun. They moved along in silence, passing no other traffic. Kedzie had also taken this into account in his plan. It was common in the desert for people to avoid being out in the noonday heat. Kedzie had counted on having the desert all to themselves.

A half-hour later, they passed a wide place in the road called

Separ. Kedzie had remembered that name for ten years—had kept it in his mind by spelling it backward; what it spelled backward made it easier to remember.

"You'll come to a turn in the road up ahead," he said. "About three miles past that is where we turn off. First road on the right."

Maxie didn't answer. He had not spoken a word since Lordsburg. When they came to the road Kedzie had indicated, he turned off the highway. The blacktop was pitted, rough. Maxie looked at Kedzie for instructions. "Just keep going," said Kedzie. "It's not far now."

They bumped along for eight miles. The terrain around them began to rise slightly in places, forming low knolls and finally small hills. Kedzie watched the mileage dial intently, glancing ahead from time to time for familiar landmarks. Finally he saw the old dirt road cutting off at an angle from the blacktop. "Turn there," he said, pointing ahead.

Maxie turned off. The dirt road was smoother than the blacktop had been and the car settled down to a level ride again. The road curved down into a washed-out gully that had once been excavated for mining. Kedzie watched through the rear window until the blacktop passed from sight. Then he turned to Maxie and said, "Pull over, partner."

When the car stopped, Kedzie got out quickly. Maxie stepped out on the driver's side. The two men faced each other across the hood of the car.

"You know, don't you, Joe?" said Maxie simply.

"Yeah, Maxie, I know." Kedzie drew the automatic from beneath his shirt and held it loosely.

"I don't know what made me do it, Joe," began Maxie. "I just—"

"I'll tell you why you did it, rat," interrupted Kedzie harshly. "Two things—Madge and a hundred grand!"

"I don't know what came over me, Joe," continued Maxie desperately. "I just didn't realize—"

"Never mind!" snapped Kedzie. He waved the gun toward the car. "Get that rope and shovel out."

Maxie dragged the heavy rope out, threw it over his shoulder, and picked up the shovel. Kedzie directed him down a narrow path, following a few feet behind. The path ended at the entrance to a mine shaft that was near the gully bottom. Twenty feet off to one side was the dry well. It had once been surrounded by a three-foot brick and clay wall, but most of the wall had deteriorated and fallen. Only one beam remained of a pair that once had held a small roof over the then-precious supply of water. The wheel that had raised and lowered a bucket now lay broken and rotted in the dust.

"There it is, Judas," said Kedzie sardonically. "That's Joe Kedzie's private bank."

Maxie stopped and half turned when Kedzie spoke. "Keep walking," warned Kedzie, raising the gun. Maxie resumed his pace. Kedzie lowered the gun again.

When Maxie got to the edge of the well, he dropped the rope to the ground. For a moment he stood staring down into the deep hole; his right hand gripped the small shovel tightly. Suddenly he whirled and hurled the shovel at Joe Kedzie's face.

Kedzie stepped easily aside and the shovel slammed into the wall of the mine shaft. He laughed and said, "Nice try, rat." Then he leveled the target pistol and pulled the trigger.

The bullet struck Maxie in his stomach. He stumbled back, grasping the wound with both hands, but did not fall. Kedzie fired a second time, and a third. Both bullets smashed into Maxie's chest. He fell backward, dropping headfirst into the well.

Kedzie stuck the gun in his belt and walked slowly to the edge of the well. He calmly lighted a cigarette, then took out the flashlight and directed its beam into the dark pit. The well was so deep that the beam failed to reach the bottom.

When he had finished his cigarette, Kedzie bent down and picked up the rope. He dragged one end to a large boulder, around which he wrapped it securely, tying it. Then he walked back to the well and dropped the rest of the rope into the blackness. He heard a thud as it struck bottom.

Carefully, he sat down on the well's edge and began to lower himself into the hole. He braced his feet flat against the wall, arching his body, descending one cautious step at a time. Soon the darkness of the well surrounded him. He edged farther and farther below the surface.

The rope snapped just before his feet reached the halfway mark. Kedzie screamed; the darkness rushed up past him for a fleeting second; then he slammed into the hard ground at the bottom.

He rolled over, dazed, his head spinning. He reached out in the darkness and felt the wall. His body ached all over and his head was beating wildly. The rope had fallen on top of him and was tangled around him. He pulled it away from his body and forced himself up into a sitting position. As he leaned back against the wall of the well, he felt very sick. For a moment he thought he was going to faint. He sat very still and sucked in deep breaths of air to calm himself.

It's all right, he thought over and over again, it's all right. I can get back up without the rope. The well isn't too wide. I can brace my feet against one side and my back against the other and I can work my way back up. It'll be hard and it'll take awhile, but I can do it. I can make it back up without a rope. I can make it.

He rested for a moment until the nausea passed, then fumbled in his pocket for the flashlight. He felt pain, too, but the excitement of his fall and of his predicament did not allow him to dwell on it. He was relieved when he switched on the flashlight and saw that the fall had not damaged it. He found the piece of rope that had fallen with him, gathered it up until he had the broken end. He was puzzled that such a strong rope would break under so little weight. He examined the end carefully under the light. Only a few strands, he saw, had been torn apart. The rest had been neatly and evenly cut—and on an angle so that it could not be easily noticed.

Maxie was the only other person who had handled the rope. He must have cut it while he had been in the car alone!

Kedzie flashed the light around until it shined on Maxie's face. He cursed the dead man aloud. Then he laughed. It won't work,

Maxie, he thought. I can still make it. I can still get out—rope or no rope!

Kedzie pushed himself to his feet. Excruciating pain shot up through his right leg, and he fell back to the ground moaning. He tried again, staggered, and fell a second time. He groaned in agony. The pain in his leg was unbearable. Desperately he twisted into a sitting position again and drew up his trouser leg. He shined the light on his leg and saw that the flesh between his knee and ankle was split apart and that a jagged bone protruded through the opening.

He leaned back against the wall, feeling fear well up in his body and overshadow the pain. His hand dropped to the ground beside him and he felt a hard, square object. He shined the flashlight down on it and saw the plastic-wrapped package he had dreamed of for ten years. Tears ran down his face and he began to tremble. Suddenly he grabbed up the package, swore. To hell with his broken leg, Maxie hadn't beat him yet out of that hundred grand. He had one good leg; he'd make it out of there.

Clutching the package, Kedzie worked his back up the wall in an attempt to get upright. He made it, panting hard, sweating. Now he had to shift his weight onto his broken leg. He waited a moment before trying, waiting for his breathing to still.

Terrific pain knifed through him the instant he tried to place a little bit of his weight on his broken leg. He fell to the ground in pain and despair. He still held to the package, but the flashlight had fallen from his hand, its beam of light unextinguished and directed straight along the ground to Maxie's face.

The way it looked to Kedzie, the dead man was smiling at him.

"Enough Rope for Two." *Alfred Hitchcock Presents,* November 17, 1957. Directed by Paul Henreid. Teleplay by Joel Murcott, based on Clark Howard's short story "Enough Rope for Two" *(Manhunt,* February 1957). With Steven Hill (Joe), Jean Hagen (Madge), Steve Brodie (Maxie).

This was the first short story I ever sold to television. It was the eighteenth story I had written, the fifth I had sold. When it appeared on Sunday night in prime time, I was thrilled to see that its stars were Steven Hill, Jean Hagen, and

Steve Brodie. Not only that, but the segment had been directed by Paul Henreid, a longtime favorite actor of mine who had recently moved behind the camera. As I watched the show, I was pleased to see that the scriptwriter not only followed the original story very closely, but also used a great deal of the dialogue I had written. The only major change was that the female role had been expanded for Jean Hagen, who was a popular TV star at the time *(Make Room for Daddy)*. All in all, this first adaptation of a story of mine for television was a thoroughly pleasant experience.

                                                                    Clark Howard

LAWRENCE TREAT

Suburban Tigress

MARGOT SLIPPED OFF HER SHOES and rubbed her toes against the stiff, braided edging of her chair. She'd fixed a tray with a couple of sandwiches and a glass of milk, and she was curled up next to the telephone, dreaming a little, nibbling at a sandwich and waiting for Lewis to call.

She was certain he would; he'd want to tell her he'd gotten the appointment. Special investigator in charge of the bribery investigation. It would be Lewis's first big step into the limelight.

She closed her eyes and thought of what the adoption agency had said last week. She and Lewis were of good character, with an adequate income. There remained only a final interview, and a few formalities. "I'm sure there's no scandal or moral turpitude in your background," the social worker had said, smiling.

Margot kept wondering whether the baby had been born yet, what sex it would be, how she'd feel when she first held it. I'm like an expectant mother, she thought, sensitive and edgy, full of secret little fears.

She opened her eyes, and the microphone of Lewis's tape recorder was in her line of vision. The machine was in the next room, but he liked to dictate here, talking into the microphone that had been built into the radio cabinet.

At breakfast, he'd said, "I've got some stuff on that I want to finish tonight," in the course of telling her how busy he was.

She had an impulse to flick the switch and play the tape back, just to hear his voice. Or maybe she'd talk nonsense into it, about Lewis and herself—about the baby. How she felt, what she hoped for.

Why was she so jittery?

At the sound of a motor outside, she put on her shoes and stood up. She was tall and slim and serene, with lips that curved softly. Her dark eyes were quiet, but they held a suggestion of deep, obstinate turbulence.

She walked to the window and saw the truck parked at the beginning of the driveway, near the street. A light delivery truck, painted green. On the side of it was the name, "Jack Staley, Plumbing and Heating, 483 East Bay Street."

She went back to her tray, took a sip of milk, and glanced hopefully at the phone. But it was the front doorbell that rang.

On opening the door, her first impression was astonishment. Jack Staley was a jovial, husky man, and he laughed with the full exuberance of bursting health. His cheeks were red, round and padded, and his eyes alive with vitality. He was wearing a beige sport shirt.

"Mrs. Brenner?" he said. His hoarse, tenor voice seemed to challenge her. "You called up about a leak?"

She hesitated, catching some subtle, hidden threat. The phrase, *like an expectant mother,* crossed her mind again. She realized she was being absurd. She was here in her own home with a telephone in the living room and with neighbors next door. Nothing could be safer.

"Why, yes," she said, in her slow, soothing voice. "Down in the cellar."

"Fine," he said. He picked up his canvas kit of tools. "Just show me, huh?"

"This way," she said. But she was vaguely disturbed as she opened the door to the cellar stairs, switched on the light, and went down.

He followed, and he kept talking. "Nice place you got, Mrs. Brenner. Lots of people would have ripped out them boulders in front, but you got it fixed nice. I always did go for a rock garden. What's the name of that stuff with the reddish leaves, just off the path?"

"That's my ajuga," she said.

She kept listening for the phone. If it rang, she'd excuse herself and answer it immediately. She'd know if it was Lewis, she could always tell from the sound. Just as she knew Lewis would get the appointment. She had no doubts.

She stopped in front of the furnace and pointed. "There," she said. "In that space behind. You can see the puddle."

Staley nodded cheerfully. "Sure, I'll take care of that. You know where the turn-off valve is?"

"No," she said. He was standing too close to her, grinning down at her, and she tensed up. Alone here in the cellar with him, she thought. I don't like it.

She slipped past him, barely touching his shirt, and she cringed at the contact. She could feel his big, cavernous chest inflate. He laughed.

"I'll be upstairs," she said in a low voice.

She almost ran. Her heart was pounding, and she panted. She was silly for feeling as she did, just because a plumber wore a beige sport shirt and laughed. But there could be danger; the things that were in her mind did happen.

She saw her tray on the telephone table, and she sat down. I can always call the police, she told herself. And I'll stay here, next to the phone. Lewis should be calling.

She picked up her sandwich, put it down. She wasn't hungry anymore. She took a few sips of milk, but had no taste for it either.

She brought the tray to the kitchen, dumped the remnants of the sandwich in the garbage pail, and turned on the hot water. She was glad that she'd left the breakfast dishes.

With a tense eagerness, she kept listening for the phone.

Maybe that was why her hands trembled a little. Maybe that was why a glass slipped and broke.

She finished the dishes and went back to the living room. She hadn't heard the plumber come upstairs, yet there he was standing in front of the fireplace. He was smoking, and staring at the Maine woods picture that she'd done last year. Her signature in the corner was neat and legible.

"That's pretty nice," he said. "You painted it, huh?"

"Yes," she said. "Thank you." She was polite, and she pretended it was perfectly natural for him to take possession of the room and discuss her painting.

"Say," he said, "you're all right. Talent, looks. I bet you got brains, too."

"I thought you were fixing the leak," she said stiffly.

"Just hanging around while the pipe drains," he said. "You got a Manson valve on it, for safety, and it takes a little time. I got to go up and turn the valve in the bathroom, too. Been waiting for you to show me."

"You have to go upstairs," she said, "to fix a leak in the cellar?"

He nodded, and he smiled with superior knowledge. "Sure. With a Manson valve, you got to equalize the pressure. That's the trouble with 'em, but otherwise they're good. Without one of them, your cellar would have been flooded out." He grinned. "You got any more of your paintings in here?"

"No," she said. "And the bathroom's upstairs, through the bedroom on your right."

He tamped out his cigarette. "Sure," he said. "I'll find it."

"Maybe I'd better show you."

She didn't like the idea of leaving him alone upstairs. She went up swiftly, entered the bedroom and pointed to the bath. "There," she said.

He merely looked around the bedroom and admired it. "Say," he said, "you got real good taste. Wallpaper, furniture—the works. Now me, I didn't get educated too good, but I got an artistic side. Them pictures on the wall—you paint them too?"

"Yes."

He studied them with a kind of awe. "Well, whadda you know! A real artist. I always wanted to meet an artist. I'm just a plumber, the guy they make jokes about. But I got appreciation, huh?"

In a way Margot felt flattered, but she was uneasy. She still shrank from offending him directly. She tried to convince herself that he was merely a character, bluff and hearty and unpolished. An overgrown boy who meant no harm.

"Everyone has appreciation," she said, "but most people are untrained and don't really see things."

He nodded vigorously. "Yeah," he said. "That's it. A lot of people go through life with their eyes closed. But me—you'd be surprised what I see."

He rolled his big shoulders under the beige shirt. Then he stepped to the bed and picked up a corner of the patchwork quilt with the pink and gold design. As he touched it, she felt numb.

"Please," she said sharply.

He looked up. He was still holding the corner of the quilt. Slowly, as if he thoroughly understood her meaning, his smile faded into a dark sullenness. Then, just as slowly, the darkness went and the grin returned.

"How much do you pay for a thing like this?"

"I thought you wanted to fix the valve," she said.

He shrugged. "I'm just friendly," he said. "Like a big, friendly dog. And I guess I got too much curiosity. That's what they tell me, anyhow. And you know what I answer? I say you got to have curiosity to be a good plumber."

She just stared at him. She felt as if he were desecrating something. The stocky, grinning man; the broad, thick hands rubbing the corner of the quilt; the words spilling out of him . . .

"Yeah," he said. "I talk too much. But don't pay no attention. I'm just naturally friendly. If everybody in the world was like that, it would be pretty good, huh? Love thy neighbor. I guess I was born loving—everybody."

She tried to stare him down. He merely took her stare and enjoyed it.

"You got nice eyes," he said. But he didn't approach her. Not yet.

He noticed her red slippers with the fluffy white pompons, and he stooped down to touch them. "Style," he said. His blunt fingers caressed a slipper, and she blushed crimson.

"Please put it down," she said.

He paid no attention. "I got an old pair of slippers I been wearing every night for ten years. They're all wore out, but you get fond of a slipper. It gets so it means something."

He crushed the fragile toe in his big, chunky hand. "Thread's ripped along the edge," he observed. Then he dropped the slipper. It hit the floor with a soft thud. "You look scared," he said.

She lifted her head to convey defiance and said coldly, "Please tend to your work."

He stiffened, opened the drawer of the night table, shoved it shut. He did it a couple of times, automatically, before he moved forward. She felt the attack coming, foresaw it in all its horror. She sidled toward the doorway, ready to dash down the stairs and run out screaming.

"I was just shooting my big mouth off, like usual," he said. "I better get busy, huh?"

He went into the bathroom.

She started listening for the telephone again. She wondered whether to call Anne Warren. Anne could be over in a couple of minutes. Between the two of them, they'd be safe.

But it seemed foolish. He hadn't done anything. He was just a character. He talked, and the rest was in her mind. Nevertheless, she wasn't at all sure that she'd convinced herself.

When he came out, he drove her down the stairs ahead of him. She held onto the bannister. Behind her, he was speaking. Pictures, art, the patchwork quilt. Some kind of a valve.

She turned to the safety of the telephone, planting herself next to it, thinking it extremely odd that Lewis hadn't called.

The plumber poked his head through the doorway and said, "I'm going down to the cellar, Mrs. Brenner."

"Yes," she said.

Why had he told her that? Was he inviting her to follow? She tried to remember what she'd read about sex maniacs. They were normal until something set them off. They committed minor nuisances. They acted queerly—admiring her art would come under that heading. Then something broke, and there were headlines.

Lewis, she thought. Lewis, please, why don't you call?

She lost all sense of time. The plumber came up the cellar stairs, walked through the living room, lit a cigarette. He mentioned something he had to do.

To escape him, she went into the kitchen and made herself a cup of tea. She drank it too hot and scalded her lips. She put the cup down and walked with a display of determination to the telephone. She heard Staley banging away lustily, in the cellar.

She felt baffled. She couldn't ask him to leave in the middle of a job, with the water turned off. She couldn't call the police, there was nothing to tell them. And phoning Lewis was out of the question.

Anne? But Margot felt that Lewis must certainly be about to call her, and she didn't want to block the line, even for a moment.

The phone did not ring. Some time after four, the plumber came into the living room.

"All fixed," he said, rubbing his hands. "You want to pay now?"

"Yes," she said, standing up. She was only too glad to settle, and get rid of him. "How much?"

"Five hundred dollars."

Very slowly, she said, "What?" Her heart seemed to freeze, and his purpose began to dawn on her.

"Five hundred dollars," he repeated. "Look—you wouldn't want people to hear about it, would you?"

She gripped the back of the chair. "Hear about—what?" she whispered.

"Us. Upstairs. The patchwork quilt, the red slippers with the worn thread, the stuff you keep in the night table. How would I know all about that, huh?''

"This is extortion," she said, "and it's ridiculous."

"Look—I fixed up a leak that takes five minutes to repair. My truck's outside there, where everybody can see. Been there three hours. You and me, we're in here alone. Maybe somebody calls. No answer."

He grinned and moved toward the phone. She stepped out of his way and watched him stoop and pull a thick wad of paper from the phone bell. She remembered how she'd found him here just after she'd washed the dishes. He'd done it then. That was why the phone hadn't rung all afternoon.

Lewis. Lewis had undoubtedly tried to get her.

Staley showed her the wad of paper. He licked his lips and said, almost dreamily, "Maybe somebody phoned. It just rang and rang and rang."

"I'll call the police," she said.

"Go ahead. But Mrs. Warren didn't. And Mrs. Herzog and Mrs. Forbes didn't. They figured they'd end up paying off the cop, too."

Anne Warren? she thought. And Rhoda Forbes? Then he's done this before. He planned it from the beginning.

"My husband's a lawyer," she said in a low, angry voice. "I'll tell him."

The plumber threw back his heavy shoulders and laughed. She realized exactly what he meant. He was big, powerful, and he knew all the angles.

Margot closed her eyes and pressed her fingers against her forehead. She thought of what the adoption service would say. "We're sorry about the trouble, Mrs. Brenner, but—" And yet, every fiber of her being rebelled at the idea of blackmail. She simply refused to be victimized. Or to saddle Lewis with the problem, which might cause him to lose his coveted appointment.

"I won't give you a cent," she said, and her eyes widened with her anger.

"You're asking for it," Staley said. "You want to get sued for damages, on account I slipped and fell in the upstairs bathroom and hurt my back? While I was getting dressed.''

She gasped. "You wouldn't dare!''

"Try me," he said. "And remember, I know this game. I do it about once a week. Twenty-five G's a year, tax free. I'd love to go to court and describe your quilt and slippers and stuff, when I was supposed to fix a leak in the cellar. And think of the worry and disgrace for a sensitive type like you. I hear you're trying to adopt a kid, too.''

She sat down heavily with a jolt. "I don't have five hundred dollars," she said feebly.

"Get it.''

"I—I can't. I don't have a checking account. My husband handles everything.''

The lie was too transparent. Staley said, "Don't ask me to swallow that one.''

She kept shaking her head. "I can't. I won't. I tell you, I just won't.''

"Think it over," he said serenely. "You're a little upset now, that's natural. The trouble is, you should have thought about it before you took me upstairs.''

"You're perfectly contemptible," she said, and trembled violently.

"I'll tell you what," he said. "I'll give you till tomorrow to get the dough. Time to get used to the idea, huh? In the morning, after the banks are open.''

He strode past her. The door slammed, a motor started up, a truck pulled out of the driveway. She leaned back in her chair and felt faint.

When the five-forty-two came in, she was at the station. Anne Warren was there and Rhoda Forbes was there, and they smiled and looked happy and talked about the new supermarket. Margot saw that you could pay a blackmailer and keep on with a normal life.

But not she.

She saw Lewis on the steps of the second car, as usual, and she saw his long, sharp face seeking her out. She waved, and then she went running to him and threw her arms around him.

"You did, didn't you?" she said. "Lewis—you got it!"

"Of course," he said, smiling. "But how did you find out?"

"I just knew," she said. "It had to be."

"Well, you might have been home so I could let you know." She linked her arm in his. "I was home. Did you call?"

"Did I!" he said. He opened the car door for her, climbed in on the other side and turned on the motor. "I called you at one-thirty, the minute after I heard from the governor. There was no answer, so I told Mary to neglect letters she was doing for me and to keep trying. She worked on it until after four."

"Well, the plumber came, and I had to go down in the cellar and show him what had to be done."

"And that took all afternoon?" Lewis said, teasing her.

"Oh, no." She swallowed hard. She had to lie. "Later on I was in the garden, and then I took a dress to the cleaner's."

"A nice, peaceful day," he said. "Can see it was by just the way you look. The beautiful Margot Brenner, who stokes the home fires with her own quiet magic." This was all part of his jubilation over his appointment. Then he said, "Did he fix the leak?"

"Oh, yes," she said. "It wasn't much."

As soon as Lewis had left the house the following morning, Margot called the police department. She explained briefly that she was being blackmailed and would like a police witness to the payment. She said the story against her was trumped up, and that she could prove it. Then she went to the bank.

When she returned home, a tall, ruddy man was waiting for her. He showed her his badge and announced that he was Detective Thompson. She brought him into the living room. Over a cup of coffee, she told him what had happened.

"Staley?" he said in surprise. "I didn't know he went in for that kind of stuff."

"Well, he does," she said curtly. "You'll see."

"Okay. Let me mark the money, so I can prove he got it from

you. I'll sit behind the kitchen door. Just keep your voice up, and try to bring him over to this side of the room so I can hear good.''

About twenty minutes later, Margot heard a car, and through the window she saw the green panel truck. She thought of the role she had to play, and her heart hammered with great, thudding strokes. She had trouble walking.

She brought Staley to the corner of the room near the kitchen door, and she picked up the money. She had to draw a long, deep breath and then exhale it before she could speak. She phrased her words carefully.

"Here," she said. "I decided to pay you your blackmail. To avoid the nuisance."

Staley looked surprised. "Lady, I don't get it."

"You asked for five hundred dollars," she said. Her nervousness was so apparent that she wanted to cry. "Here."

He didn't touch the money. "Look," he said, "you don't have to be scared. You had a weak moment, sweetheart, but don't worry. Our little secret's safe."

"But you said—"

He waved her aside, and he gave her a big broad grin. "Look," he said, "I'm just a plumber. I'd feel funny taking all that dough. If I get a big medical bill, on account of my back, you probably got insurance to cover it, regular and proper. But I wouldn't bother *you.*"

She gasped. The door opened and Detective Thompson came in.

"Hello, Staley," he said, "I've been in there, listening. This lady claims you tried to get five hundred dollars out of her. Extortion, she says. What's the story?"

Staley shrugged and rubbed his foot on the carpet. "It's just one of those things," he said. "Between me and the lady."

"How about her charge?"

Staley grunted. "Hell," he said. "Forget it."

The detective turned to Margot. "Can I call your husband about all this?"

"No, no, you mustn't! He—I—'' She broke off, aghast, realizing that the detective now believed Staley's story.

After she watched the two men leave together, she sat down on the couch and dug her nails into her palms. Now that the police believed Staley, they wouldn't help her. And if the matter should come to court, the detective's evidence would damn her.

She was sick with exasperation. Her nervousness had given her away; she'd been too tense, too obvious in leading Staley across the room. He'd guessed immediately. She was shy, timid, inept, and unable to cope with a real problem.

Nevertheless, she rejected the idea of telling Lewis. This was her job, her responsibility, and she had to assume it. And deep down, she knew that she was also afraid to tell him.

When the phone rang, she picked it up. Jack Staley's voice said, "Mrs. Brenner? That was a dirty trick you tried to pull. You're going to make me sore."

She answered calmly. "I'll pay whenever you want me to."

"This afternoon," he said. "And no more tricks."

She hung up. After a few moments, she called Anne Warren, then Rhoda Forbes and Myra Herzog. A half hour later, Margot was in the kitchen preparing lunch.

Jack Staley arrived at three. He was still wearing the beige shirt; it was still clean and pressed. "Hello, Mrs. Brenner," he said cheerfully. "I never would have thought it of you. And you an artist."

"Come in," she said.

"Sure. And if it's all the same with you, I'll take a look around."

She nodded nervously and watched him circle the room, look at the microphone in the radio cabinet. "Them tape recorders," he remarked. "Some dame tried that on me once, but she sure landed in the soup." He faced Margot amiably. "Well, let's have it."

"I'm not going to give you the money. I—I've decided to tell the District Attorney."

Staley put his hands on his hips. "Lady, if I got to teach you a lesson, I'll teach it to you good. This is all fixed. You ain't got a chance. Remember?''

"I know the D.A.; he's a friend of my husband's. I'll invite him for dinner and that's when I'll tell him."

"Him?" Staley said, with blistering contempt. "He wouldn't do nothing to me; I got too much on him."

"I don't believe you," Margot said. "And Mrs. Forbes, Mrs. Warren, others—we'll all tell the same story."

Staley's face reddened, and his small, dark eyes went sullen. "Go ahead," he said with repressed anger. "I figured this would happen someday, the bunch of you ganging up on me. So go ahead, but you're going to bust up Mrs. Forbes's home for her, and you wouldn't do that. You're too nice, too soft. You don't hurt people. You can't."

Margot caught her breath. Rhoda Forbes? Had she really been—been involved with him? Or was he bluffing, slashing out with wild, unfounded accusations?

"Soft," he repeated in a singsong voice, and he was smirking.

Her pulses pounded as she retreated slowly until she was pressed against the door of Lewis's study. Behind her back, her hand scratched along the woodwork until she found the knob.

"Every word," she said, in a voice barely above a whisper, "is recorded on tape, in the next room."

"Yeah?" he said, still smirking, not believing her.

She pushed the door open and slipped into the study. Rhoda Forbes, Anne Warren, and Myra Herzog stood in a solid phalanx in front of the recorder. Margot ranged herself alongside them.

Staley halted in his tracks. He said in a hoarse, menacing voice, "Let's have it, and no fuss about it, either."

No one answered him. He took a step forward. "You know damn well I can take it," he said, "so hand it over." His big, rough palm was extended, and his powerful fingers closed slowly into a fist. "Come on," he said, "before I get rough."

They still didn't speak. Four women facing him, all of them nervous, terrified, but resolved to stand up to him.

His hand dropped slowly, and a bead of sweat oozed out on his forehead. "Okay," he said harshly. "Let's call it quits. No more worries, Mrs. Brenner. Give me the tape, and we're even."

"You can't have it," Margot said.

Myra Herzog, short, plump, solid, whispered to Margot. "Make him give us our money back."

Anne Warren plucked Myra's sleeve. "Tell him what we decided about the school."

Staley loomed above Margot. She sensed he was balanced on a knife-edge, uncertain, dangerous, weighing consequences.

"Mr. Staley," she said, and it was as though she were a child reciting something memorized, "we'd like you to contribute your services for the plumbing work on the new preschool nursery. And then we'll promise not to use the tape."

He stepped back in astonishment and gripped the jamb of the doorway. He appeared to be tensing his muscles, getting ready to lunge, but instead he let out a roar of laughter.

"For free?" he exclaimed. "Say, I could tell the paper about that. And the Chamber of Commerce, maybe they give me a scroll, I stick it in the window of the shop. You girls got class; you ought to go in business with me. Man, what publicity I'll get!"

He slapped his hands together with a sound like a shot, spun around, and strutted out. The front door slammed, and a few moments later a motor roared defiantly. But it was all too loud, and it all had the hollowness of bravado.

Margot rubbed her forehead. She felt weak, dizzy, at loose ends, until she noticed the smudge on the doorjamb. "He dirtied it," she said with distaste. "I'd better get a damp cloth, and then I'll make some tea."

At five-forty-two that evening, Margot was waiting on the platform. Next to her were Anne Warren and Rhoda Forbes and Myra Herzog. Their eyes were bright; their mouths were laughing. When the train ground to a stop, they separated and went forward to their husbands.

Margot put her arms around Lewis. "Hello, darling," she said. "Did you have a nice day?"

"Fine. Everybody's been congratulating me. And you?"

"I had some friends over this afternoon, and we had tea."

Lewis chuckled. "Sounds exciting. Anything else?"

She smiled and gave him a quick, impulsive hug. "Yes," she said, "I settled with the plumber."

Then she slipped her arm through Lewis's, and together they walked to the car.

"The Deadly." *Alfred Hitchcock Presents,* December 15, 1957. Directed by Don Taylor. Teleplay by Robert C. Dennis, based on Lawrence Treat's short story "Suburban Tigress" *(Alfred Hitchcock's Mystery Magazine,* July 1957). With Phyllis Thaxter (Margot Brenner), Craig Stevens (Lewis Brenner), Lee Philips (Staley), Frank Gerstle (Police Officer), Anabel Shaw (Rhoda Forbes), Peggy McCay (Myra).

Besides the obvious pleasure of seeing a story of mine acted out on TV and being able to tell everybody, "Sure, I've had stuff on TV," my chief reaction was astonishment. Astonishment that practically all the dialogue was repeated verbatim from my own script, and that all the action had already been limned out in that same story of mine. For which somebody had been paid handsomely. And for which I got nothing. Or at least, nothing extra.

Lawrence Treat

HENRY SLESAR

The Day of
the Execution

WHEN THE JURY FOREMAN STOOD UP and read the verdict, Warren Selvey, the prosecuting attorney, listened to the pronouncement of guilt as if the words were a personal citation of merit. He heard in the foreman's somber tones, not a condemnation of the accused man who shriveled like a burnt match on the courtroom chair, but a tribute to Selvey's own brilliance. *"Guilty as charged . . ."* No, Warren Selvey thought triumphantly, guilty as I've proved. . . .

For a moment, the judge's melancholy eye caught Selvey's and the old man on the bench showed shock at the light of rejoicing that he saw there. But Selvey couldn't conceal his flush of happiness, his satisfaction with his own efforts, with his first major conviction.

He gathered up his documents briskly, fighting to keep his mouth appropriately grim, though it ached to smile all over his thin, brown face. He put his briefcase beneath his arm, and when he turned, faced the buzzing spectators. "Excuse me," he said soberly, and pushed his way through to the exit doors, thinking now only of Doreen.

He tried to visualize her face, tried to see the red mouth that could be hard or meltingly soft, depending on which one of her many moods happened to be dominant. He tried to imagine how she would look when she heard his good news, how her warm body would feel against his, how her arms would encompass him.

But this imagined foretaste of Doreen's delights was interrupted. There were men's eyes seeking his now, and men's hands reaching toward him to grip his hand in congratulation. Garson, the district attorney, smiling heavily and nodding his lion's head in approval of his cub's behavior. Vance, the assistant D.A., grinning with half a mouth, not altogether pleased to see his junior in the spotlight. Reporters too, and photographers, asking for statements, requesting poses.

Once, all this would have been enough for Warren Selvey. This moment, and these admiring men. But now there was Doreen too, and thought of her made him eager to leave the arena of his victory for a quieter, more satisfying reward.

But he didn't make good his escape. Garson caught his arm and steered him into the gray car that waited at the curb.

"How's it feel?" Garson grinned, thumping Selvey's knee as they drove off.

"Feels pretty good," Selvey said mildly, trying for the appearance of modesty. "But, hell, I can't take all the glory, Gar. Your boys made the conviction."

"You don't really mean that." Garson's eyes twinkled. "I watched you through the trial, Warren. You were tasting blood. You were an avenging sword. You put him on the waiting list for the chair, not me."

"Don't say that!" Selvey said sharply. "He was guilty as sin, and you know it. Why, the evidence was clear-cut. The jury did the only thing it could."

"That's right. The way you handled things, they did the only thing they could. But let's face it, Warren. With another prosecutor, maybe they would have done something else. Credit where credit's due, Warren."

Selvey couldn't hold back the smile any longer. It illumined his long, sharp-chinned face, and he felt the relief of having it relax his features. He leaned back against the thick cushion of the car.

"Maybe so," he said. "But I thought he was guilty, and I tried to convince everybody else. It's not just A-B-C evidence that counts, Gar. That's law-school sophistry, you know that. Sometimes you just *feel . . .*"

"Sure." The D.A. looked out of the window. "How's the bride, Warren?"

"Oh, Doreen's fine."

"Glad to hear it. Lovely woman, Doreen."

She was lying on the couch when he entered the apartment. He hadn't imagined this detail of his triumphant homecoming.

He came over to her and she shifted slightly on the couch to let his arms surround her.

He said, "Did you hear, Doreen? Did you hear what happened?"

"I heard it on the radio."

"Well? Don't you know what it means? I've got my conviction. My first conviction, and a big one. I'm no junior anymore, Doreen."

"What will they do to that man?"

He blinked at her, tried to determine what her mood might be. "I asked for the death penalty," he said. "He killed his wife in cold blood. Why should he get anything else?"

"I just asked, Warren." She put her cheek against his shoulder.

"Death is part of the job," he said. "You know that as well as I do, Doreen. You're not holding that against me?"

She pushed him away for a moment, appeared to be deciding whether to be angry. Then she drew him quickly to her, her breath hot and rapid in his ear.

They embarked on a week of celebration. Quiet, intimate celebration, in dim supper clubs and with close acquaintances. It wouldn't do for Selvey to appear publicly gay under the circumstances.

On the evening of the day the convicted Murray Rodman was sentenced to death, they stayed at home and drank hand-warmed

brandy from big glasses. Doreen got drunk and playfully passionate, and Selvey thought he could never be happier. He had
parlayed a mediocre law-school record and an appointment as a
third-class member of the state legal department into a position of
importance and respect. He had married a beautiful, pampered
woman and could make her whimper in his arms. He was proud
of himself. He was grateful for the opportunity Murray Rodman
had given him.

It was on the day of Rodman's scheduled execution that Selvey
was approached by the stooped, gray-haired man with the grease-
spotted hat.

He stepped out of the doorway of a drugstore, his hands shoved
into the pockets of his dirty tweed overcoat, his hat low over his
eyes. He had white stubble on his face.

"Please," he said. "Can I talk to you a minute?"

Selvey looked him over, and put a hand in his pocket for
change.

"No," the man said quickly. "I don't want a handout. I just
want to talk to you, Mr. Selvey."

"You know who I am?"

"Yeah, sure, Mr. Selvey. I read all about you."

Selvey's hard glance softened. "Well, I'm kind of rushed right
now. Got an appointment."

"This is important, Mr. Selvey. Honest to God. Can't we go
someplace? Have coffee maybe? Five minutes is all."

"Why don't you drop me a letter, or come down to the office?
We're on Chambers Street—"

"It's about that man, Mr. Selvey. The one they're executing
tonight."

The attorney examined the man's eyes. He saw how intent and
penetrating they were.

"All right," he said. "There's a coffee shop down the street.
But only five minutes, mind you."

It was almost two-thirty; the lunchtime rush at the coffee shop
was over. They found a booth in the rear, and sat silently while a
waiter cleared the remnants of a hasty meal from the table.

Finally, the old man leaned forward and said, "My name's Arlington, Phil Arlington. I've been out of town, in Florida, else I wouldn't have let things go this far. I didn't see a paper, hear a radio, nothing like that."

"I don't get you, Mr. Arlington. Are you talking about the Rodman trial?"

"Yeah, the Rodman business. When I came back and heard what happened, I didn't know what to do. You can see that, can't you? It hurt me, hurt me bad to read what was happening to that poor man. But I was afraid. You can understand that. I was afraid."

"Afraid of what?"

The man talked to his coffee. "I had an awful time with myself, trying to decide what to do. But then I figured—hell, this Rodman is a young man. What is he, thirty-eight? I'm sixty-four, Mr. Selvey. Which is better?"

"Better for what?" Selvey was getting annoyed; he shot a look at his watch. "Talk sense, Mr. Arlington. I'm a busy man."

"I thought I'd ask your advice." The gray-haired man licked his lips. "I was afraid to go to the police right off; I thought I should ask you. Should I tell them what I did, Mr. Selvey? Should I tell them I killed that woman? Tell me. Should I?"

The world suddenly shifted on its axis. Warren Selvey's hands grew cold around the coffee cup. He stared at the man across from him.

"What are you talking about?" he said. "Rodman killed his wife. We proved that."

"No, no, that's the point. I was hitchhiking east. I got a lift into Wilford. I was walking around town, trying to figure out where to get food, a job, anything. I knocked on this door. This nice lady answered. She didn't have no job, but she gave me a sandwich. It was a ham sandwich."

"What house? How do you know it was Mrs. Rodman's house?"

"I know it was. I seen her picture, in the newspapers. She was a nice lady. If she hadn't walked into that kitchen after, it would have been okay.''

"What, what?'' Selvey snapped.

"I shouldn't have done it. I mean, she was real nice to me, but I was so broke. I was looking around the jars in the cupboard. You know how women are; they're always hiding dough in the jars, house money they call it. She caught me at it and got mad. She didn't yell or anything, but I could see she meant trouble. That's when I did it, Mr. Selvey. I went off my head.''

"I don't believe you,'' Selvey said. "Nobody saw any— anybody in the neighborhood. Rodman and his wife quarreled all the time—''

The gray-haired man shrugged. "I wouldn't know anything about that, Mr. Selvey. I don't know anything about those people. But that's what happened, and that's why I want your advice.'' He rubbed his forehead. "I mean, if I confess now, what would they do to me?''

"Burn you,'' Selvey said coldly. "Burn you instead of Rodman. Is that what you want?''

Arlington paled. "No. Prison, okay. But not that.''

"Then just forget about it. Understand me, Mr. Arlington? I think you dreamed the whole thing, don't you? Just think of it that way. A bad dream. Now get back on the road and forget it.''

"But that man. They're killing him tonight—''

"Because he's guilty.'' Selvey's palm hit the table. "I *proved* him guilty. Understand?''

The man's lip trembled.

"Yes, sir,'' he said.

Selvey got up and tossed a five on the table.

"Pay the bill,'' he said curtly. "Keep the change.''

That night, Doreen asked him the hour for the fourth time.

"Eleven,'' he said sullenly.

"Just another hour.'' She sank deep into the sofa cushions. "I wonder how he feels right now. . . .''

"Cut it out!''

"My, we're jumpy tonight."

"My part's done with, Doreen. I told you that again and again.
Now the State's doing its job."

She held the tip of her pink tongue between her teeth thoughtfully. "But you put him where he is, Warren. You can't deny
that."

"The jury put him there!"

"You don't have to shout at *me,* attorney."

"Oh, Doreen . . ." He leaned across to make some apologetic
gesture, but the telephone rang.

He picked it up angrily.

"Mr. Selvey? This is Arlington."

All over Selvey's body, a pulse throbbed.

"What do you want?"

"Mr. Selvey, I been thinking it over. What you told me today.
Only I don't think it would be right, just forgetting about it. I
mean—"

"Arlington, listen to me. I'd like to see you at my apartment.
I'd like to see you right now."

From the sofa, Doreen said, "Hey!"

"Did you hear me, Arlington? Before you do anything rash, I
want to talk to you, tell you where you stand legally. I think you
owe that to yourself."

There was a pause at the other end.

"Guess maybe you're right, Mr. Selvey. Only I'm way downtown, and by the time I get there—"

"You can make it. Take the IRT subway, it's quickest. Get off
at Eighty-sixth Street."

When he hung up, Doreen was standing.

"Doreen, wait. I'm sorry about this. This man is—an important witness in a case I'm handling. The only time I can see him is
now."

"Have fun," she said airily, and went to the bedroom.

"Doreen—"

The door closed behind her. For a moment, there was silence.
Then she clicked the lock.

Selvey cursed his wife's moods beneath his breath, and stalked over to the bar.

By the time Arlington sounded the door chimes, Selvey had downed six inches of bourbon.

Arlington's grease-spotted hat and dirty coat looked worse than ever in the plush apartment. He took them off and looked around timidly.

"We've only got three-quarters of an hour," he said. "I've just got to do something, Mr. Selvey."

"I know what you can do," the attorney smiled. "You can have a drink and talk things over."

"I don't think I should—" But the man's eyes were already fixed on the bottle in Selvey's hands. The lawyer's smile widened.

By eleven-thirty, Arlington's voice was thick and blurred, his eyes no longer so intense, his concern over Rodman no longer so compelling.

Selvey kept his visitor's glass filled.

The old man began to mutter. He muttered about his childhood, about some past respectability, and inveighed a string of strangers who had done him dirt. After a while, his shaggy head began to roll on his shoulders, and his heavy-lidded eyes began to close.

He was jarred out of his doze by the mantel clock's chiming.

"Whazzat?"

"Only the clock." Selvey grinned.

"Clock? What time? What time?"

"Twelve, Mr. Arlington. Your worries are over. Mr. Rodman's already paid for his crime."

"No!" The old man stood up, circling wildly. "No, that's not true. I killed that woman. Not him! They can't kill him for something he—"

"Relax, Mr. Arlington. Nothing you can do about it now."

"Yes, yes! Must tell them—the police—"

"But why? Rodman's been executed. As soon as that clock struck, he was dead. What good can you do him now?"

"Have to!" the old man sobbed. "Don't you see? Couldn't live with myself, Mr. Selvey. Please—"

He tottered over to the telephone. Swiftly the attorney put his hand on the receiver.

"Don't," he said.

Their hands fought for the instrument, and the younger man's won easily.

"You won't stop me, Mr. Selvey. I'll go down there myself. I'll tell them all about it. And I'll tell them about you—"

He staggered toward the door. Selvey's arm went out and spun him around.

"You crazy old tramp! You're just asking for trouble. Rodman's dead—"

"I don't care!"

Selvey's arm lashed out and his hand cracked across the sagging, white-whiskered face. The old man sobbed at the blow, but persisted in his attempt to reach the door. Selvey's anger increased and he struck out again, and after the blow, his hands dropped to the old man's scrawny neck. The next idea came naturally. There wasn't much life throbbing in the old throat. A little pressure, and Selvey could stop the frantic breathing, the hoarse, scratchy voice, the damning words . . .

Selvey squeezed, harder and harder.

And then his hands let him go. The old man swayed and slid against Selvey's body to the floor.

In the doorway, rigid, icy-eyed: Doreen.

"Doreen, listen—"

"You choked him," she said.

"Self-defense!" Selvey shouted. "He broke in here, tried to rob the apartment."

She slammed the door shut, twisted the inside lock. Selvey raced across the carpet and pounded desperately on the door. He rattled the knob and called her name, but there was no answer. Then he heard the sound of a spinning telephone dial.

It was bad enough, without having Vance in the crowd that

jammed the apartment. Vance, the assistant D.A., who hated his guts anyway. Vance, who was smart enough to break down his burglar story without any trouble, who had learned that Selvey's visitor had been expected. Vance, who would delight in his predicament.

But Vance didn't seem delighted. He looked puzzled. He stared down at the dead body on the floor of Selvey's apartment and said, "I don't get it, Warren. I just don't get it. What did you want to kill a harmless old guy like that for?"

"Harmless? *Harmless?*"

"Sure. Harmless. That's old Arlington, I'd know him any place."

"You know him?" Selvey was stunned.

"Sure, I met up with him when I was working out of Bellaire County. Crazy old guy goes around confessing to murders. But why kill him, Warren? What for?"

"Night of the Execution." *Alfred Hitchcock Presents,* December 29, 1957. Directed by Justus Addiss. Teleplay by Bernard C. Schoenfeld, based on Henry Slesar's short story "The Day of the Execution" *(Alfred Hitchcock's Mystery Magazine,* June 1957; collected in Slesar's *Clean Crimes and Neat Murders,* Avon, 1960). With Pat Hingle (Warren Selvey), Russell Collins (Ed Barnes), Georgann Johnson (Doreen Selvey), Harry Jackson (Vance).

I've always had a debt of gratitude to Alfred Hitchcock, who was the first to dramatize a story I had written. Eventually, he dramatized so many that I was able to bargain for the rights to self-adaptation, and this led to the TV writing career that is now the main supplier of food, fuel, and fineries in the Slesar home. But my gratitude extends beyond the pecuniary. Because there is another, perhaps greater reward for writers in seeing good, intelligent adaptations of their work in a dramatic medium. It enables us to start *seeing* the people we are writing about; to visualize the action we have plotted only in our heads; to hear the dialogue which seemed "real" enough on paper but might not be so convincing when it becomes the spoken word. The process results in a kind of "feedback," helping writers to "see" and "hear" the action of their stories while they're still ink on paper (or pixels on a word processor).

When "The Day of the Execution" was written, I thought it was a good story, a clear and eventually ironic exposition on the subject of Ambition. When it became an episode on *Alfred Hitchcock Presents,* something changed. It was the same story; the events occurred just as they had on paper; even most of the dialogue was intact. But there was one difference. Suddenly, the minor people of the story, who had been only pawns in the fictional chess game played between the two main characters, became flesh and blood. The prosecutor's beautiful wife became not just a symbol of his acquisitiveness, but a human being with a stake in the circumstances. The prosecutor's rival, only a name on paper, made a brief appearance that gave emphasis to the prosecutor's own motivations.

It's been a long time since I have reread "The Day of the Execution." But I have to admit that, when I did, I saw Warren Selvey and Phil Arlington and all the rest on my old black-and-white TV screen, followed shortly by that familiar rotundity whose sly concluding remarks ended with "Good Evening." It was definitely a good evening for me.

Henry Slesar

HAROLD Q. MASUR

The $2,000,000 Defense

THE TRIAL HAD GONE WELL for the prosecution. Strand by strand, a web of guilt had been woven around the defendant, Lloyd Ashley. Now, late in the afternoon of the fifth day, District Attorney Herrick was tying up the last loose ends with his final witness.

Understandably, the case had made headlines. An avid public kept clamoring for more and more details, and the newspapers obligingly supplied whatever revelations they could find. For all the elements of a *cause célèbre* were present—a beautiful wife, allegedly unfaithful; a dashing Casanova, now dead; and a millionaire husband, charged with murder.

Beside Ashley at the counsel table sat his lawyer, Mark Robison, seemingly unconcerned by the drama unfolding before him. His lean face was relaxed, chin resting on the palm of his hand. To a casual observer he seemed preoccupied, almost disinterested; yet nothing would be further from the truth. Robison's mind was keenly attuned, ready to pounce on any error the district attorney might commit.

Defense counsel was a formidable opponent, as the district attorney well knew—they had both trained in the same school, Robison having served as an assistant prosecutor through two administrations. In this capacity he had been tough and relentless, doing more than his share to keep the state prison at Ossining well populated.

As a muskrat takes to water, so Robison found his natural habitat in the courtroom. He had a commanding presence, the ego and voice of a born actor, and the quick, searching brain so essential to a skilled cross-examiner. He had, too, an instinct with jurors. Unerringly he would spot the most impressionable members of a panel, playing on their emotions and prejudices. And so, where his defenses were inadequate, he would often wind up with a hung jury.

But the Ashley case was more serious. Robison's defense was more than inadequate, it was virtually nonexistent.

Robison sat motionless, studying the prosecution's final witness. James Keller, police-department specialist in ballistics, was a pale, heavyset man, stolid and slow-spoken. District Attorney Herrick had taken him through the preliminaries, qualifying him as an expert, and was now extracting the final bit of testimony that should send Lloyd Ashley to eternity, the whine of a high-voltage electric current pounding in his ears.

The district attorney picked up a squat black pistol whose ownership by the accused had already been established. "And now, Mr. Keller," Herrick said, "I show you State's Exhibit B. Can you tell us what kind of gun this is?"

"Yes, sir. That is a thirty-two-caliber Colt automatic."

"Have you ever seen this gun before?"

"Yes, sir, I have."

"Under what circumstances?"

"It was handed to me in the performance of my duties as a ballistics expert to determine whether or not it had fired the fatal bullet."

"And did you make the necessary tests?"

"I did."

"Will you tell the jury what you found?"

Keller faced the twelve talesmen, who were now leaning forward in their chairs. There were no women in the jury box—

Robison had used every available challenge to keep them from being empaneled. It was his theory that men would be more sympathetic to acts of violence by a betrayed husband.

Keller spoke in a dry, somewhat pedantic voice. "I fired a test bullet to compare with the one recovered from the deceased. Both bullets had overall dimensions of three-tenths of an inch, and a weight of seventy-four grams, placing them in a thirty-two-caliber class. They both bore the imprint of six spiral grooves with a leftward twist which is characteristic of Colt firearms. In addition, every gun develops with usage certain personality traits of its own, and all these are impressed on the shell casing as it passes through the barrel. By checking the two bullets with a comparison microscope—"

Robison broke into Keller's monologue with a casual gesture.

"Your Honor, I think we can dispense with a long technical dissertation on the subject of ballistics. The defense concedes that Mr. Ashley's gun fired the fatal bullet."

The judge glanced at Herrick. "Is the prosecution agreeable?"

Grudgingly Herrick said, "The State has no desire to protract this trial longer than necessary."

Secretly, however, he was not pleased. Herrick preferred to build his case carefully and methodically, laying first the foundation, then each plank in turn, until the lid was finally clamped down, with no loophole for escape and no error that could be reversed on appeal. There were times, of course, when he might welcome a concession by the defense, but with Robison—well, you never knew; the man had to be watched, his every move had to be scrutinized.

When Robison resumed his seat, Lloyd Ashley turned to him, his eyes troubled. "Was that wise, Mark?" With his life at stake, Ashley felt that every point should be hotly contested.

"It was never in dispute," Robison said, smiling assurance.

But the smile had no effect, and seeing Ashley's face now, Robison felt a twist of compassion. How radically changed the man was! Ashley's usual arrogance had crumbled, his sarcastic tongue was now humble and beseeching. Not even his money, those vast sums solidly invested, could give him any sense of security.

Robison could not deny a certain feeling of responsibility for Ashley's plight. He had known Ashley for years, in a business way and socially. He could recall that day only two months ago when Ashley had come to him for advice, grim with repressed anger, suspecting his wife of infidelity.

"Have you any proof?" Robison had asked.

"I don't need any proof. This is something a man knows. She's been cold and untouchable."

"Do you want a divorce?"

"Never." The word had been charged with feeling. "I love Eve."

"Just what do you want me to do, Lloyd?"

"I want you to give me the name of a private detective. I'm sure you know someone I can trust. I'd like him to follow Eve, keep track of her movements. If he can identify the man for me, I'll know what to do."

Yes, Robison knew a reliable private detective—a lawyer sometimes needs the services of a trained investigator to check the background of hostile witnesses whose testimony he might later want to impeach.

So Ashley retained the man, and within a week had his report. The detective had trailed Eve Ashley to a rendezvous with Tom Ward, an investment counselor in charge of Ashley's securities. He had watched them in obviously intimate conversation in an obscure cocktail lounge in the Village.

The one thing he had never anticipated, Robison told himself, was violence. Not that Ashley was a coward. But Ashley's principal weapon in the past had been words—sharp, barbed, insulting. When the call came through from police headquarters that Ashley was being held for murder, Robison had been genuinely shocked, and he had felt a momentary pang of guilt. But Robison was not the kind of man who would long condemn himself for lack of omniscience. And Ashley, allowed one telephone call, demanded that Robison appear for him.

At the preliminary hearing in felony court, Robison had made a quick stab at getting the charge dismissed, presenting Ashley's version with shrewdness and skill. The whole affair had been an accident, Robison had maintained. No premeditation, no malice, no intent to kill. Ashley had gone to Ward's office and drawn his gun, brandishing it, trying to frighten the man, to extract a promise that Ward would stay away from Ashley's wife. He had been especially careful to check the safety catch, not to release it before entering Ward's office.

But instead of suffering paralysis or pleading for mercy, Ward had panicked, thrown himself at Ashley, and grappled for the gun. It had fallen to the desk, Ashley swore, and been accidentally discharged. He had been standing over the body when discovered.

Hearing this version, the district attorney had scoffed, promptly labeling it as a bald fiction. The State, Herrick contended, could prove motive, means, and opportunity. So the magistrate had no choice. Lloyd Ashley was bound over for action by the Grand Jury, which quickly returned an indictment for murder in the first degree.

And now, in general sessions, Judge Felix Cobb presiding, on the fifth day of testimony, Herrick was engaged in destroying Ashley's last hope. He held up the gun so that Keller and the jury could see it—a small weapon which had erased a man's life in the twinkling of an eye.

He said, "You are acquainted with the operation of this gun, Mr. Keller, are you not?"

"I am."

"In your opinion as a ballistics expert, could a gun of this type be accidentally discharged—with the safety catch on?"

"No, sir."

"You're certain of that?"

"Absolutely."

"Could it be discharged—with the safety on—if it were dropped from a height of several feet?"

"It could not."

"If it were slammed down on a hard surface?"

"No, sir."

"In all your experience—twenty years of testing and handling firearms—have you ever heard of any such incident?"

"Not one, sir."

Herrick headed back to the prosecution table. "The defense may cross-examine."

"It is now five minutes to four," the judge said. "I think we can recess at this point." He turned to the jury. "You will remember my instructions, gentlemen. You are admonished not to discuss this case among yourselves, and not to permit anyone to discuss it in your presence. Do not form or express any opinions until all the evidence is before you. Court stands adjourned until ten o'clock tomorrow morning."

He straightened his black robes and strode off. Everyone else remained seated until a tipstaff had led the jurors through a side door. A court officer moved up and touched Ashley's shoulder.

Ashley turned to Robison, his face drawn and tired. He had lost considerable weight during these last few weeks, and the flaccid skin hung loose under his chin. His sunken eyes were veined and red, and a vagrant muscle kept twitching at the corner of his right temple.

"Tomorrow's the last day, isn't it, Mark?"

"Almost." Robison doubted if the whole defense would require more than a single session. "Except for the summation and the judge's charge."

The guard said, "Let's go, Mr. Ashley."

"Listen, Mark." There was sudden intensity in Ashley's voice. "I've got to talk to you. It—it's absolutely vital."

Robison studied his client. "All right, Lloyd. I'll be up in about fifteen minutes."

Ashley left with the guard and disappeared through a door behind the judge's bench. A few spectators still lingered in the courtroom. Robison gathered his papers and notes, slid them into his briefcase. He sat back, fingertips stroking his closed eyelids, still seeing Ashley's face. The man was terrified—and with considerable justification, Robison thought. Despite the judge's admonition to the jurors, advising them not to reach any decision, Robison's experience told him they had done just that.

He could read the signs. He could tell from the way they filed out, the way they averted their eyes, not looking at the defendant. Nobody really enjoys sending another human being to the electric chair. Ashley must have felt it, too, this sense of doom.

When Robison reached the corridor, he saw Eve Ashley waiting at the south bank of elevators. She seemed small and lost, the very bones of her body cringing against themselves. Robison started forward, but she was swallowed up in the descending throng before he could reach her.

Eve's reaction had surprised him. She was taking it hard, ill with self-condemnation and remorse. He remembered her visit to his office directly after the murder. "I knew he was jealous," she said, her eyes full of pain, "but I never expected anything like this. Never." She kept clasping and unclasping her hands. "Oh, Mark, they'll send him to the chair! I know they will and it's all my fault."

He had spoken to her sharply. "Listen to me. You had no way of knowing. I want you to get hold of yourself. If you go to pieces, you won't be any good to yourself—or to Lloyd. It's not your fault."

"It *is* my fault." Her lips were trembling. "I should have known. Just look what I've done. Two men. Tom is already dead, and Lloyd soon will—"

"Now, stop that!" He had gripped her shoulders.

"You must get him off," she cried fiercely. "Please, Mark. If you don't I'll never forgive myself."

"I'll do my best."

But he knew the odds. The State had a solid case. Motive, means, and opportunity. . . .

The elevator took him down, and he went around to the detention cells at the White Street entrance. After the usual routine, he gained admittance to the counsel room, and a moment later Lloyd

Ashley was brought in. They sat on opposite sides of the table, the board between them.

"All right, Mark." Ashley's clenched hands rested on the table. "I want the truth. How does it look?"

Robison shrugged. "The case isn't over. Nobody can tell what a jury will do."

"Stop kidding, Mark. I saw those men—I saw their faces."

Robison shrugged again.

"Look, Mark, you've been my lawyer for a long time. We've been through a lot of deals together. I've seen you operate. I know how your mind works. You're smart. You're resourceful. I have the utmost respect for your ability, but I—well, I . . ." He groped for words.

"Aren't you satisfied with the way I'm handling your defense?"

"I didn't say that, Mark."

"Don't you think I'm exploiting every possible angle?"

"Within legal limitations, yes. But I've seen you try cases before. I've watched you handle juries. And I've seen you pull some rabbits out of a hat. Now, all of a sudden, you're so damn scrupulous I hardly recognize the same man. Why, Mark, what's happened?"

"I can't find a single loophole, Lloyd, that's why. Not one crack in the State's case. My hands are tied."

"Untie them."

"How?" Robison asked quietly.

"Listen, Mark"—Ashley's fingers were gripping the edge of the table—"you know almost as much about my financial affairs as I do. You know how much money I inherited, how much I've made. As of now, I'm worth about four million dollars." He compressed his lips. "Maybe that's why Eve married me; I don't know. Anyway, it's a lot of loot and I'd like a chance to spend some of it. But I won't have that chance, not if they convict me."

Ashley moistened his lips, then went on. "Dead, the money will do me no good. Alive, I can do all I want to do on a lot less. If anybody can get me off the hook, even at this stage of the game, it's you. I don't know how, but I have a feeling—hunch, intuition, call it what you will. You can think of *something*. You've got the imagination. I know you can pull it off."

Robison felt a stir of excitement.

Ashley leaned forward. "Down the middle," he said, his voice hoarse. "An even split, Mark, of everything I own. Half for you, half for me. A two-million-dollar fee, Mark. You'll be financially independent for life. Just figure out an angle! I want an acquittal."

Robison said promptly, "Will you put that in writing, Lloyd?"

"Of course!"

Robison took a blank sheet of paper from his briefcase. He wrote swiftly, in clear, unmistakable language. He passed the paper to Ashley, who scanned it briefly, reached for the pen, and scratched his signature. Robison, his fingers a trifle unsteady, folded the document and put it away.

"Have you any ideas, Mark?"

The lawyer sat motionless, his flat-cheeked face devoid of expression. He did have an idea, one that was not entirely new to him. He remembered, three nights ago, sitting bolt upright in bed when the brainstorm suddenly struck him. He had considered the idea for a moment, weighed its possibilities; then, putting his head back, he had laughed aloud in the darkness.

It was ingenious, even amusing in a macabre way, but nothing he would actually use. Now, abruptly, his thinking had changed, all scruples gone. There was considerable persuasive power in a fee of $2,000,000. Men had committed serious crimes—including murder—for much less.

Now the possibilities of his idea stood out, sharp and clear and daring. There was no guarantee of success. He would have to cope with certain imponderables—most of them in the minds of twelve men, the twelve men in the jury box.

"Leave it to me," Robison said, rising abruptly. "Relax, Lloyd. Try to get some sleep tonight." He swung toward the door with a peremptory wave at the guard.

The declining sun had cooled the air, and Robison walked

briskly, details of the plan churning in his mind. Ethical? He would hardly call it that. But then Robison was not often troubled by delicate moral considerations. As a trial lawyer he had been consistently successful. His voice was a great asset: it could be gentle and sympathetic or blistering and contemptuous. Neophytes around the Criminal Courts Building still talked about Robison's last case as an assistant district attorney, remembering his savage cross-examination of the defendant, a man accused of armed robbery. He had won a conviction, and upon pronouncement of a maximum sentence, the enraged defendant had turned on him, swearing revenge. Later he had received venomous, threatening letters from the man's relatives.

So Mark Robison had acquired a pistol permit. And each year he had had it renewed. He always carried the permit in his wallet.

His first stop was on Centre Street, not far from police headquarters—at a small shop that specialized in firearms. He examined the stock, carefully selected a Colt automatic, pocket model, caliber .32, and a box of shells. The proprietor checked his permit and wrapped the package.

Robison then took a cab to his office. His secretary, Miss Graham, paused in her typing to hand him a list of calls. Seeing the abstracted look on his face, she did not bother to ask him about the trial. He went on through to the inner room.

It had recently been refurnished, and Robison was pleased with the effect. Hanging on the far wall, facing the desk, was a picture of the nine Justices of the United States Supreme Court. The extraordinary occurrence that now took place before these venerable gentlemen was probably unparalleled in all their collective histories.

Mark Robison unwrapped his package and balanced the gun for a moment in his hand. Then, without further hesitation, he inserted three bullets into the clip and rammed the clip into the butt. His jaw was set as he lifted the gun, aimed it at his left arm, slightly above the elbow, and pulled the trigger.

The echoing explosion left his ears ringing. Robison was no stoic. He felt the stab of pain, like a branding iron, and cried out.

The next instant he gritted his teeth while his thumb reached for the safety catch and locked it into position.

A moment later the door burst open and Miss Graham's apprehensive face poked through. With sudden dismay she saw Robison's pallor and the widening stain on his sleeve. She stifled a scream.

"All right," Robison told her harshly. "It was an accident. Don't stand there gaping. Call a doctor. There's one down the hall."

Miss Graham fled. Her urgent story stopped whatever the doctor was doing and brought him on the double with his rumpled black bag.

"Well," he said, sparing the gun a brief look of distaste, "what have we here, another one of those I didn't-know-it-was-loaded accidents?"

"Not quite," Robison said dryly.

"Here, let's get the coat off." The doctor helped him, then ripped the lawyer's shirt-sleeve from cuff to shoulder, exposing the wound, and probed the inflamed area. The bullet had scooped out a shallow trench of flesh.

"Hmm," said the doctor. "Looks worse than it is. You're a lucky man, Counselor. No muscles or arteries severed. Loss of tissue, yes, and some impairment of articulation—"

He reached into his bag and brought out some antiseptic. It burned Robison's arm like a flame. Then, having dressed and bandaged the wound, the doctor stepped back to appraise his handiwork.

He looked faintly apologetic. "You know the law, Counselor. Whenever a doctor is called in for the treatment of a gunshot wound, he is required to notify the police. I really have no choice."

Robison repressed a smile. Had the doctor been ignorant of the law, Robison would have immediately enlightened him. Most assuredly he *wanted* the police here. They were an essential part of his plan.

He could already picture the headlines: *Robison Accidentally*

Wounded. Defense Counsel Shot Making Test—and the stories telling how he had tried to simulate the conditions that had existed in Tom Ward's office—by deliberately dropping a gun on his desk. . . .

Promptly at ten o'clock the following morning, a court officer arose and began to intone the ritual. "All rise, the Honorable Judge of the Court of General Sessions in and for the County of New York."

A door behind the bench opened and Justice Cobb emerged briskly, his black robe billowing behind him.

"Be seated, please," the attendant said, tapping his gavel. "This court is now in session."

The judge looked curiously at Robison, eyeing the wounded arm supported by a black silk sling knotted around the lawyer's neck. "Call the witness," he said.

James Keller was duly sworn and resumed his seat on the stand.

The twelve jurors bent forward, stirred by excitement and anticipation. District Attorney Herrick sat at the prosecution table, vigilant, wary. Robison smiled to himself, remembering the district attorney's tight-lipped greeting. Did Herrick suspect? Possibly.

"The defense may cross-examine," Judge Cobb said.

There was a murmur from the spectators as Robison pushed erect. He half turned, letting everyone have a look at his wounded arm in its silken cradle. He saw Eve Ashley in the first row, her eyes eloquent with appeal.

Robison walked to the clerk's table and picked up Ashley's gun. Holding it, he advanced toward Keller and addressed the witness. "Now, Mr. Keller, if I remember correctly, you testified yesterday that you fired a test bullet from this gun, did you not?"

"Yes, sir, I did." Keller's tone was guarded.

"You wanted to prove that this gun and no other fired the fatal bullet."

"That is correct."

"I assume that you released the safety catch before making the test?"

"Naturally. Otherwise I would still be standing there in my laboratory pulling the trigger."

Someone in the courtroom tittered, and one of Herrick's assistants grinned. Keller's self-confidence mounted visibly.

Robison regarded him sternly. "This is hardly a moment for humor, Mr. Keller. You realize that your testimony may send an innocent man to the chair?"

Herrick's hand shot up. "I move that last remark be stricken."

"Yes," said the judge. "It will be stricken and the jury will disregard it."

"Then you're absolutely sure," Robison said, "that the safety catch must be released before the gun can be fired?"

"Positive."

"Are you equally positive that the safety catch on a gun of this type cannot be joggled loose under certain circumstances?"

Keller hesitated. "Well, yes, to the best of my knowledge."

"Have you ever made any such test?"

"What do you mean?"

"Did you ever load this gun—State's Exhibit B—and try dropping it on a hard surface?"

"I—I'm afraid not, sir."

"Even though you knew what the basis of our defense here in court would be?"

Keller shifted uncomfortably and glanced at Herrick, but he found no help in the district attorney's expressionless face.

"Please answer the question." Robison's voice was no longer friendly.

"No, sir. I did not."

"Why, Mr. Keller? Why didn't you make such a test? Wouldn't it seem the obvious thing to do? Were you afraid it might confirm the defendant's story?"

"No, sir, not at all."

"Then why?"

Keller said lamely, "It just never occurred to me."

"It never occurred to you. I see. A man is accused of first-degree murder; he is being tried for his life, facing the electric chair; and it never occurred to you to make that one simple test to find out if by any chance he might be telling the truth."

A flush rose from Keller's neck up to his cheeks. He sat silent, squirming in the witness chair.

"Let the record note that the witness did not answer," Robison said. "Now, sir, you testified yesterday that a gun of this type could never be discharged by dropping it on a hard surface, did you not?"

"With the safety catch on."

"Of course."

"I—yes, I believe I did."

"There is no doubt in your mind?"

Keller swallowed uncomfortably, glancing at Robison's arm. "Well . . . no."

"Let us see." Robison tranferred the gun to his left hand, jutting out of the sling, its fingers slightly swollen. His right hand produced a .32-caliber shell from the pocket of his coat. His movements were awkward as he loaded the gun and jacked a shell into firing position. He stepped closer to the witness and started to offer the gun with his left hand, but he stopped short with a sudden grimace of pain. The expression was telling and dramatic. Then ruefully he shifted the gun to his right hand and extended it to the witness.

In distinct, deliberate tones he said, "Now, Mr. Keller, will you please look at the safety device on State Exhibit B and tell us if it is in the proper position to prevent firing?"

"It is."

"Then will you kindly rise, sir? I would like you to prove to His Honor, and to these twelve jurors, and to the spectators in this courtroom, that the gun in question *cannot possibly be discharged by dropping on the judge's dais.* Just lift it, if you please, or slap it down."

A murmur rustled through the courtroom as Herrick landed on both feet in front of the bench. The muscles around his jaw were contracted with anger. "I object, your Honor. This is highly irregular, a cheap grandstand play, inherently dangerous to every—" He caught himself, swallowing the rest of his sentence. His own words, uttered impulsively, had implied a possibility, however remote, that the gun might go off.

In contrast, Robison sounded calm and reasonable. "If it please the court, this witness made a statement under oath as a qualified expert. I am merely asking him to prove his confidence in his own expert statement."

Judge Cobb spoke without pleasure. "Objection overruled."

"Go ahead, if you please, Mr. Keller," Robison said. "Demonstrate to the court and to the jury that State Exhibit B could not *possibly* have been fired in the manner claimed by the defendant."

A hush fell over the courtroom as Keller rose. He lifted the gun slowly and held it suspended over the bench, his face a mixture of anxiety and misgiving. Lloyd Ashley was gripping his knees, the knuckles on his hands bone-white.

Robison held his breath as Keller's arm twitched. The judge, trying to look inconspicuous, started to slide down his chair, as if to minimize himself as a target. The foreman's face was pale, and the other jurors seemed ready to duck.

"We're waiting," Robison said softly, clearly.

Beads of moisture formed along Keller's temples. Had he flexed his muscles? Had he lifted the gun a little higher? No one in the courtroom could be sure.

"Please proceed, Mr. Keller," Robison said, sharply now. "The court hasn't got all day."

Their eyes met and locked. Deliberately Robison rearranged his sling. Keller took a long breath; then without warning he dropped back into his seat. The gun hung loose between his knees.

A sigh of relief swelled in the courtroom.

The verdict, everyone conceded, was a foregone conclusion. Robison's closing speech was a model of forensic law, and the judge, charging the jury to be satisfied beyond a reasonable doubt, left them little choice. They were out for less than an hour before returning a verdict of not guilty.

Lloyd Ashley showed no jubilation—the strain had left him on the edge of nervous exhaustion. He sat like a man anesthetized, slowly shaking his head from side to side. Robison touched his shoulder.

"All right, Lloyd. It's over. You're free now. Let's go back to my office. I believe we have some business to transact."

Ashley roused himself. "Yes, of course," he said with a stiff smile.

They got through the crowd, acknowledging congratulations, and hailed a cab. The closing speeches and the judge's charge had taken all afternoon, so it was growing dark when they reached Robison's office. He ushered the way into his private room and snapped on the light.

By way of celebration, the lawyer produced a bottle and poured two drinks. Both men emptied their glasses in single gulps. Robison passed the humidor and snapped a lighter for his client. Ashley settled back, inhaling the rich smoke of a long, thin cigar.

"Well, Mark," he said, "I knew you could to it. You performed your share of the bargain. I suppose now you'd like me to fulfill mine."

Robison made a deprecating gesture.

"Have you a blank check, Mark?"

There was a pad of blank checks somewhere in the outer office, Robison knew. He kept it handy for clients who needed legal representation but who came to him with insufficient funds. He went out to the reception room, rummaged through a storage cabinet, and finally located the pad.

Lloyd Ashley had shifted chairs and was now seated behind Robison's desk. He accepted the blank check and Robison's pen. Without flicking an eyelash he wrote out a check for $2,000,000.

"I said fifty-fifty, Mark. There may even be more coming to you. We'll know after my accountant goes over the books."

Robison held the check, his eyes transfixed by the string of figures. There was a faint throbbing in his wounded arm, but he didn't mind. Ashley's voice came back to him, sounding soft and strange.

"Oh, yes, Mark, there's more coming to you. Perhaps I can arrange to let you have it now."

Robison looked up and saw the .32-caliber automatic in Ashley's hand, his thumb on the safety catch.

"I found this in your desk," Ashley said. "It must be the gun you used last night. Ironic, isn't it, Mark? You now have the one thing that means more to you than anything else in this world—money—and you'll never be able to spend a penny of it."

Robison did not like the look in Ashley's eyes. "What are you talking about?"

"Remember that private detective you recommended? Funny thing, after that trouble with Ward I never had a chance to take him off the case. So he kept watching Eve all the time I was in jail. As a matter of fact, he brought me a report only two days ago. I don't suppose I have to tell you about it—who she's been seeing, who the other man really is?"

Robison had gone white.

The gun in Ashley's hand was very steady. "You know, Mark, I feel you're almost as responsible for Ward's death as I am. After all, who persuaded Eve to use him as a decoy, so that you and she could be safe? It must have been you. Eve never had that much imagination."

Perspiration now bathed Robison's face, and his voice went down to a whisper. "Wait, Lloyd, listen to me—"

"No, I'd rather not. You're too good at winning people over. I saw a demonstration of your powers in court today, remember? I've been planning on this for two days. Finding your gun merely accelerated the timetable. There's a kind of justice in this, I think. You forced me into killing the wrong man. Now I see no reason why I shouldn't kill the right one."

Of the two shots that rang out, Mark Robison heard only the first.

180 Harold Q. Masur

"The $2,000,000 Defense." *Alfred Hitchcock Presents,* November 2, 1958. Directed by Norman Lloyd. Teleplay by William Fay, based on Harold Q. Masur's short story "The $2,000,000 Defense" *(Ellery Queen's Mystery Magazine,* May 1958). With Barry Sullivan (Mark Robison), Leslie Nielsen (Lloyd Ashley), Lori March (Eve Ashley).

Few authors would fault the TV version of a story when gifted performers like Barry Sullivan and Leslie Nielsen interpret the principal roles. Since the adaptation and dialogue closely followed the original, I was inclined to applaud an industry that often in the past had disappointed. I lament only the lack of a video recorder at that time to immortalize my favorite yarn.

Harold Q. Masur

HARRY MUHEIM

The Dusty Drawer

NORMAN LOGAN PAID for his apple pie and coffee, then carried his tray toward the front of the cafeteria. From a distance, he recognized the back of William Tritt's large head. The tables near Tritt were empty, and Logan had no desire to eat with him, but they had some unfinished business that Logan wanted to clear up. He stopped at Tritt's table and asked, "Do you mind if I join you?"

Tritt looked up as he always looked up from inside his teller's cage in the bank across the street. He acted like a servant—like a fat, precise butler that Logan used to see in movies—but behind the film of obsequiousness was an attitude of vast superiority that always set Logan on edge.

"Why, yes, Mr. Logan. Do sit down. Only please, I must ask you not to mention that two hundred dollars again."

"Well, we'll see about that," said Logan, pulling out a chair and seating himself. "Rather late for lunch, isn't it?"

"Oh, I've had lunch," Tritt said. "This is just a snack." He cut a large piece of roast beef from the slab in front of him and thrust it into his mouth. "I don't believe I've seen you all summer," he added, chewing the meat.

"I took a job upstate," Logan said. "We were trying to stop some kind of blight in the apple orchards."

"Is that so?" Tritt looked like a concerned bloodhound.

"I wanted to do some research out West," Logan went on, "but I couldn't get any money from the university."

"You'll be back for the new term, won't you?"

"Oh, yes," Logan said with a sigh, "we begin again tomorrow." He thought for a moment of the freshman faces that would be looking up at him in the lecture room. A bunch of high-strung, mechanical New York City kids, pushed by their parents or by the army into the university, and pushed by the university into his botany class. They were brick-bound people who had no interest in growing things, and Logan sometimes felt sad that in five years of teaching he had communicated to only a few of them his own delight with his subject.

"My, one certainly gets a long vacation in the teaching profession," Tritt said. "June through September."

"I suppose," Logan said. "Only trouble is that you don't make enough to do anything in all that spare time."

Tritt laughed a little, controlled laugh, and continued chewing. Logan began to eat the pie. It had the drab, neutral flavor of all cafeteria pies.

"Mr. Tritt," he said, after a long silence.

"Yes?"

"When are you going to give me back my two hundred dollars?"

"Oh, come now, Mr. Logan. We had this all out ten months ago. We went over it with Mr. Pinkson and the bank examiners and everyone. I did *not* steal two hundred dollars from you."

"You did, and you know it."

"Frankly, I'd rather not hear any more about it."

"Mr. Tritt, I had three hundred and twenty-four dollars in my hand that day. I'd just cashed some bonds. I know how much I had."

"The matter has all been cleared up," Tritt said coldly.

"Not for me, it hasn't. When you entered the amount in my

checking account, it was for one hundred and twenty-four, not three hundred twenty-four.''

Tritt put down his fork and carefully folded his hands. "I've heard you tell that story a thousand times, sir. My cash balanced when you came back and complained.''

"Sure it balanced," Logan exploded. "You saw your mistake when Pinkson asked you to check the cash. So you took my two hundred out of the drawer. No wonder it balanced!''

Tritt laid a restraining hand on Logan's arm. "Mr. Logan, I'm going a long, long way in the bank. I simply can't afford to make mistakes.''

"You also can't afford to admit it when you do make one.''

"Oh, come now," said Tritt as though he were speaking to a child. "Do you think I'd jeopardize my entire career for two hundred dollars?'

"You didn't jeopardize your career," Logan snapped. "You knew you could get away with it. And you took my money to cover your error.''

Tritt sat calmly and smiled a fat smile at Logan. "Well, that's your version, Mr. Logan. But I do wish you'd quit annoying me with your fairy tale.'' Leaving half his meat untouched, Tritt stood up and put on his hat. Then he came around the table and stood looming over Logan. "I will say, however, from a purely hypothetical point of view, that if I *had* stolen your money and then staked my reputation on the lie that I hadn't, the worst thing I could possibly do would be to return the money to you. I think you'd agree with that.''

"I'll get you, Tritt," said Logan, sitting back in the chair. "I can't stand to be had.''

"I know, I know. You've been saying that for ten months, too. Good-bye, now.''

Tritt walked out of the cafeteria. Norman Logan sat there motionless, watching the big teller cross the street and enter the bank. He felt no rage—only an increased sense of futility. Slowly, he finished his coffee.

A few minutes later, Logan entered the bank. Down in the safe-deposit vaults, he raised the lid of his long metal box and took out three twenty-five-dollar bonds. With a sigh, he began to fill them out for cashing. They would cover his government insurance premium for the year. In July, too, he'd taken three bonds from the box, when his father had overspent his pension money. And earlier in the summer, Logan had cashed some more of them, after slamming into a truck and damaging his Plymouth. Almost every month there was some reason to cash bonds, and Logan reflected that he hadn't bought one since his navy days. There just wasn't enough money in botany.

With the bonds in his hand, he climbed the narrow flight of stairs to the street floor, then walked past the long row of tellers' cages to the rear of the bank. Here he opened an iron gate in a low marble fence and entered the green-carpeted area of the manager and assistant manager. The manager's desk was right inside the gate, and Mr. Pinkson looked up as Logan came in. He smiled, looking over the top of the glasses pinched on his nose.

"Good afternoon, Mr. Logan." Pinkson's quick eyes went to the bonds, and then, with the professional neutrality of a branch-bank manager, right back up to Logan's face. "If you'll just sit down, I'll buzz Mr. Tritt."

"Mr. Tritt?" said Logan, surprised.

"Yes. He's been moved up to the first cage now."

Pinkson indicated a large, heavy table set far over against the side wall in back of his desk, and Logan sat in a chair next to it.

"Have a good summer?" The little man had revolved in his squeaky executive's chair to face Logan.

"Not bad, thanks."

"Did you get out of the city?"

"Yes, I had a job upstate. I always work during my vacations."

Mr. Pinkson let out a controlled chuckle, a suitable reply when he wasn't sure whether the customer was trying to be funny. Then he revolved again; his chubby cue-ball head bobbed down, and he was back at his figures.

Logan put the bonds on the clean desk blotter and looked over at Tritt's cage. It was at the end of the row of cages, with a door opening directly into the manager's area. Tritt was talking on the telephone inside, and for a long, unpleasant minute Logan watched the fat, self-assured face through the greenish glass. I'll get him yet, Logan thought. But he didn't see how. Tritt had been standing firmly shielded behind his lie for nearly a year now, and Norman Logan didn't seem to know enough about vengeance to get him.

Restive, Logan sat back and tipped the chair onto its hind legs. He picked ineffectually at a gravy stain on his coat; then his eye was attracted to a drawer hidden under the overhang of the table-top. It was a difficult thing to see, for it had no handle, and its face was outlined by only a thin black crack in the dark-stained wood. Logan could see faintly the two putty-filled holes that marked the place where the handle had once been. Curious, he rocked forward a little and slipped his fingernails into the crack along the bottom of the drawer. He pulled gently, and the drawer slid smoothly and silently from the table.

The inside was a dirty, cluttered mess. Little mounds of gray-ish mold had formed on the furniture glue along the joints. A film of dust on the bottom covered the bits of faded yellow paper and rusted paper clips that were scattered about. Logan rocked the chair back farther, and the drawer came far out to reveal a delicate spiderweb. The spider was dead and flaky, resting on an old page from a desk calendar. The single calendar sheet read October 2, 1936. Logan pushed the drawer softly back into the table, wondering if it had actually remained closed since Alf Landon was running against Roosevelt.

The door of Tritt's cage clicked open, and he came out, carrying a large yellow form. William Tritt moved smoothly across the carpet, holding his fat young body erect and making a clear effort to keep his stomach in.

"Why hello, Mr. Logan," he said. "I'm sorry for the delay. The main office called me. I can't hang up on them, you know."

"I know," Logan said.

The teller smiled as he lowered himself into the chair opposite Logan. Logan slid the bonds across the table.

"It's nice to see you again," Tritt said pleasantly as he opened his fountain pen. "Preparing for the new semester, I suppose?" There was no indication of their meeting across the street. Logan said nothing in reply, so Tritt went to work, referring rapidly to the form for the amount to be paid on each bond. "Well, that comes to sixty-seven dollars and twenty-five cents," he said, finishing the addition quickly.

Logan filled out a deposit slip. "Will you put it in my checking account, please?" He handed his passbook across the table. "And will you please enter the right amount?"

"Certainly, Mr. Logan," Tritt said, smiling indulgently. Logan watched carefully as Tritt made the entry. Then the teller walked rapidly back to his cage, while Logan, feeling somehow compelled to do so, took another glance into the dusty drawer. He kept thinking about the drawer as he got on a bus and rode up to the university. It had surprised him to stumble upon a dirty, forgotten place like that in a bank that was always so tidy.

Back in the biology department, Logan sat down at his desk, planning to prepare some roll sheets for his new classes. He stayed there for a long time without moving. The September sun went low behind the New Jersey Palisades, but he did not prepare the sheets, for the unused drawer stayed unaccountably in his mind.

Suddenly he sat forward in his chair. In a surprising flash of creative thought, he had seen how he could make use of the drawer. He wasn't conscious of having tried to develop a plan. The entire plan simply burst upon him all at once, and with such clarity and precision that he hardly felt any responsibility for it. He would rob the bank and pin the robbery on Tritt. That would take care of Tritt. . . .

In the weeks that followed, Norman Logan remained surprisingly calm about his plan. Each time he went step by step over the mechanics of the robbery, it seemed more gemlike and more workable. He made his first move the day he got his November paycheck.

Down on Fifty-first Street, Logan went into a novelty-and-trick store and bought a cigarette case. It was made of a dark, steel-blue plastic, and it looked like a trim thirty-eight automatic. When the trigger was pressed, a section of the top of the gun flipped upon a hinge, revealing the cigarettes inside the handle.

With this in his pocket, Logan took a bus way down to the lower part of Second Avenue and entered a grimy little shop displaying pistols and rifles in the window. The small shopkeeper shuffled forward, and Logan asked to see a thirty-eight.

"Can't sell you a thing until I see your permit," the man said. "The Sullivan law."

"Oh, I don't want to buy a weapon," Logan explained. He took out his plastic gun. "I just want to see if the real thing looks like mine here."

The little man laughed a cackle laugh and brought up a thirty-eight from beneath the counter, placing it next to Logan's. "So you'll just be fooling around, eh?"

"That's right," said Logan, looking at the guns. They were almost identical.

"Oh, they look enough alike," said the man. "But lemme give you a little tip. Put some Scotch tape over that lid to keep it down. Friend of mine was using one of those things, mister. He'd just polished off a stickup when he pulled the trigger and the lid flopped open. Well, he tried to offer the victim a cigarette, but the victim hauled off and beat the hell out of him."

"Thanks," Logan said with a smile. "I'll remember that."

"Here, you can put some Scotch tape on right now."

Logan walked over to the Lexington Avenue line and rode uptown on the subway. It was five minutes to three when he got to the bank. The old, gray-uniformed guard touched his cap as Logan came through the door. The stand-up desks were crowded, so it was natural enough for Logan to go through the little iron gate and across to the table with the drawer. Mr. Pinkson and the new assistant manager had already left; their desks were clear. As Logan sat down, Tritt stuck his head out the door of his cage.

"More bonds, Mr. Logan?" he asked.

"No," said Logan. "Just a deposit."

Tritt closed the door and bent over his work. Logan took out his wallet, removed the paycheck, then looked carefully the length of the bank. No one was looking in his direction. As he put the wallet back into his inside coat pocket, he withdrew the slim plastic gun and eased open the drawer. He dropped the gun in, shut the drawer, deposited the check, and went home to his apartment. In spite of the Sullivan law, he was on his way.

Twice during November he used the table with the drawer. Each time he checked on the gun. It had not been moved. By the time he deposited his December check, Logan was completely certain that nobody ever looked in there. On the nineteenth of the month, he decided to take the big step.

Next morning, after his ten-o'clock class, Logan walked six blocks through the snow down the hill to the bank. He took four bonds out of his safe-deposit box and filled them out for cashing. The soothing sound of recorded Christmas carols floated down from the main floor.

Upstairs, he seated himself at the heavy table to wait for Tritt. Pinkson had nodded and returned to his figuring; the nervous assistant manager was not around. The carols were quite loud here, and Logan smiled at this unexpected advantage. He placed the bonds squarely on the blotter. Then he slipped open the drawer, took out the gun with his left hand, and held it below the table.

Tritt was coming toward him, carrying his bond chart. They said hello, and Tritt sat down and went to work. He totaled the sum twice and said carefully, still looking at the figures, "Well, Mr. Logan, that comes to eighty-three fifty."

"I'll want something in addition to the eighty-three fifty," said Logan, leaning forward and speaking in an even voice.

"What's that?" asked Tritt.

"Ten thousand dollars in twenty-dollar bills."

Tritt's pink face smiled. He started to look up into Logan's face, but his eyes froze on the muzzle of the gun poking over the edge of the table. He did not notice that Scotch tape.

"Now just go to your cage and get the money," Logan said. It was William Tritt's first experience with anything like this. "Mr. Logan. Come now, Mr. Logan . . ." He swallowed and tried to start again, but his self-assurance had deserted him. He turned toward Pinkson's back.

"Look at me," snapped Logan.

Tritt turned back. "Mr. Logan, you don't know what you're doing."

"Keep still."

"Couldn't we give you a loan or perhaps a—"

"Listen to me, Tritt." Logan's voice was just strong enough to carry above "The First Noel." He was amazed at how authoritative he sounded. "Bring the money in a bag. Place it on the table here."

Tritt started to object, but Logan raised the gun slightly, and the last resistance drained from Tritt's fat body.

"All right, all right. I'll get it." As Tritt moved erratically toward his cage, Logan dropped the gun back into the drawer and closed it. Tritt shut the door of the cage, and his head disappeared below the frosted part of the glass. Immediately, Mr. Pinkson's telephone buzzed, and he picked it up. Logan watched his back, and after a few seconds, Pinkson's body stiffened. Logan sighed, knowing then that he would not get the money on this try.

Nothing happened for several seconds; then suddenly the little old guard came rushing around the corner of the cages, his big pistol drawn and wobbling as he tried to hold it on Logan.

"Okay. Okay. Stay there! Put your hands up, now!"

Logan raised his hands, and the guard turned to Pinkson with a half-surprised face. "Okay, Mr. Pinkson. Okay, I've got him covered now."

Pinkson got up as Tritt came out of the cage. Behind the one gun, the three men came slowly toward Logan.

"Careful, Louie, he's armed," Tritt warned the guard.

"May I ask what this is all about?" Logan said, his hands held high.

"Mr. Logan," said Pinkson, "I'm sorry about this, but Mr. Tritt here tells me that—that—"

"That you tried to rob me of ten thousand dollars," said Tritt, his voice choppy.

"I—I *what?*"

"You just attempted an armed robbery of this bank," Tritt said slowly. "Don't try to deny it."

Logan's face became the face of a man so completely incredulous that he cannot speak. He remembered not to overplay it, though. First he simply laughed at Tritt. Then he lowered his hands, regardless of the guard's gun, and stood up, the calm, indignant faculty member.

"All I can say, Mr. Tritt, is that I do deny it."

"Goodness," said Pinkson.

"Better take his gun, Louie," Tritt ordered the guard.

The guard stepped gingerly forward to Logan and frisked him, movie-style. "Hasn't got a gun, Mr. Tritt," he said.

"Of course he's got a gun," snapped Tritt. He pushed the guard aside. "It's right in his coat." Tritt jammed his thick hand into Logan's left coat pocket and flailed it about. "It's not in that pocket," he said after a moment.

"It's not in any pocket," Logan said. "I don't have one."

"You do. You *do* have a gun. I saw it," Tritt answered, beginning to sound like a child in an argument. He spun Logan around and pulled the coat off him with a jerk. The sleeves turned inside out. Eagerly, the teller pulled the side pockets out, checked the inside pocket and the breast pocket, then ran his hands over the entire garment, crumpling it. "The—the gun's not in his coat," he said finally.

"It's not in his pants," the guard added.

Tritt stepped over to the table quickly. "It's around here somewhere," he said. "We were sitting right here." He stood directly in front of the closed drawer, and his hands began to move meaninglessly over the tabletop. He picked up the neat stack of deposit slips, put them down again, then looked under the desk blotter as though it could have concealed a gun.

Logan knew he had to stop this. "Is there anyplace I can remove the rest of my clothes?" he asked loudly, slipping the suspenders from his shoulders. Several depositors had gathered on the other side of the marble fence to watch, and Mr. Pinkson had had enough.

"Oh, no, no," he said, almost shouting. "That won't be necessary, Mr. Logan. Louie said you were unarmed. Now, Louie, put *your* gun away, and for goodness' sake, request the customers to please move on."

"But Mr. Pinkson, you must believe me," Tritt said, coming over to the manager. "This man held a gun on me and—"

"It's hard to know what to believe," said Pinkson. "But no money was stolen, and I don't see how we can embarrass Mr. Logan further with this matter. Please, Mr. Logan, do pull up your suspenders."

It was a shattering moment for the teller—the first time his word had ever been doubted at the bank.

"But sir, I insist that this man—"

"I must ask you to return to your cage now, Mr. Tritt," Pinkson said, badly agitated. Tritt obeyed.

The manager helped Logan put on his coat, then steered him over to his desk. "This is all a terrible mistake, Mr. Logan. Please do sit down now, please." The friendly little man was breathing heavily. "Now, I just want you to know that if you should press this complaint, it—it would go awfully bad for us down in the main office downtown, and I—"

"Please don't get excited, Mr. Pinkson," Logan said with a smile. "I'm not going to make any complaint." Logan passed the whole thing off casually. Mr. Tritt imagined he saw a gun, that's all. It was simply one of those aberrations that perfectly normal people get occasionally. Now, could Mr. Pinkson finish cashing his bonds? The manager paid him the eighty-three fifty, continuing to apologize.

Logan left the bank and walked through the soft snowfall, whistling a Christmas carol. He'd handled himself perfectly.

In the weeks that followed, Logan continued to do business with Tritt, just as though nothing had happened. The teller tried to remain aloof and calm, but he added sums incorrectly and his hands shook. One day late in January, Tritt stood up halfway through a transaction, his great body trembling. "Excuse me, Mr. Logan," he murmured, and rushed off into the corridor behind the cages. Pinkson followed him, and Logan took advantage of the moment to check on the gun. It lay untouched in the drawer. Then Pinkson came back alone. "I'm awfully sorry to delay you again, sir," he said. "Mr. Tritt doesn't feel too well."

"Did he imagine he saw another gun?" Logan asked quietly.

"No. He just upsets easily now. Ever since that incident with you last month, he's been like a cat on a hot stove."

"I've noticed he's changed."

"He's lost that old, calm banking touch, Mr. Logan. And of course, he's in constant fear of a new hallucination."

"I'm sorry to hear that," Logan said, looking genuinely concerned. "It's very sad when a person loses his grip."

"It's particularly disappointing to me," the manager said sadly. "I brought Tritt into the bank myself, you see. Had him earmarked for a big spot downtown someday. Fine man. Intelligent, steady, accurate—why, he's been right down the line on everything. But now—now he's—well, I *do* hope he gets over this."

"I can understand how you feel," Logan said sympathetically. He smiled inside at the precision of his planning. Fat William Tritt had been undermined just enough—not only in Pinkson's mind, but in his own.

On the tenth of March, Norman Logan acted again. When Tritt was seated across the table from him, Logan said, "Well, here we go again, Mr. Tritt." Tritt's head came up, and once more he was looking into the barrel of the toy automatic. He did not try to speak. "Now go get the ten thousand," ordered Logan. "And this time, do it."

Without objecting, the teller moved quickly to his cage. Logan slipped the gun back into the drawer; then he took his briefcase from the floor and stood it on the edge of the table. Pinkson's telephone didn't buzz, and the guard remained out of sight. After a few moments, Tritt came out of the cage, carrying a small cloth bag.

"All right, continue with the bonds," Logan said. "The bag goes on the table between us." Logan shifted forward and opened the bag, keeping the money out of sight behind the briefcase. The clean new bills were wrapped in thousand-dollar units, each package bound with a bright yellow strip of paper. Logan counted through one package, and with Tritt looking right at him, he placed the package of money carefully in the briefcase.

"There," he said. "Now finish with the bonds." Tritt finished filling out the form and got Logan's signature. He was not as flustered as Logan had thought he'd be. "Now listen, Tritt," Logan went on, "my getaway is all set, of course, but if you give any signal before I'm out of the bank, I'll put a bullet into you—right here." Logan pointed to the bridge of his own nose. "Please don't think I'd hesitate to do it. Now get back to your cage."

Tritt returned to the cage. While his back was turned, Logan slipped the bag of money from his briefcase and dropped it into the drawer, next to the gun. He eased the drawer into the table, took the briefcase, and walked out of the bank.

Outside, he stood directly in front of the entrance, as though he were waiting for a bus. After just a few seconds, the burglar alarm went off with a tremendous electrical shriek, and the old guard came running out of the door after him.

He was followed immediately by Pinkson, the assistant manager, and Tritt.

"Well, gentlemen," said Logan, his hands raised again in front of the guard's gun, "here we are again, eh?"

A crowd was gathering, and Pinkson sent the assistant to turn off the alarm. "Come, let's all go inside," he said. "I don't want any fuss out here."

It was the same kind of scene that they'd played before, only now Logan—the twice-wronged citizen—was irate, and now ten thousand dollars was missing from William Tritt's cage. Tritt was calm, though.

"I was ready for him this time," he said proudly to Pinkson. "I marked ten thousand worth of twenties. My initial is on the band. The money's in his briefcase."

"Oh, for heaven's sake, Tritt," Logan shouted suddenly, "who ever heard of making a getaway by waiting for a bus? I don't know what your game is, but—"

"Never mind my game," said Tritt. "Let's just take a look in your briefcase."

He wrenched it from Logan's hand, clicked the lock, and turned the briefcase upside down. A group of corrected examination books fell out. That was all.

"See?" said Logan. "Not a cent." The guard put away his gun as Pinkson began to pick up the scattered books.

Tritt wheeled, threw the briefcase against the wall, and grabbed Logan by the lapels. "But I gave you the money. I did. I did!" His face was a pasty gray, and his voice high. "You put it in the briefcase. I saw you. I *saw* you do it!" He began to shake Logan in a kind of final attempt to shake the ten thousand dollars out of him.

Pinkson straightened up with the exam books and said, "For goodness' sake, Mr. Tritt. Stop it. Stop it."

Tritt stopped shaking Logan, then turned wildly to Pinkson. "You don't believe me!" he shouted. "You don't believe me!" he shouted. "You don't believe me!"

"It's not a question of—"

"I'll find that money. I'll show you who's lying." He rushed over to the big table and swept it completely clear with one wave of his heavy arm. The slips fluttered to the floor, and the inkwell broke, splattering black ink over the carpet. Tritt pulled the table in a wild, crashing arc across the green carpet, smashing it into Pinkson's desk. Logan saw the dusty drawer come open about a half-inch.

The big man dropped clumsily to his knees and began to pound on the carpet with his flattened hands as he kept muttering, "It's around here someplace—a cloth bag." He grabbed a corner of the carpet and flipped it back with a grunt. It made a puff of dust and revealed only a large triangle of empty, dirty floor. A dozen people had gathered outside the marble fence by now, and all the tellers were peering through the glass panes of the cages at Tritt.

"I'll find it! I'll find it!" he shouted. A film of sweat was on his forehead as he stood up, turned, and advanced again toward the table. The slightly opened drawer was in plain sight in front of him, but everyone's eyes were fixed on Tritt, and Tritt did not see the drawer under the overhang of the table.

Logan turned quickly to Pinkson and whispered, "He may be dangerous, Mr. Pinkson. You've got to calm him." He grabbed Pinkson by the arm and pushed him backward several feet, so that the manager came to rest on the edge of the table, directly over the drawer. The exam books were still in his hand.

"Mr. Tritt, you *must* stop this!" Mr. Pinkson said.

"Get out of my way, Pinkson," said Tritt, coming right at him, breathing like a bull. "You believe him, but I'll show you. I'll find it!" He placed his hands on Pinkson's shoulders. "Now get away, you fool."

"I won't take that from anyone," snapped Pinkson. He slapped Tritt's face with a loud, stinging blow. The teller stopped, stunned, and suddenly began to cry.

"Mr. Pinkson. Mr. Pinkson, you've *got* to trust me."

Pinkson was immediately ashamed of what he had done. "I'm sorry, my boy. I shouldn't have done that."

"I tell you he held a gun on me again. A real gun—it's not my imagination."

"But why didn't you call Louie?" Pinkson said. "That's the rule, you know."

"I wanted to catch him myself. He—he made such a fool of me last month."

"But that business last month was hallucination," said Pinkson, looking over at Logan. Logan nodded.

"It's no hallucination when ten thousand dollars is missing," Tritt shouted.

"That's precisely where the confusion arises in my mind," Mr. Pinkson said slowly. "We'll get it straight, but in the meantime, I must order your arrest, Mr. Tritt."

Logan came and stood next to Pinkson, and they both looked sympathetically at the teller as he walked slowly, still sobbing, back to the cage.

"I'm just sick about it," Pinkson said.

"I think you'll find he's not legally competent," said Logan, putting a comforting thought into Pinkson's head.

"Perhaps not."

Logan showed his concern by helping to clean up the mess that Tritt had made. He and the assistant manager placed the table back into its position against the far wall, Logan shoving the dusty drawer firmly closed with his fingertips as they lifted it.

Norman Logan returned to the bank late the next day. He sat at the table to make a deposit, and he felt a pleasantly victorious sensation surge through him as he slipped the gun and the ten thousand dollars out of the drawer and into his overcoat pocket. As he walked out the front door past the guard, he met Mr. Pinkson, who was rushing in.

"Terrible. Terrible," the little man said, without even pausing to say hello.

"What's that?" Logan asked calmly.

"I've just been talking to the doctors at Bellevue about Tritt," Pinkson said. "He seems all right, and they've released him. Unfortunately, he can answer every question except 'Where's the money?' " Logan held firmly to the money in his pocket and continued to extend his sympathies.

Back at his apartment, Logan borrowed a portable typewriter from the man upstairs. Then he sat down and wrote a note:

Dear Mr. Pinkson:
   I'm returning the money. I'm so sorry. I guess I didn't

know what I was doing. I guess I haven't known for some time.

After looking up Tritt's initials on an old deposit slip, he forged a small, tidy *W.T.* to the note.

Logan wiped his fingerprints from the bills and wrapped them, along with the note, in a neat package. For one delicious moment he considered how nice it would be to hang on to the money. He could resign from the university, go out West, and continue his research on his own. But that wasn't part of the plan, and the plan was working too well to tamper with it now. Logan drove to the post office nearest Tritt's apartment and mailed the money to Pinkson at the bank.

In the morning, Mr. Pinkson telephoned Logan at the university. "Well, it's all cleared up," he said, relieved but sad. "Tritt returned the money, so the bank is not going to press the charges. Needless to say, we're dropping Tritt. He not only denies having taken the money, he also denies having returned it."

"I guess he just doesn't know what he's doing," Logan said.

"Yes. That's what he said in the note. Anyway, Mr. Logan, I—I just wanted to call and apologize for the trouble we've caused you."

"Oh, it was no trouble for me," Logan replied, smiling.

"And you've been very helpful, too," Pinkson added.

"I was glad to be of help," Logan said quietly. "Delighted, in fact."

They said good-bye then, and Logan walked across the hall to begin his ten-o'clock botany lecture.

"The Dusty Drawer." *Alfred Hitchcock Presents*, May 31, 1959. Directed by Herschel Daugherty. Teleplay by Halsted Welles, based on Harry Muheim's short story "The Dusty Drawer" (*Collier's*, May 3, 1952). With Dick York (Norman Logan), Philip Coolidge (Mr. Tritt), Wilton Graff (Mr. Pinkson).

The Hitchcock script was based on a short story of mine of the same name that appeared in the late *Collier's* magazine in 1952. I subsequently adapted it into a one-hour script for presentation on the *Philco Television Playhouse*—"live from New York" as they used to say.

My Philco script used the device of the performer-as-narrator. William Prince played the lead, and he would play a scene, turn from the scene to comment to the camera, then turn back into the scene. It was a complex device that worked against the essential simplicity of the prose piece. But I liked it. Maybe because I had written it!

I had no connection with the making of the Hitchcock version, and I remember seeing it some years later with no *freshness* in my view. I was just looking to see how it differed from "my" versions. It was an unfair way to look at a perfectly substantial show. But that's the way I was in those days—back in the Pleistocene era. Matter of fact, I would like to see it again sometime.

Harry Muheim

DOROTHY SALISBURY DAVIS

Backward, Turn Backward

SHERIFF ANDREW WILLETS STOOD at the living-room window and watched his deputies herd back from the lawn another surge of the curious, restive people of Pottersville. Some had started out from their houses, shops, or gardens at the first sound of his siren, and throughout the long morning the crowd had swelled, winnowed out, and then swelled again.

Behind him in the kitchen, from which the body of Matt Thompson had been recently removed, the technical crew of the state police were at work with microscope and camera, ultraviolet lamp and vacuum cleaner. He had full confidence in them, but grave doubts that their findings would add much weight to, or counterbalance by much, the spoken testimony against Phil Canby. They had not waited, some of those outside, to give it to police or state's attorney; they passed it one to another, neighbor to stranger, stranger sometimes back again to neighbor.

It was possible to disperse them, the sheriff thought, just as a swarm of flies might be waved from carrion; but they would as quickly collect again, unless it were possible to undo murder—unless it were possible to go out and say to them: "It's all a mistake. Matt

Thompson fell and hit his head. His daughter Sue got hysterical when she found him . . ." Idle conjecture. Even had he been able to say that to the crowd, they would not have dispersed. They would not have believed it. Too many among them were now convinced that they had been expecting something like this to happen.

There was one person in their midst responsible in large measure for this consensus, a lifetime neighbor of both families, Mrs. Mary Lyons, and she was prepared also to give evidence that Phil Canby was not at home with his grandson the night before, at the hour he swore he was at home and asleep.

Sheriff Willets went outdoors, collected Mrs. Lyons, and led her across the yard between the Thompson house and the house where Phil Canby lived with his daughter and son-in-law, and up her own back steps. From the flounce of her skirts and the clack of her heels, he could tell she didn't want to come. She smiled when she looked up at him, a quick smile in which her eyes had no part.

"I hope this won't take long, Andy," she said when he deliberately sat down, forcing her hospitality. "I should give the poor girl a hand."

"In what way, Mrs. Lyons?"

"With the house," she said, as though there would be nothing unusual in her helping Sue Thompson with the house. "It must be a terrible mess."

"You've lots of time," he said. "There's nobody going to be in that house for quite a while except the police."

Mrs. Lyons made a noise in her throat, a sort of moan, to indicate how pained she was at what had happened across her backyard.

"You were saying over there," Willets went on, "that you knew something terrible was going to happen."

"Something terrible did happen, even before this," she said. "Phil Canby taking after that girl. Sue Thompson's younger than his own daughter."

"Just what do you mean, taking after her?"

"I saw him kiss her," she said. Then, as though it had hurt her to say it in the first place, she forced herself to be explicit. "A week ago last night I saw Phil Canby take Sue in his arms and kiss her. He's over sixty, Andy.''

"He's fifty-nine,'' the sheriff said, wondering immediately what difference a year or two made, and why he felt it necessary to defend the man in the presence of this woman. It was not that he was defending Canby, he realized: he was defending himself against the influence of a prejudiced witness. ''And he gave it out the next day that he was going to marry her, and she gave it out she was going to marry him. At least, that's the way I heard it.''

"Oh, you heard it right,'' Mrs. Lyons said airily, folding her hands in her lap.

If it had been of her doing, he should not have heard it right, the sheriff thought. But Phil Canby had passed the age in life, and had lived too much of that life across the hedge from Mary Lyons, to be either precipitated into something or forestalled from it by her opinions. Had he looked up on the night he proposed to Sue Thompson and seen her staring in the window at them, likely the most he would have done would be to pull the window shade in her face.

"Would you like your daughter to marry a man of fifty-nine, Andy?''

"My daughter's only fifteen,'' the sheriff said, knowing the answer to be stupid as soon as he had made it. He was no match for her, and what he feared was that he would be no match for the town, with her sentiments carrying through it as they now were carrying through the crowd across the way. They would want Phil Canby punished for courting a young girl, whatever Canby's involvement in her father's murder. ''How old is Sue Thompson, Mrs. Lyons?''

"Nineteen, she must be. Her mother died giving birth to her the year after I lost Jimmie.''

"I remember about Jimmie,'' the sheriff said, with relief. Remembering that Mary Lyons had lost a boy of four made her more tolerable. He wondered now how close she had got to Matt Thompson when his wife died. Nobody had been close to him from then on that Willets could remember. He had been as sour a man as ever gave the devil credence. A gardener by trade, Thompson had worked for the town of Pottersville, tending its landscape. A lot of people said that whatever tenderness he had went into the care of his flowers. One thing was agreed upon by all of them, it didn't go into the care of his daughter. As he thought about it now, Willets caught a forlorn picture from memory: Sue as a child of five or six trotting to church at her father's side, stopping when he stopped, going on when he went on, catching at his coattail when she needed balance but never at his hand, because it was not offered to her. Would no one but him remember these things now?

"How long has it been since you were in the Thompson house, Mrs. Lyons?"

Her eyes narrowed while she weighed his purpose in asking it. "I haven't been in the house in fifteen years," she said finally.

He believed her. It accounted in part for her eagerness to get into it now. "She isn't much of a housekeeper, Sue," he said, to whet her curiosity further and to satisfy his own on what she knew of her neighbors. "Or maybe that's the way Matt Thompson wanted it."

She leaned forward. "What way?"

"It has a funny dead look about it," he said. "It's not dirty, but it just looks like nothing has been put in or taken out in fifteen years."

"He never got over his wife's death," Mrs. Lyons said, "and he never looked at another woman."

Her kind had no higher praise for any man, he thought. "Who took care of Sue when she was a baby?"

"Her father."

"And when he was working?"

"I don't know."

"From what I've heard," he lied, for he had not yet had the opportunity to inquire elsewhere, "you were very good to them, and so was Phil Canby's wife in those days."

"Mrs. Canby was already ailing then," she snapped. "I was good to both families, if I say it myself."

"And if you don't," the sheriff murmured, "nobody else will."

"What?"

"People have a way of being ungrateful," he explained.

"Indeed they do."

"You know, Mrs. Lyons, thinking about it now, I wonder why Matt didn't offer Sue for adoption."

"You might say he did to me once." A bit of color tinged her bleached face after the quick, proud answer. She had probably been at the Thompson house night and day then with solicitudes and soups, when Matt was home and when he wasn't home.

Assuming Thompson to have been sarcastic with her—and he had had a reputation for sarcasm even that far back—the sheriff said, "Would you have taken the child? You must've been lonesome . . . after Jimmie."

For once she was candid with him, and soft as he had not known her to be since her youth. "I'd have thought a good deal about it. I had a feeling there was something wrong with her. She was like a little old maid, all to herself. She's been like that all her life—even in school, they say."

"It makes you understand why she was willing to marry Phil Canby," the sheriff said quietly. "Don't it?"

"Oh, I don't blame her," Mrs. Lyons said. "This is one case where I don't blame the woman."

Willets sighed. Nothing would shake her belief that there was something immoral in Phil Canby's having proposed marriage to a girl younger than his own daughter. "Last night," he said, "your husband was away from home?"

"He was at the Elks' meeting. I was over at my sister's and then I came home about ten-thirty. I looked at the clock. I always do. It takes me longer to walk home than it used to."

"And that was when you heard the baby crying?"

"It was crying when I came up the back steps."

Phil Canby had been baby-sitting with his grandson while his daughter, Betty, and his son-in-law, John Murray, were at the movies. It was his custom to stay with young Philip every Thursday night, and sometimes oftener, because he lived with them; but on Thursdays Betty and her husband usually went to the movies.

"And you're sure it was the Murray baby?"

"Who else's would it be over that way? I couldn't hear the Brady child from here. They're five houses down."

The sheriff nodded. Phil Canby swore that he was in bed and asleep by that time, and he swore that the baby had not cried. He was a light sleeper, in the habit of waking up if little Philip so much as whimpered. The neighbors to the south of the Murray house had not heard the crying, nor for that matter the radio in the Murray house, which Canby said he had turned on at ten o'clock for the news. But they had been watching television steadily until eleven-thirty. By that time the Murrays had come home and found Phil and the baby Philip each asleep in his own bed.

But to the north of the Murrays, in the corner house where Sue Thompson claimed she was asleep upstairs, her father Matt had been bludgeoned to death sometime between ten o'clock and midnight.

"And you didn't hear anything else?" the sheriff asked.

"No, but I didn't listen. I thought maybe the baby was sick and I was on the point of going down. Then I remembered it was Thursday night and Mr. Canby would be sitting with him. He wouldn't take the time of day from me."

Not now he wouldn't, the sheriff thought. "Have you any idea how long the baby was crying, Mrs. Lyons?"

"I was getting into bed when he stopped. That was fifteen minutes later, maybe. I never heard him like that before, rasping like for breath. I don't know how long the poor thing was crying before I got home."

If Phil Canby had murdered Matt Thompson and then reached home by a quarter to eleven, he would have had time to quiet baby Philip and to make a least a pretense of sleep himself before his family came home. Betty Murray admitted that her father was in the habit of feigning sleep a good deal these days, his waking presence was so much of an embarrassment to all of them. Scarcely relevant except as a practiced art.

Willets took his leave of Mrs. Lyons. What seemed too relevant to be true, he thought, striding over the hedge which separated her yard from the Thompsons', was that Phil Canby admitted quarreling with Thompson at nine o'clock that night, and in the Thompson kitchen.

After the first exchange of violent words between the two households, when Phil Canby and Sue Thompson made known their intentions of marriage, an uneasy, watchful quiet had fallen between them. Sue Thompson had not been out of the house except with her father, and then to Sunday prayer meeting. Matt Thompson had started his vacation the morning his daughter told him. Vacation or retirement: he had put the hasty choice up to the town supervisor. Thompson then had gone across to Betty Murray. He had never been in Betty's house before, not once during her mother's long illness or at her funeral; and if he had spoken to Betty as a child, she could not remember it. But that morning he spoke to her as a woman, and in such a manner and with such words that she had screamed at him, "My father is not a lecher!" To which he had said, "And my daughter is not a whore. Before she takes to the bed of an old man, I'll shackle her!" When John Murray came home from the office that night and heard of it, he swore that he would kill Matt Thompson if ever again he loosed his foul tongue in Betty's presence.

But Matt Thompson had gone into his house and pulled down all the shades on the Murray side, and Phil Canby had gone about the trade he had pursued in Pottersville since boyhood. He was a plumber, and busier that week for all the talk about him in the town. All this the sheriff got in bits and pieces, mostly from Betty Murray. When Thursday night had come around again, she told him, she felt that she wanted to get out of the house. Also, she had begun to feel that if they all ignored the matter, the substance of it might die away.

So she and John had gone to the movies, leaving her father to sit with the baby. About eight-thirty, Sue Thompson had come into the yard and called to Phil. He went out to her. She had asked him to come over and fix the drain to the kitchen sink. Her father was sleeping, she told him, but he had said it would be all right to ask him. Canby had gone back into the house for his tools and then had followed her into the Thompson house, carrying a large plumber's wrench in his hand. When Phil Canby had told this to the sheriff that morning—as frankly, openly, as he spoke of the quarrel between him and Thompson, a quarrel so violent that Sue hid in the pantry through it—Willets got the uncanny feeling that he had heard it all before and that he might expect at the end of the recitation as candid and calm a confession of murder.

But Canby had not confessed to the murder. He had taken alarm, he said, when Matt Thompson swore by his dead wife to have him apprehended by the state and examined as a mental case. He knew the man to do it, Thompson had said, and Canby knew the man of whom he spoke: Alvin Rhodes, the retired head of the state hospital for the insane. Thompson had landscaped Rhodes's place on his own time when Rhodes retired, borrowing a few shrubs from the Pottersville nursery to do it. This the sheriff knew. And he could understand the extent of Canby's alarm when Canby told about the confinement of a friend on the certification of his children, and on no more grounds apparent to Canby than that the man had become cantankerous, and jealous of the house which he had built himself and in which he was becoming, as he grew older, more and more of an unwelcome guest. Phil Canby had bought the house in which he now lived with his daughter. He had paid for it over thirty years, having had to add another mortgage during his wife's invalidism. Unlike his friend, he did not feel a stranger in it. The baby had even been named after him, but he was well aware of the tax his wooing of Sue Thompson put upon his daughter and her husband.

All this the sheriff could understand very well. The difficulty was to reconcile it with the facts of the crime. For example, when Canby left the Thompson house, he took with him all his tools save the large wrench with which Thompson was murdered. Why leave it then—or later—except that to have taken it from beside the murdered man and to have had it found in his possession (or without it when its ownership was known) was to leave no doubt at all as to the murderer? All Canby would say was that he had forgotten it.

Willets went to the back door of Canby's house. He knocked, and Betty Murray called out to him to come in. Little Philip was in his high chair, resisting the apple sauce his mother was trying to spoon into him. The sheriff stood a moment watching the child, marveling at the normalcy that persists through any crisis when there is a baby about. Every blob of sauce spilled on the tray Philip tried to shove to the floor. What he couldn't get off the tray with his hands, he went after with his tongue.

The sheriff grinned. "That's one way to get it into him."

"He's at that age now," his mother said, cleaning up the floor. She looked at Willets. "But I'm very grateful for him, especially now."

The sheriff nodded. "I know," he said. "Where's your father?"

"Up in his room."

"And the Thompson girl?"

"In the living room. Sheriff, you're not going to take them . . ."

"Not yet," he said, saving her the pain of finishing the sentence. He started for the inside door and paused. "I think Mrs. Lyons would be willing to have her there for a bit."

"I'll bet she would," Betty said. "I had to close the front windows, with people gaping in to see her. Some of them, and they weren't strangers either, kept asking . . . where her boyfriend was."

"It won't be for long," Willets said; and then because he had not quite meant that, he added: "It won't be this way for long."

"Then let her stay. I think she feels better here, poor thing, just knowing Papa's in the house." She got up then and came to him. She was a pretty girl, and like her father's, her eyes seemed darker when they were troubled. "Mr. Willets, I was talking to Papa a while ago. He was trying to tell me about . . . him and

Sue. He told her when he asked her to marry him that he was going to be as much a father to her . . . as a husband.'' Betty colored a bit. ''As a lover,'' she corrected. ''That's what he really said.''

''And did he tell you what she had to say to that?''

''She said that's what she wanted, because she'd never had either one.''

The sheriff nodded at the obvious truth in that.

''I thought I'd tell you,'' Betty went on, ''because I know what everybody says about Papa and her. They think he's peculiar. Almost like what I told you Matt Thompson said. And he's not. All the time mother was sick, until she died, he took care of her himself. He even sent me away to school. Most men would have said that was my job, and maybe it was, but I was terribly glad to go. Then when mother died, and I got married, it must have seemed as though . . . something ended for him. And fifty-nine isn't really very old.''

''Not very,'' Willets said, being so much closer to it than she was.

''I'm beginning to understand what happened to him,'' Betty said. ''I wish I'd thought about it sooner. There might have been something . . . somebody else.''

The sheriff shook his head. ''That's a man's own problem till he's dead.''

''You're right,'' she said after a moment. ''That's what really would have been indecent.''

The sheriff nodded.

''I wish it was possible to separate the two things,'' Betty said as he was leaving, ''him and Sue—and Mr. Thompson's murder. I wish to God it was.''

''So do I,'' the sheriff said, thinking again of the pressures that would be put upon him because it was not possible to separate them, not only by the townspeople but by the state's attorney, who would find it so much more favorable to prosecute a murderer in a climate of moral indignation.

On the stairway, with its clear view of the living room, he

paused to watch Sue Thompson for a moment, unobserved. She was sitting with a piece of crochet work in her lap, at which she stitched with scarcely a glance. Whatever her feelings, the sheriff thought, she was not grieving. She had the attitude of waiting. All her life she had probably waited—but for what? Her father's death? A dream lover? A rescuer? Surely her girlish dreams had not conjured up Phil Canby in that role. The strange part of it was that it seemed unlikely to the sheriff she had dreamed of rescue at all. However she felt about her father, she did not fear him. Had she been afraid of him, she could not have announced to him that she intended to marry Phil Canby. And because she was not afraid of him, Willets decided, it was difficult to imagine that she might have killed him. She was a soft, plump girl, docile-eyed, and no match for her father physically. Yet she was the one alternate to Phil Canby in the deed, and he was the only one who knew her well enough to say if she was capable of it.

The sheriff went on and knocked at Canby's door. "I've got to talk to you some more, Phil."

Canby was lying on the bed staring at the ceiling. "I've told you all I know," he said, without moving.

The sheriff sat down in the rocker by the open window. The radio, which Canby claimed to have been listening to at ten o'clock the night before, was on a table closer to the window; and across the way, no more than fifteen yards, the neighbors had not heard it.

"Mrs. Lyons says that little Philip was crying at ten-thirty last night, Phil."

"Mrs. Lyons is a liar," Canby said, still without rising. His thin gray hair was plastered to his head with sweat, and yet he lay on his back where no breeze could reach him. A pulse began to throb at his temple. The skin over it was tight and pale; it reminded Willets of a frog's throat.

"Betty admits you didn't change the baby. That wasn't like you, Phil, neglecting him."

"He was sleeping. I didn't want him to wake up. I had to think of my plans."

"What plans?"

"My marriage plans."

"What were they?"

Finally Canby rose and swung his slippered feet over the side of the bed. He looked at Willets. "We're going to be married in Beachwood." It was a village a few miles away. "I've got a house picked out on the highway and I'll open a shop in the front of it."

It was fantastic, Willets thought: both Canby and the girl behaved as though they were not in any way suspected of Matt Thompson's death—as though nothing in the past should interfere with the future. This angered Willets as nothing save Mrs. Lyons's judgments had. "You're in trouble, Phil, and you're going to hang higher than your fancy plans if you don't get out of it. The whole damn town's against you."

"I know that," Canby said. "That's why I'm not afraid."

The sheriff looked at him.

"If I didn't know what everybody was saying," Canby went on, "I wouldn't of run off home last night when Matt Thompson said he was going to get me certified."

"Phil," the sheriff said with great deliberateness, "the state's attorney will maintain that's why you *didn't* run home, why you *weren't* in this house to hear the baby crying, why you *weren't* home in time to change him, why you *can't* admit Mrs. Lyons heard Philip crying! Because, he'll say, you were over in the Thompson kitchen, doing murder and cleaning up after murder."

Canby was shaking his head. "That baby don't cry. He don't ever cry with me around."

The sheriff got up and walked the length of the room and back, noting that Phil Canby was careful in his things, their arrangement, their repair. He was a tidy man. "You're still planning to marry her, then?" he said when he reached Canby.

"Of course. Why shouldn't I?"

The sheriff leaned down until he was face-to-face with the man. "Phil, who do *you* think killed her father?"

Canby drew back from him, his eyes darkening. "I don't

know," he said, "and I guess I never rightly cared . . . till now."

Willets returned to the rocker and took a pipe from his shirt pocket. He didn't light it; he merely held it in his hand as though he might light it if they could talk together. "When did you fall in love with Sue Thompson?"

Canby smoothed the crumpled spread. "Sounds funny, saying that about somebody my age, don't it?" Willets didn't answer and Canby went on: "I don't know. Whatever it was, it happened last spring. She used to stop by ever since she was a little girl, when I was out working in the yard, and watch me. Never said much. Just watched. Then when little Philip came, she used to like to see him. Sometimes I'd invite her in. If I was alone she'd come. Kind of shy of Betty, and whenever John'd speak to her she'd blush. John don't have a good opinion of her. He's like all the young fellows nowadays. They look at a girl's ankles, how she dances, what clothes she puts on. It's pure luck if they get a decent wife, what they look for in a girl . . ."

"You and Sue," the sheriff prompted, when Canby paused.

"Well, I was holding Philip one night and she was watching. He was puckering up to cry, so I rocked him to and fro and he just went off to sleep in my arms. I remember her saying, 'I wish I could do that,' so I offered her the baby. She was kind of scared of it." The man sank back on his elbows and squinted a bit, remembering. "It struck me then all of a sudden how doggone rotten a life Matt had give her as a kid."

"How, rotten?" the sheriff said.

"Nothing. No affection, no love at all. He bought her what she needed, but that was all. She was in high school before she knew people was different, what it was like to . . . to hold hands even."

"I wonder what got into him," Willets said. "Most men, losing a wife like he did, would put everything into the kid till they got another woman."

"He didn't want another woman. He liked his hurt till it got to mean more to him than anything else."

The sheriff shook his head. It might be so, although he could not understand it. "Go on about you and Sue," he said.

Canby took a moment to bring himself back to the contemplation of it. He sat up so that he could illustrate with his hands, the strong, calloused, black-nailed hands. "I put Philip into his cradle and she was standing there, and I just sort of put out my arms to her like she was maybe a little girl which'd lost something or was hurt, and she came to me." He paused, moistened his lips, and then plunged on. "While I was holding her . . . Oh, Jesus, what was it happened then?"

He sprang up from the bed and walked, his hands behind his back. "I thought that was all over for me. I hadn't felt nothing like it, not for years." He turned and looked down at Willets. "I was young again, that's all, and she wasn't a little girl. I was ashamed at first, and then I thought—what am I ashamed of? Being a man? I waited all summer thinking maybe it'd go away. But it didn't. It just got inside me deeper and quieter so's I wasn't afraid of it, and I wasn't ashamed. And when I asked her and she was willing to marry me, I explained to her that it couldn't be for long because I'm fifty-nine, but she didn't care." He opened his hands as if to show they were empty. "That's how it was, Andy. That's how. I can't explain it any more than that."

"That's how it was," the sheriff repeated, getting up, "but look how it is right now."

Willets went downstairs to Sue Thompson where she still sat, crochet work in hand, a bit back from the window yet with the people outside within her view.

"Know any of those folks, Miss Thompson?"

"No," she said, "I don't think I do."

He could believe that, although some of them had lived in the neighborhood all her lifetime. He sat down opposite her so that the light would be in her face. "Last night, Miss Thompson, why did you tell Mr. Canby your father said it would be all right to ask him to fix the drain?"

"Because I wanted him to come over. It was the only excuse I could think of."

"Your father didn't say it would be all right?"

"No."

"Didn't you expect trouble between them?"

"I didn't think my father would wake up."

"I see," the sheriff said. A pair, the two of them, he thought, unless their guilt was black as night: one as naïve as the other. The marks of Canby's wrench were on the drainpipe where he had actually commenced to work. "When did you and Mr. Canby expect to be married?"

"Soon. Whenever he said."

"Were you making plans?"

"Oh, yes," she said, smiling then. "I've been doing a lot of work." She held up the crocheting by way of illustration.

"Didn't you expect your father to interfere—in fact, to prevent it?"

"No," she said.

The sheriff rested his chin upon his hand and looked at her. "Miss Thompson, I'm the sheriff of this county. Your father was murdered last night, and I'm going to find out why, and who murdered him. You'd better tell me the truth."

"I'm telling you the truth, Mr. Willets. I know who you are."

"And you didn't expect your father to interfere with your marriage?"

"He never interfered with anything I did," she said.

"Did you know he told Betty Murray that he would chain you up rather than see you marry her father?"

"I didn't know that. He never said it to me."

"Just what did he say when you told him?"

"He laughed. I think he said something like, 'Well, doesn't that beat everything.'"

The sheriff sat up. "He was treating you like a half-wit. You're an intelligent girl. Didn't you resent it?"

"Of course," she said, as though surprised that he should ask. "That's one reason why I'm so fond of Phil . . . Mr. Canby."

"You resented it," Willets repeated, "and yet you did nothing about it?"

"I was waiting," she said.

"For what? For him to die? To be murdered?"

"No," she said, "just waiting."

"Have you always got everything you wanted by waiting, Miss Thompson?"

She thought about that for a moment. "Yes, I think I have . . . or else I didn't want it anymore."

Passive resistance, that's what it amounted to, the sheriff thought. If nations could be worn down by it, Matt Thompson was not invulnerable. But his murder was not passive resistance. "Last night you hid in the pantry during the quarrel?"

"Yes. Phil told me to go away, so I hid in there."

"Did you hear what they were saying?"

"Not much. I put my fingers in my ears."

"What did you hear exactly?"

She looked at him and then away. "I heard my father say 'insane asylum.' That's when I put my fingers to my ears."

"Why?"

"I was there once with him when I was a little girl."

"Can you tell me about it?" the sheriff said.

"Yes," she said thoughtfully. "There was a man working for him in the garden. I liked him, I remember. He would tickle me and laugh just wonderful. When I told my father that I liked him, he took me inside to see the other people. Some of them screamed at us and I was frightened."

"I see," the sheriff said, seeing something of Matt Thompson and his use of the afflicted to alarm the timid. "Last night, when did you come out of the pantry?"

"When my father told me to. He said it was all over and I could go up to bed."

"And you did? No words with him about the quarrel?"

"I went upstairs and went to bed, like I told you this morning."

"And you went to sleep right away because you felt so badly," he said, repeating her earlier account of it. He could see how sleep must have been her salvation many times. She had slept soundly through the night, by her account, and had wakened only to the persistent knocking of Phil Canby—who, when he was about to start his day's work, had remembered, so he said, the plumber's wrench. Going downstairs to answer Canby's knocking, she had discovered her father's body.

The sheriff took his hat. "You can have the funeral tomorrow, Miss Thompson," he said. "I'd arrange it quickly if I were you, and see to it there's a notice of it in the paper."

He went out the front door and across the yard, ignoring the questions pelted at him from the crowd. The technician in charge of the state crew was waiting. "I don't have much for you, Willets. Whoever did the job scrubbed up that kitchen afterwards. But good."

"Canby's clothes?"

"Nothing from that job on them. We'll run some more tests to be dead sure, if you want us to."

"I want you to. What about hers?"

"Not even a spot to test. I put them back in her room, night clothes and day clothes."

The sheriff thought for a moment. "What was the kitchen cleaned up with?"

"A bundle of rags. Left in the sink. They came out of a bag hanging beside the stove."

"Handy," the sheriff said, and went upstairs.

After the male sparsity and drabness in the rest of the house—and that was how Willets thought of it, as though a woman's hand had not touched it in years—Sue's room screamed with color. Her whole life in the house was in this one room. There was crochet work and needlework of multi- and clashing colors, laces and linens, stacked piece on piece. She had fashioned herself a fancy lamp shade that almost dripped with lace. At some time not too long before, she had tried her hand at painting, too. It was crude, primitive, and might very well be art for all he knew, but in his reckoning it was in contrast to the exact work of her needle. In a small rocker, left over from her childhood—perhaps even from her mother's childhood, by its shape and age—sat two dolls, faded and matted and one with an eye that would never close

again. The dust of years was ground into them, and he wondered
if they had been sitting there while she grew into womanhood, or
if upon her recent courtship—if Phil Canby's attentions could be
called that—she, a timid girl, and likely aware of her own igno-
rance, had taken them out to help her bridge the thoughts of marriage.

The bed was still unmade, Sue's pajamas lying on it. Not a button on the tops, he noticed, and the cloth torn out. The technician
had put them back where he had found them. Her dress lay with
its sleeves over the back of the chair, just as she had flung it on
retiring. She had, no doubt, put on a fresh dress to go out to the
fence and call Phil Canby. There was scarcely a crease in it. The
sheriff trod upon her slippers, a button, a comb. The rug, as he
looked at it, was dappled with colored thread from her sewing.
Not the best of housekeepers, Sue Thompson, he thought, going
downstairs and locking up the house; but small wonder, keeping
house only for herself and in one room.

George Harris, the state's attorney, was in the sheriff's office
when he returned to the county building. He didn't want to seem
too eager, Willets thought, since obviously the sheriff had not yet
made an arrest. He spoke of the murder as a tragedy and not a
case, and thus no doubt he had spoken of it in town.

"I've had a lot of calls, Andy," he said, "a lot of calls."

The sheriff grunted. "Did you answer them?"

Harris ignored the flippancy. "Not enough evidence yet, eh?"

"I'm going to put it all together now," Willets said. "When I
get it in a package I'll show it to you. Maybe in the morning."

"That's fine by me," Harris said. He started for the door and
then turned back. "Andy, I'm not trying to tell you how to run
your office, but if I were you, I'd call the local radio station and
give them a nice handout on it—something good for the nerves."

"Like what?"

"Oh, something to the effect that any suspect in the matter is
under police surveillance."

He was right, of course, Willets thought. The very mention of
such surveillance could temper would-be vigilantes. He called the

radio station and then worked through most of the night. His last tour of duty took him past the two darkened houses where his deputies kept sullen vigil.

Fifty or so people attended the funeral service and as many more were outside the chapel. Among them were faces he had seen about the town most of his life. With the murder they seemed to have become disembodied from the people who clerked, drove delivery trucks, or kept house. They watched him with the eyes of ghouls to see how long it would take him to devour his prey.

The minister spoke more kindly of Matt Thompson than his life deserved, but the clergyman had the whole orbit of righteousness, frugality, and justice to explore and, under the circumstances in the presence of those attending, the word *love* to avoid.

Phil Canby stood beside the girl as tall as he could, with the hard stoop of his trade upon his back. His head was high, his face grim. Sue wept as did the other women, one prompted by another's tears. Behind Canby stood his daughter and his son-in-law, John Murray—who, when the sheriff spoke to him at the chapel door, said he had taken the day off to "see this thing finished." It would be nice, Willets thought, if it could be finished by John Murray's taking the day off.

When the final words were said, people shuffled about uneasily. It was customary to take a last look at the deceased, but Matt Thompson's coffin remained unopened. Then his daughter leaned forward and fumbled at a floral wreath. Everyone watched. She caught one flower in her hand and pulled it from the rest, nearly upsetting the piece. She opened her hand and looked at the bloom. Willets glanced at Mrs. Lyons, who was on tiptoe watching the girl. She too was moved to tears by that. Then the girl looked up at the man beside her. If she did not smile, there was the promise of it in her round, blithe face. She offered him the flower. Phil Canby took it, but his face went as gray as the tie he wore. Mrs. Lyons let escape a hissing sound, as sure a condemnation as any words she might have cried aloud, and a murmur of wrathful shock went through the congregation. Willets stepped quickly to

Canby's side and stayed beside him until they returned to the Murray house, outside which he then doubled the guard.

He went directly to the state's attorney's office, for George Harris had had the report on his investigation since nine o'clock that morning.

"Everything go off all right?" Harris offered Willets a cigarette, shaking four or five out on the desk from the package. He was feeling expansive, the sheriff thought.

"Fine," he said, refusing the cigarette.

The attorney stacked the loose cigarettes. "I'll tell you the truth, Andy, I'm damned if I can see why you didn't bring him in last night." He patted the folder closest to him. It chanced to be the coroner's report. "You've done a fine job all the way. It's tight, neat."

"Maybe that's why I didn't bring him in," Willets said.

Harris cocked his head and smiled his inquisitiveness. At forty-five he was still boyish, and he had the manner of always seeming to want to understand fully the other man's point of view. He would listen to it, weigh it, and change his tactics—but not his mind.

"Because," the sheriff said, "I haven't really gone outside their houses to look for a motive."

The attorney drummed his fingers on the file. "Tell me the God's truth, Andy, don't you think it's here?"

"Not all of it," the sheriff said doggedly.

"But the heart of it?"

"The heart of it's there," he admitted.

" 'All of it' to you means a confession. Some policemen might have got it. I don't blame you for that."

"Thanks," Willets said dryly. "I take it, Mr. Harris, you feel the case is strong against him?"

"I don't predict the outcome," the attorney said, his patience strained. "I prosecute and I take the verdict in good grace. I believe the state has a strong case, yes." He shrugged off his irritation. "Much hinges, I think, on whether Canby could feel secure from interruption while he did the job, and afterward while he cleaned up."

Willets nodded.

Harris fingered through the folder and brought out a paper. "Here. The girl hid in the pantry when he told her to leave. She went upstairs to bed when her father told her to. Now I say that if she came downstairs again, all Canby had to do was tell her to go up again. She's the amenable type. Not bright, not stupid, just willing and obedient."

That from his documentation, Willets thought. If ever Harris had seen the girl it was by accident. "Then you think she was an accessory?" Certainly most people did now, having seen or heard of her conduct at the funeral.

The attorney pursed his lips. "I wouldn't pursue that right now. You haven't turned up anything to prove it. But he could feel secure about being able to send her upstairs again before she saw anything. That's what was important: that he could feel safe, secure. That's how I'd use it. Put that together with the Lyons woman's testimony and his own daughter's. No jury will take his word that he was home with his grandson between ten and eleven."

"Did he strip naked to do the job?" said Willets. "His clothes went through the lab."

"Old work clothes." The attorney looked him in the eyes. "There's been cleaner jobs than this before, and I'll prove it. I don't expect to go in with the perfect case. There's no such thing."

"Then all I have to do," Willets said, "is get the warrant and bring him in."

"That's all. The rest is up to me." The sheriff had reached the door when Harris called after him. "Andy . . . I'm not the s.o.b. you seem to think I am. It's all in here." He indicated the file. "You'll see it yourself when you get to where you can have some perspective."

Harris might very well be right, the sheriff thought as he walked through the county court building. He had to accept it. Either Harris was right and he had done his job as sheriff to the best of his ability and without prejudice, making the facts stand

out from sentiments . . . or he had to accept something that logic
would not sanction: Sue Thompson as the murderer of her own father. That this amenable girl, as Harris called her, who by the
very imperturbability of her disposition had managed a life for
herself in the house of her father—that she, soft and slovenly,
could do a neat and terrible job of murder, he could not believe.
But even granting that she could have done it, could someone as
emotionally untried as she withstand the strain of guilt? He
doubted it. Such a strain would crack her, he thought, much as an
overripe plum bursts while yet hanging on the tree.

But the motive, Canby's motive: it was there and it was not
there, he thought. It was the thing which so far had restrained him
from making the arrest—that, and his own stubborn refusal to be
pressured by the followers of Mary Lyons.

The sheriff sat for some time at his desk, and then he telephoned Matt Thompson's friend, Alvin Rhodes. The appointment made, he drove out to see the former superintendent of the
state hospital for the insane.

Rhodes, as affable as Thompson had been dour, told of Matt
Thompson's visiting him the previous Wednesday, the day before
his death. "We were not friends, Willets," the older man said,
"although his visit implies that we were. He was seeking advice
on his daughter's infatuation with a man three times her age."

As Thompson had grown more sullen with the years, the sheriff
thought, Rhodes had mellowed into affability upon retirement.
Such advice was not sought of someone uncongenial to the
seeker. "And did you advise him, Mr. Rhodes?"

"I advised him to do nothing about it. I recounted my experience with men of Canby's age who were similarly afflicted. The
closer they came to consummation, shall we say, the more they
feared it. That's why the May-and-December affairs are rare indeed. I advised him to keep close watch on the girl, to forestall an
elopement, and leave the rest to nature. In truth, Willets, although
I did not say it to him, I felt that if they were determined, he could
not prevent it."

"He cared so little for the girl," Willets said, "I wonder why he interfered at all. Why not let her go and good riddance?"

Rhodes drew his white brows together while he phrased the words carefully. "Because as long as he kept her in the house, he could atone for having begot her, and in those terms for having caused his wife's death." Willets shook his head. Rhodes added then: "I told him frankly that if anyone in the family should be examined, it was he and not the girl."

Willets felt the shock like a blow. "The girl?"

Rhodes nodded. "That's why he came to me, to explore the possibility of confining her—temporarily. In his distorted mind he calculated the stigma of such proceedings to be sufficient to discourage Canby."

And the threat of such proceedings, Willets thought, was sufficient to drive Canby to murder—as such threats against his own person were not. "I should think," he said, preparing to depart, "you might have taken steps against Matt Thompson yourself."

Rhodes rose with him. "I intended to," he said coldly. "If you consult the state's attorney, you will discover that I made an appointment with him for two o'clock yesterday afternoon. By then Thompson was dead. I shall give evidence when I am called upon."

The sheriff returned to the courthouse and swore out the warrant before the county judge. At peace with his conscience at last, he drove again to the Murray house. Betty Murray was staring out boldly at the watchers who had reconvened—as boldly as they were again staring in at her.

There would be a time now, Willets thought, when they could stare their fill and feel righteous in their prejudgment of the man. Only then would they be willing to judge the full story, only then would they be merciful, vindicating their vindictiveness. He ordered his deputies to clear the street. John Murray opened the door when the sheriff reached the steps.

"Better take Betty upstairs," Willets said to her husband. He could see the others in the living room, Sue and Phil Canby sitting at either end of the couch, their hands touching as he came.

"The old man?" John whispered. Willets nodded and Murray called to his wife. Betty looked at him over her shoulder but did not move from the window.

"You too, Miss Thompson," Willets said quietly. "You both better go upstairs with John."

Betty lifted her chin. "I shall stay," she said. "This is my father's house and I'll stay where I want to in it."

Nor did Sue Thompson make any move to rise. Willets strode across to Canby. "Get up," he said. "I'm arresting you, Phil Canby, for the willful murder of Matt Thompson."

"I don't believe it," Betty said from behind them, her voice high, tremulous. "If God's own angel stood here now and said it, I still wouldn't believe it."

"Betty, Betty," her husband soothed, murmuring something about good lawyers.

Canby's eyes were cold and dark upon the sheriff. "What's to become of her?" he said, with a slight indication of his head toward Sue.

"I don't know," Willets said. No one did, he thought, for she looked completely bemused, her eyes wide upon him as she tried to understand.

"You're taking him away?" she said as Canby rose. Willets nodded.

"It won't be for long," John Murray said in hollow comfort, and more to his wife than to the girl.

"Don't lie to her," Canby said. "If they can arrest me for something I didn't do, they can hang me for it." He turned to Willets. "If you're taking me, do it now."

"You can get some things if you want."

"I don't want no things."

Willets started to the door with him. Betty looked to her husband. He shook his head. She whirled around then on Sue Thompson. "Don't you understand? They're taking him to jail. Because of you, Sue Thompson!"

Canby stiffened at the door. "You leave her alone, Betty. Just leave her alone."

"I won't leave her alone and I won't leave Sheriff Willets alone. What's the matter with everyone? My father's not a murderer." Again she turned on Sue. "He's not! He's a good man. You've got to say it, too. We've got to shout it out at everybody, do you hear me?"

"Betty, leave her alone," her father repeated.

"Then get her out of here," John Murray said, his own fury rising with his helplessness. "She sits like a bloody cat and you don't know what's going on in her mind . . ."

The sheriff cut him off. "That's enough, John. It's no good." He looked at the girl. Her face was puckered up almost like an infant's about to cry. "You can go over home now, Miss Thompson. I'll send a deputy in to help you."

She did not answer. Instead she seemed convulsed with the effort to cry, although there was no sound to her apparent agony. Little choking noises came then. She made no move to cover her face, and as Willets watched, the face purpled in its distortion. All of them stared at her, themselves feeling straitened with the ache of tears they could not shed. Sue's body quivered and her face crinkled up still more, like a baby's.

Then the sound of crying came—a high, gurgling noise—and it carried with the very timbre and rasp of an infant's. Willets felt Phil Canby clutch his arm and he felt terror icing its way up his own spine; he heard a sick, fainting moan from Betty Murray between the girl's spasms, but he could not take his eyes from the sight. Nor could he move to help her. Sue hammered her clenched fists on her knees helplessly. Then she tried to get up, rocking from side to side. Finally she rolled over on the couch and, her backside in the air, pushed herself up as a very small child must. Her first steps were like a toddle when she turned and tried to balance herself. Then, catching up an ash stand which chanced to stand in her way, she ran headlong at Willets with it, the infantile screams tearing from her throat. . . .

In time it would be told that Sue Thompson reverted to the infancy she coveted at least once before her attack on Willets, rising from sleep as a child on the night of her father's quarrel with

Canby, ripping off her nightclothes when she could not manage the buttons, and in a rage with her father—when, perhaps, he berated her for nudity, immodesty, or some such thing a child's mind cannot comprehend—attacking him with a child's fury and an adult's frenzied strength . . . using the weapon at hand, Phil Canby's wrench.

Sheriff Willets could document much of it when the sad horror had been manifest before him: the crying Mrs. Lyons heard, even the cleaning up after murder, for he had watched Canby's grandson clean off the tray of his high chair. And he could believe she had then gone upstairs to fall asleep again and waken in the morning as Sue Thompson, nineteen years old and the happy betrothed of Phil Canby.

"Backward, Turn Backward." *Alfred Hitchcock Presents,* January 31, 1960. Directed by Stuart Rosenberg. Teleplay by Charles Beaumont, based on Dorothy Salisbury Davis' short story "Backward, Turn Backward" (*Ellery Queen's Mystery Magazine,* June 1954; collected in Davis' *Tales for a Stormy Night,* Countryman/Foul Play Press, 1984). With Tom Tully (Phil Canby), Alan Baxter (Sheriff Willett), Phyllis Love (Sue Thompson), Raymond Bailey (Harris), Paul Maxwell (Saul), David Carlile (Betty Murray), Peggy Converse (Miss Lyons), Selmer Jackson (Clergyman).

I watched with fascination a story that was totally foreign to me. That didn't matter. I enjoyed it. The cast was excellent, the suspense was gripping. Alas, it was still gripping when the show was over and Mr. Hitchcock was saying his inimitable adieus. Friends called to ask what happened. I wasn't sure myself. Then I remembered how the story ended as I had written it. It ought to have been an actress's dream, and a director's, but as Charles Beaumont, the screenwriter, wrote me afterward, it came across as a writer's nightmare: nobody in the audience understood the ending. Shall I say that Mr. Hitchcock himself proved its dramatic worth? In a picture, some years later, a picture which shall be nameless here. Mercifully, for more reasons than one.

Dorothy Salisbury Davis

JOHN D. MACDONALD

Hangover

HE DREAMED THAT HE HAD DROPPED SOMETHING, lost something of value in the furnace, and he lay on his side trying to look down at an angle through a little hole, look beyond the flame down into the dark guts of the furnace for what he had lost. But the flame kept pulsing through the hole with a brightness that hurt his eyes, with a heat that parched his face, pulsing with an intermittent husky rasping sound.

With this awakening, the dream became painfully explicable—the pulsing roar was his own harsh breathing, the parched feeling was a consuming thirst, the brightness was transmuted into pain intensely localized behind his eyes. When he opened his eyes, a long slant of early morning sun dazzled him, and he shut his eyes quickly again.

This was a morning time of awareness of discomfort so acute that he had no thought for anything beyond the appraisal of the body and its functions. Though he was dimly aware of psychic discomforts that might later exceed the anguish of the flesh, the immediacy of bodily pain localized his attentions. Even without the horizontal brightness of the sun, he would have known it was early. Long sleep would have muffled the beat of the taxed heart to a softened, sedate, and comfortable rhythm. But it was early

225

and the heart knocked sharply with a violence and in a cadence almost hysterical, so that no matter how he turned his head, he could feel it, a tack hammer chipping away at his mortality.

His thirst was monstrous, undiminished by the random nausea that teased at the back of his throat. His hands and feet were cool, yet where his thighs touched he was sweaty. His body felt clotted, and he knew that he had perspired heavily during the evening, an oily perspiration that left an unpleasant residue when it dried. The pain behind his eyes was a slow bulging and shrinking, in contrapuntal rhythm to the clatter of his heart.

He sat on the edge of the bed, head bowed, eyes squeezed shut, cool trembling fingers resting on his bare knees. He felt weak, nauseated, and acutely depressed.

This was the great joke. This was a hangover. Thing of sly wink, of rueful guffaw. This was death in the morning.

He stood on shaky legs and walked into the bathroom. He turned the cold water on as far as it would go. He drank a full glass greedily. He was refilling the glass when the first spasm came. He turned to the toilet, half falling, cracking one knee painfully on the tile floor, and knelt there and clutched the edge of the bowl in both hands, hunched, miserable, naked. The water ran in the sink for a long time while he remained there retching, until nothing more came but flakes of greenish bile. When he stood up, he felt weaker but slightly better. He mopped his face with a damp towel, then drank more water, drank it slowly and carefully, and in great quantity, losing track of the number of glasses. He drank the cold water until his belly was swollen and he could hold no more, but he felt as thirsty as before.

Putting the glass back on the rack, he looked at himself in the mirror. He took a quick, overly casual look, the way one glances at a stranger, the eye returning for a longer look after it is seen that the first glance aroused no undue curiosity. Though his face was grayish, eyes slightly puffy, jaws soiled by beard stubble, the long face with its even, undistinguished features looked curiously unmarked in relation to the torment of the body.

The visual reflection was a first step in the reaffirmation of identity. You are Hadley Purvis. You are thirty-nine. Your hair is turning gray with astonishing and disheartening speed.

He turned his back on the bland image, on the face that refused to comprehend his pain. He leaned his buttocks against the chill edge of the sink, and a sudden unbidden image came into his mind, as clear and supernaturally perfect as a colored advertisement in a magazine. It was a shot glass full to the very brim with dark brown bourbon.

By a slow effort of will, he caused the image to fade away. Not yet, he thought, and immediately wondered about his instinctive choice of mental phrase. Nonsense. This was a part of the usual morbidity of hangover—to image oneself slowly turning into an alcoholic. The rum sour on Sunday mornings had become a ritual with him, condoned by Sarah. And that certainly did not speak of alcoholism. Today was, unhappily, a working day, and it would be twelve-thirty before the first martini at Mario's. If anyone had any worries about alcoholism, it was Sarah, and her worries resulted from her lack of knowledge of his job and its requirements. After a man has been drinking for twenty-one years, he does not suddenly become a legitimate cause for the sort of annoying concern Sarah had been showing lately.

In the evening when they were alone before dinner, they would drink, and that certainly did not distress her. She liked her few knocks as well as anyone. Then she had learned somehow that whenever he went to the kitchen to refill their glasses from the martini jug in the deep freeze, he would have an extra one for himself, opening his throat for it, pouring it down in one smooth, long, silvery gush. By mildness of tone she had trapped him into an admission, then had told him that the very secrecy of it was "significant." He had tried to explain that his tolerance for alcohol was greater than hers, and that it was easier to do it that way than to listen to her tiresome hints about how many he was having.

Standing there in the bathroom, he could hear the early morning sounds of the city. His hearing seemed unnaturally keen. He realized that it was absurd to stand there and conduct mental argu-

ments with Sarah and become annoyed at her. He reached into the
shower stall and turned the faucets and waited until the water was
the right temperature before stepping in, just barely warm. He
made no attempt at first to bathe. He stood under the roar and
thrust of the high nozzle, eyes shut, face tilted up.

As he stood there he began, cautiously, to think of the previous
evening. He had much experience in this sort of reconstruction.
He reached out with memory timorously, anticipating remorse
and self-disgust.

The first part of the evening was, as always, easy to remember.
It had been an important evening. He had dressed carefully yesterday morning, knowing that there would not be time to come
home and change before going directly from the office to the hotel
for the meeting, with its cocktails, dinner, speeches, movie, and
unveiling of the new model. Because of the importance of the
evening, he had taken it very easy at Mario's at lunchtime, limit-
ing himself to two martinis before lunch, conscious of virtue—
only to have it spoiled by Bill Hunter's coming into his office at
three in the afternoon, staring at him with both relief and approval
and saying, "Glad you didn't have one of those three-hour
lunches, Had. The old man was a little dubious about your joining
the group tonight."

Hadley Purvis had felt suddenly and enormously annoyed.
Usually he liked Bill Hunter, despite his aura of opportunism, despite the cautious ambition that had enabled Hunter to become
quite close to the head of the agency in a very short time.

"And so you said to him, 'Mr. Driscoll, if Had Purvis can't go
to the party, I won't go either.' And then he broke down."

He watched Bill Hunter flush. "Not like that, Had. But I'll tell
you what happened. He asked me if I thought you would behave
yourself tonight. I said I was certain you realized the importance
of the occasion, and I reminded him that the Detroit people know
you and like the work you did on the spring campaign. So if you
get out of line, it isn't going to do me any good either."

"And that's your primary consideration, naturally."

Hunter looked at him angrily, helplessly. "Damn it, Had . . ."

"Keep your little heart from fluttering. I'll step lightly."

Bill Hunter left his office. After he was gone, Hadley tried very hard to believe that it had been an amusing little interlude. But he could not. Resentment stayed with him. Resentment at being treated like a child. And he suspected that Hunter had brought it up with Driscoll, saying very casually, "Hope Purvis doesn't put on a floor show tonight."

It wasn't like the old man to have brought it up. He felt that the old man genuinely liked him. They'd had some laughs together. Grown-up laughs, a little beyond the capacity of a Boy Scout like Hunter.

He had washed up at five, then gone down and shared a cab with Davey Tidmarsh, the only one of the new kids who had been asked to come along. Davey was all hopped up about it. He was a nice kid. Hadley liked him. Davey demanded to know what it would be like, and in the cab Hadley told him.

"We'll be seriously outnumbered. There'll be a battalion from Detroit, also the bank people. It will be done with enormous seriousness and a lot of expense. This is a pre-preview. Maybe they'll have a mockup there. The idea is that they get us all steamed up about the new model. Then, all enthused, we whip up two big promotions. The first promotion is a carnival deal they will use to sell the new models to the dealers and get them all steamed up. That'll be about four months from now. The second promotion will be the campaign to sell the cars to the public. They'll make a big fetish of secrecy, Davey. There'll be uniformed company guards. Armed."

It was as he had anticipated, only a bit bigger and gaudier than last year. Everything seemed to get bigger and gaudier every year. It was on the top floor of the hotel, in one of the middle-size convention rooms. They were carefully checked at the door, and each was given a numbered badge to wear. On the left side of the room was sixty feet of bar. Along the right wall was the table where the buffet would be. There was a busy rumble of male conversation, a blue haze of smoke. Hadley nodded and smiled at the people he knew as they worked their way toward the bar. With drink in hand, he went into the next room—after being checked again at the door—to look at the mockup.

Hadley had to admit that it had been done very neatly. The mockup was one-third actual size. It revolved slowly on a chest-high pedestal, a red-and-white convertible with the door open, with the model of a girl in a swimming suit standing beside it, both model girl and model car bathed in an excellent imitation of sunlight. He looked at the girl first, marveling at how cleverly the sheen of suntanned girl had been duplicated. He looked at the mannequin's figure and thought at once of Sarah and felt a warm wave of tenderness for her, a feeling that she was his luck and, with her, nothing could ever go wrong.

He looked at the lines of the revolving car and, with the glibness of long practice, he made up phrases that would be suitable for advertising it. He stood aside for a time and watched the manufactured delight on the faces of those who were seeing the model for the first time. He finished his drink and went out to the bar. With the first drink, the last traces of irritation at Bill Hunter disappeared. As soon as he had a fresh drink, he looked Bill up and said, "I'm the man who snarled this afternoon."

"No harm done," Hunter said promptly and a bit distantly. "Excuse me, Had. There's somebody over there I have to say hello to."

Hadley placed himself at the bar. He was not alone long. Within ten minutes he was the center of a group of six or seven. He relished these times when he was sought out for his entertainment value. The drinks brought him quickly to the point where he was, without effort, amusing. The sharp phrases came quickly, almost without thought. They laughed with him and appreciated him. He felt warm and loved.

He remembered there had been small warnings in the back of his mind, but he had ignored them. He would know when to stop. He told the story about Jimmy and Jackie and the punch card over at Shor's, and knew he told it well, and knew he was having a fine time, and knew that everything was beautifully under control.

But, beyond that point, memory was faulty. It lost continuity. It became episodic, each scene bright enough, yet separated from other scenes by a grayness he could not penetrate.

He was still at the bar. The audience had dwindled to one, a small man he didn't know, a man who swayed and clung to the edge of the bar. He was trying to make the small man understand something. He kept shaking his head. Hunter came over to him and took his arm and said, "Had, you've got to get something to eat. They're going to take the buffet away soon."

"Smile, pardner, when you use that word 'got.' "

"Sit down and I'll get you a plate."

"Never let it be said that Hadley Purvis couldn't cut his own way through a solid wall of buffet." As Hunter tugged at his arm, Hadley finished his drink, put the glass on the bar with great care, and walked over toward the buffet, shrugging his arm free of Hunter's grasp. He took a plate and looked at all the food. He had not the slightest desire for food. He looked back. Hunter was watching him. He shrugged and went down the long table.

Then, another memory. Standing there with plate in hand. Looking over and seeing Bill Hunter's frantic signals. Ignoring him and walking steadily over to where Driscoll sat with some of the top brass from Detroit. He was amused at the apprehensive expression on Driscoll's face. But he sat down and Driscoll had to introduce him.

Then, later. Dropping something from his fork. Recapturing it and glancing up to trap a look of distaste on the face of the most important man from Detroit, a bald, powerful-looking man with a ruddy face and small bright blue eyes.

He remembered that he started brooding about that look of distaste. The others talked, and he ate doggedly. They think I'm a clown. I'm good enough to keep them laughing, but that's all. They don't think I'm capable of deep thought.

He remembered Driscoll's frown when he broke into the con-

versation, addressing himself to the bald one from Detroit and
taking care to pronounce each word distinctly, without slur.

"That's a nice-looking mockup. And it is going to make a lot
of vehicles look old before their time. The way I see it, we're in a
period of artificially accelerated obsolescence. The honesty has
gone out of the American product. The great god is turnover. So
all you manufacturers are straining a gut to make a product that
wears out, or breaks, or doesn't last or, like your car, goes out of
style. It's the old game of rooking the consumer. You have your
hand in his pocket, and we have our hand in yours."

He remembered his little speech vividly, and it shocked him.
Maybe it was true. But that had not been the time or place to state
it, not at this festive meeting where everybody congratulated each
other on what a fine new sparkling product they would be selling.
He felt his cheeks grow hot as he remembered his own words.
What a thing to say in front of Driscoll! The most abject apologies
were going to be in order.

He could not remember the reaction of the man from Detroit, or
Driscoll's immediate reaction. He had no further memories of
being at the table. The next episode was back at the bar, a glass in
his hand, Hunter beside him speaking so earnestly you could almost see the tears in his eyes. "Good Lord, Had! What did you
say? What did you do? I've never seen him so upset."

"Tell him to go do something unspeakable. I just gave them a
few clear words of ultimate truth. And now I intend to put some
sparkle in that little combo."

"Leave the music alone. Go home, please. Just go home,
Had."

There was another gap, and then he was arguing with the drum-
mer. The man was curiously disinclined to give up the drums. A
waiter gripped his arm.

"What's your trouble?" Hadley asked him angrily. "I just
want to teach this clown how to stay on top of the beat."

"A gentleman wants to see you, sir. He is by the cloakroom.
He asked me to bring you out."

Then he was by the cloakroom. Driscoll was there. He stood

close to Hadley. "Don't open your mouth, Purvis. Just listen carefully to me while I try to get something through your drunken skull. Can you understand what I'm saying?"

"Certainly I can—"

"Shut up! You may have lost the whole shooting match for us. That speech of yours. He told me he wasn't aware of the fact that I hired Commies. He said that criticisms of the American way of life make him physically ill. Know what I'm going back in and tell him?"

"No."

"That I got you out here and fired you and sent you home. Get this straight. It's an attempt to save the contract. Even if it weren't, I'd still fire you, and I'd do it in person. I thought I would dread it. I've known you a long time. I find out, Purvis, that I'm actually enjoying it. It's such a damn relief to get rid of you. Don't open your mouth. I wouldn't take you back if you worked for free. Don't come back. Don't come in tomorrow. I'll have a girl pack your personal stuff. I'll have it sent to you by messenger along with your check. You'll get both tomorrow before noon. You're a clever man, Purvis, but the town is full of clever men who can hold liquor. Good-bye."

Driscoll turned on his heel and went back into the big room. Hadley remembered that the shock had penetrated the haze of liquor. He remembered that he had stood there, and he had been able to see two men setting up a projector, and all he could think about was how he would tell Sarah and what she would probably say.

And, without transition, he was in the Times Square area on his way home. The sidewalk would tilt unexpectedly, and each time he would take a lurching step to regain his balance. The glare of the lights hurt his eyes. His heart pounded. He felt short of breath.

He stopped and looked in the window of a men's shop that was still open. The sign on the door said OPEN UNTIL MID-NIGHT. He looked at his watch. It was a little after eleven. He had imagined it to be much later. Suddenly it became impera-tive to him to prove both to himself and to a stranger that he was not at all drunk. If he could prove that, then he would know that Driscoll had fired him not for drinking, but for his opinions. And would anyone want to keep a job where he was not permitted to have opinions?

He gathered all his forces and looked intently into the shop window. He looked at a necktie. It was a gray wool tie with a tiny figure embroidered in dark red. The little embroidered things were shaped like commas. He decided that he liked it very much. The ties in that corner of the window were priced at three-fifty. He measured his stability, cleared his throat, and went into the shop.

"Good evening, sir."

"Good evening. I'd like that tie in the window, the gray one on the left with the dark red pattern."

"Would you please show me which one, sir?"

"Of course." Hadley pointed it out. The man took a duplicate off a rack.

"Would you like this in a box, or shall I put it in a bag?"

"A bag is all right."

"It's a very handsome tie."

He gave the man a five-dollar bill. The man brought him his change. "Thank you, sir. Good night."

"Good night." He walked out steadily, carrying the bag. No one could have done it better. A very orderly purchase. If he ever needed proof of his condition, the clerk would remember him. "Yes, I remember the gentleman. He came in shortly before closing time. He bought a gray tie. Sober? Perhaps he'd had a drink or two. But he was as sober as a judge."

And somewhere between the shop and home, all memory ceased. There was a vague something about a quarrel with Sarah, but it was not at all clear. Perhaps because the homecoming scene had become too frequent for them.

He dried himself vigorously on a harsh towel and went into the bedroom. When he thought of the lost job, he felt quick panic. Another one wouldn't be easy to find. One just as good might be impossible. It was a profession that fed on gossip.

Maybe it was a good thing. It would force a change on them.

Maybe a new city, a new way of life. Maybe they could regain something that they had lost in the last year or so. But he knew he whistled in the dark. He was afraid. This was the worst of all mornings-after.

Yet even that realization was diffused by the peculiar aroma of unreality that clung to all his hangover mornings. Dreams were always vivid, so vivid that they became confused with reality. With care, he studied the texture of the memory of Driscoll's face and found therein a lessening of his hope that it could have been dreamed.

He went into his bedroom and took fresh underwear from the drawer. He found himself thinking about the purchase of the necktie again. It seemed strange that the purchase should have such retroactive importance. The clothing he had worn was where he had dropped it beside his bed. He picked it up. He emptied the pockets of the suit. There was a skein of dried vomit on the lapel of the suit. He could not remember having been ill. There was a triangular tear in the left knee of the trousers, and he noticed for the first time an abrasion on his bare knee. He could not remember having fallen. The necktie was not in the suit pocket. He began to wonder whether he had dreamed about the necktie. In the back of his mind was a ghost image of some other dream about a necktie.

He decided that he would go to the office. He did not see what else he could do. If his memory of what Driscoll had said was accurate, maybe by now Driscoll would have relented. When he went to select a necktie after he had shaved carefully, he looked for the new one on the rack. It was not there. As he was tying the one he had selected, he noticed a wadded piece of paper on the floor beside his wastebasket. He picked it up, spread it open, read the name of the shop on it, and knew that the purchase of the tie had been real.

By the time he was completely dressed, it still was not eight o'clock. He felt unwell, though the sharpness of the headache was dulled. His hands were shaky. His legs felt empty and weak.

It was time to face Sarah. He knew that he had seen her the previous evening. Probably she had been in bed, had heard him come in, had gotten up as was her custom, and no doubt there had been a scene. He hoped he had not told her of losing the job. Yet, if it had been a dream, he could not have told her. If he had told her, it would be proof that it had not been a dream. He went through the bathroom into her bedroom, moving quietly. Her bed had been slept in, turned back where she had gotten out.

He went down the short hall to the small kitchen. Sarah was not there. He began to wonder about her. Surely the quarrel could not have been so bad that she had dressed and left. He measured coffee into the top of the percolator and put it over a low gas flame. He mixed frozen juice and drank a large glass. The apartment seemed uncannily quiet. He poured another glass, drank half of it, and walked up the hallway to the living room.

Stopping in the doorway, he saw the necktie, recognized the small pattern. He stood there, glass in hand, and looked at the tie. It was tightly knotted. And above the knot, resting on the arm of the chair, was the still, unspeakable face of Sarah, a face the shiny hue of fresh eggplant.

"Hangover." *The Alfred Hitchcock Hour*, December 6, 1962. Directed by Bernard Girard. Teleplay by Lou Rambeau, based on John D. MacDonald's short story "Hangover" (*Cosmopolitan*, July 1956; collected in MacDonald's *End of the Tiger and Other Stories*, Gold Medal, 1966) and on Charles Runyon's short story "Hangover" (*Manhunt*, December 1960). With Tony Randall (Hadley Purvis), Jayne Mansfield (Marian), Dody Heath (Sandra Purvis), Robert P. Lieb (Bill Hunter), Myron Healey (Bob Blake), Tyler McVey (Driscoll), James Maloney (Cushman), June Levant (Saleswoman), William Phipps (Bartender), Chris Roman (Cliff), Richard Franchot (Albert).

The passage of years has not diminished my bafflement and annoyance at what television did to "Hangover." I was indeed pleased when I heard that it would be on the *Hitchcock Hour*. As soon as the titles came on the screen, I realized some committee of idiots had decided to combine my story with another story by Charles Runyon. The result, of course, was cluttered nonsense. The bright and shining spot was Tony Randall as Hadley Purvis. He was absolutely right. "Hangover" is, I think, a sufficiently strong story to carry the viewer along for the required fifty minutes of narrative flow. I suspect that it is decisions like this one, errors in taste and in performance, which have brought the networks to the sorry condition in which we see them today, dying and dwindling and flapping about in a hen yard of schlock.

John D. MacDonald

CHARLES RUNYON

Hangover

I COULDN'T FEEL THE HAMMERS in my head when I woke up. But I knew they were poised to thud into the base of my skull the moment I lifted my head from the pillow. My nose felt stuffed and swollen, as though someone were pinching the bridge tightly between thumb and forefinger.

I heard a noise in the kitchen. Something made of tin tipped over, rolled for what seemed like an hour, then hit the floor with a sound like the cymbals in a Wagner overture. My head began to throb. I tried to deal with the noise passively, without moving: "Marian! Are you in the kitchen?"

The only answer was a metallic echo, the kind you get from an empty house. I forced an eye open and saw that the opposite bed was empty. The spread lay neatly folded at the foot. The sheet was turned back as crisp and smooth as glass, ready to receive her body. But Marian hadn't slept there; she'd been gone for nearly two weeks.

I closed my eyes, and fragments of despair dropped like lead weights into my mind. I'd been thinking she came back last night. She smiled down at me the way she always did before coming to bed; with her eyes, hardly moving her lips. She was wearing the

pale blue nightdress I'd given her two months ago on our tenth anniversary. . . .

Hell, I must have dreamed it. I wanted her home, and that's the
kind of impossible wish that keeps distilleries in business.

I felt a warm weight pressing against my back. I turned
quickly, but it wasn't Marian. This girl's hair was the same dark
auburn color; but Marian had never let her hair get into such a tangled mess, with matted rat's nests above the ears.

I drew away from her. She frowned in her sleep and moved toward me. I slid out of bed, pulled on my robe, and looked down at
her. She was somewhere between twenty and twenty-five. If she
was pretty, I couldn't see it; not with her face lumpy and sagging
in sleep. Her upper lip arched outward to reveal two slightly protruding teeth. A line of saliva trailed from her mouth to the pillow, where it mixed with lipstick and formed a stain the color of
diluted blood.

I hated to deal with her now; even the intimacy of conversation
made my stomach queasy. But I wanted her out of my house, so I
shook her shoulder.

"Baby . . ." Without opening her eyes, she rolled her tongue
around her mouth. "Let's sleep a little longer, baby."

I could feel my patience slipping away. I hated that sticky, stupid, shopworn endearment; in thirty-five years I'd come to toler-
ate everything but being called "Baby." I shook her until her
eyes popped open. "What's your name?"

"God, did you wake me up for *that?*" She jerked the sheet
over her head. "Marian . . . you been calling me Marian."

I jerked the sheet off her head. "Dammit! That's my wife's
name."

"I know, Baby, I know." She kicked off the sheet and
stretched, her legs forming a straight line from toe to torso. "I'm
Sandra. You can call me Sandy."

She gave me a heavy-lidded smile she probably meant to be
sweet and seductive. To me it was like having syrup smeared on
my face. Her nakedness aroused me somewhat less than a tree
with the bark stripped off, though she had the fleshy, overblown

kind of figure that's supposed to be the American dream. She wasn't my dream, and that's why her presence threw me. I couldn't remember where I'd picked her up or why. My last sharp memory was coming home from the office Wednesday and feeling the emptiness of this house hit me like a fist in the stomach. I knew I couldn't spend another night talking to the furniture, so I'd gone out and started throwing down vodka martinis.

"Okay, Sandy," I said. "Where'd I meet you?"

She raised her eyebrows. "Hey, you really had a blackout. I'm a hostess at the Dolly Bar."

I frowned and shook my head. I couldn't place it.

"That's a strip joint on Fourth Street. Don't you remember *that?*"

"Would I ask if I did?"

"Aw . . . Baby's got a hangover, hasn't he?" She slid off the bed and started toward the door. "I'll get you something for that."

"Never mind. Just tell me when and why you came to my house."

She stopped in the door and turned. A hip stuck out and she cupped her palm over it. "Okay. You came into the Dolly Wednesday night. You bought me a few drinks, then a . . . former friend of mine tried to move in and you hit him. You hit him several times before they threw you out, and I liked the way you handled yourself. I took you with me to my hotel and next morning we came out here."

"What time was that?"

"About eleven."

"*Eleven?* Oh, Jesus." I saw myself staggering into my new tri/level house with a B-girl on my arm. That sort of thing wasn't done in Elysia. It was really PTA and Cub Scout country—even though its name conveyed a vision of satyrs and fat-hipped Greek women dressed in bunches of grapes. Elysia meant home and family to the men who worked in the city, and I'd broken one of the club bylaws. "Did anyone see you?"

"Well, I guess." Sandy shrugged. "You didn't tell me to

sneak in.'' She paused. ''Look, if there's any more questions, I'll be in the john.''

She walked away and slammed the bathroom door. A second later I heard a glass shatter in the kitchen.

I padded barefoot down the half-flight of stairs, walking with a bent-knee shuffle to stabilize my aching head. In the kitchen, I found that Marian's gray cat had overturned a flour canister and was anointing the room with white paw prints.

I cornered her and imprisoned her under my arm. I rubbed her behind the ears and surveyed the kitchen.

It was a mess. Odors of stale food and liquor rose from a sink piled high with dirty dishes and glasses. The stove held a stew pan filled with black pebbles which once were beans. I wondered what Marian would have said: she was the kind of woman who jumped up from the table and started washing dishes before they even cooled.

I saw two plates on the table. One held a puddle of gray grease with a slab of bacon in the center, garnished by a long auburn hair. My stomach did a half-gainer; eating with Sandy was even less appetizing than sleeping with her.

The cat mewed. ''All right, kid,'' I said. ''You first, then the other one.''

I shuffled through the long living room and found the front door open. The carpet around it was damp; the door had stood open all night and it had rained. I set the cat on the lawn and nudged her away with my toe.

Around the front steps lay proof that life in Elysia had flowed on without me. Several milk bottles warmed in the sun; I tried to count them but they kept moving. Two newspapers formed a wet, gluey mass on the sidewalk. A third lay near the door, crisp and dry and smelling of ink as I picked it up. I read the date beneath the flag: *Tuesday, July 19.*

Five days, I thought. A drop of sweat traced a cold path down my spine. *Oh, Jesus. Five days gone like bootleg liquor down the drain.*

I dropped the paper and stood there trying to remember. Nothing came but sweat, cool and clammy under my robe. The sun was a white-hot rivet tacked on a sheet of blue steel. It couldn't have been much past eight in the morning; I still had time to get to the office. But I remembered the winter sales program I was supposed to have presented to the board last Friday, and I knew that one more day would add little to the devastation.

I raised my eyes and saw my car crosswise in the drive. The back wheels rested on my neighbor's lawn. Now the whole damn town would know. Two women walked past, pushing empty grocery carts. They stared at me, then walked on with the studied concentration of students coming late to class. I was suddenly aware of my bare legs sticking out beneath my robe.

I went inside and slammed the door on the painful sunlight. I needed a drink. My nerves were rubbing together, rasping like the hind legs of a cricket.

The bar was a half-flight down in a basement room with sand-colored tile on the floor. The walls were lined with desert murals, and I reached the bar feeling I'd just trekked across the Qattara Depression on my hands and knees.

But the bar held no bourbon; no Scotch. I searched beneath it for the exotic liqueurs Marian had stocked against the day I reached the level of a party-giving executive. I wondered if she was sitting in her hotel room now, regretting that she'd ripped apart all those detailed blueprints for the future.

All the bottles were empty; we'd even drained the tall, slim containers of fiery Metaxa. Apparently we'd finished up on creme de cacao: I found two glasses containing a brown, concave residue, dry on the edge and damp in the center, like a pond in a drought.

I prowled the room and found a beer mug containing an inch of bourbon and a shredded cigarette butt. I fished out the butt, gulped down the bourbon, and shuddered like a volcano about to erupt. I swallowed three times before the bourbon gave up and decided to stay down.

After a minute I felt well enough to climb the stairs and call a cab. I felt even better when I'd done that; it would be a relief to get Sandy out of my house.

When I hung up, I found myself looking at the words I'd scrawled on the pad a week before: *Regent Hotel, CA-72700*. The number had cost me an eighty-dollar detective fee, but I'd never used it. I kept reminding myself that it was Marian who got caught cheating; not I. She had to come to me.

I got up and walked upstairs, away from the telephone. Outside the bedroom, I found my suit. It was crumpled, damp, and muddy. I lifted it with a bare toe and saw that it had bleached the hardwood beneath it, as skin is bleached by a bandage. I couldn't image what fuzz-brained impulse had driven me out into the rain. Maybe Sandy would know. . . .

I found her in the bathroom, standing under the shower with her back to me. Behind the portiere of needle-spray she looked like Marian—though a Marian drawn with thick pencil strokes that made my chest ache for the original. I felt a curious urge to shove the girl's head underwater and hold it there.

Instead, I tried to make my voice pleasant but brisk. "About finished?"

She halted in the act of lathering her belly. She turned, suds squeezing out between her fingers. "I like it slow, Baby." She smiled with one side of her mouth. "Wanta wash my back?"

I stretched out my hand and jerked the shower curtain together. Once I'd washed Marion's back; but that honeymoon ritual had been shelved several years ago. "Hurry up," I said. "I called a cab."

"A nice big Cadillac, and you use a cab?"

I could feel my tiny supply of patience seeping away. *"You'll* use it, Sandy—the minute it gets here."

"Wearing nothing but soap bubbles?" She ripped off a laugh that tweaked my nerves like a fingernail drawn across a blackboard. "Anyway, I can't leave you, Baby."

"Dammit! My name is Greg. Greg Maxwell."

"I know, Baby . . ."

"Don't call me that!"

"You liked it yesterday."

I walked to the washbasin and started throwing cold water on my face. Talking to Sandy was a pointless ordeal; she'd leave when the cab arrived. I wondered how much money she'd want. . . .

I wiped off the mirror and looked at my dripping image with detached, alcoholic disdain. I looked like someone who sang hymns in a skid row mission; a red-haired joker whose big frame hung loose inside an expensive bathrobe, as though tacked together by a hurried carpenter. The pallid face was patched here and there with red-black stubble, interspersed with tiny razor nicks.

I looked down at my hands. The knobby knuckles were scraped raw; the nails were cracked and chipped and tipped with black, dirt-filled crescents. I remembered my wet, muddy suit in the hall, and tried to recall what happened yesterday.

But yesterday was gone. So was the day before, and the day before that. Five days were lost, buried deep among three billion brain cells. A strange, violent character had taken over my body: an idiot who enjoyed being called "baby," and went for women who measured an ax-handle or more across the hips. Now he sat back in my mind and smirked from a perch atop a filing cabinet full of memories. *"Get out of here, Maxwell,"* he was saying. *"Those five days were mine, old buddy."*

"What?"

I jumped at the sound of Sandy's voice. "I didn't say anything."

"You said something about getting out of here."

"Oh, Jesus." My mind was splitting apart; I couldn't remember saying anything. I put both hands to my forehead and squeezed. "Sandy . . . what was I doing in the rain?"

"Don't you even remember *that?*"

I clamped my teeth together. "Sandy, all I know is that my suit's in a wet, muddy heap in the hall."

"Oh. Well . . ." She was silent a minute, then the shower curtain screeched. She came to stand behind me, enclosing me in her aura of scented bath soap. "You did that Friday night when the guy came to see why you hadn't come to work."

"What guy?"

"Gosh, I don't know his name—"

"Dammit! What did he look like?"

"Bug-eyed little fella. Kept eating candy."

"Candy . . ." My mouth went dry, and my skin felt hot and prickly. My boss was Harvey Reed, sales manager. His protruding eyes gave him a look of never quite believing what he saw. He chewed mints chain fashion to blunt a craving for cigarettes. "Go on," I told her.

"Well, he didn't stay long. He acted kind of teed off—didn't even taste the drink I fixed for him."

I whirled to face her. "Why the hell didn't you stay out of sight?"

She froze in the act of wiping her left ear. "Gee . . . I was trying to *help*. You said he was your boss and I wanted to treat him nice . . ."

"Oh, for God's sake!" I turned back and gripped the washbasin. Harvey was a nut on family integrity: *"A man who can't run his home has no business dealing with customers."* I remembered him saying that, looking like a surprised chipmunk with the mint tucked in his cheek. "Okay, Sandy. So he saw you. Now, how'd the rain get into the picture?"

"I . . . Are you sure you wanta hear?"

I spoke softly, watching my lips move in the mirror. "Sandy, for the last time, I wouldn't be asking if I didn't."

"Okay. Okay. Jesus, I wish you'd get drunk again. You're a lot more fun when you're drunk." She sighed. "Well . . . so when the guy left, you followed him outside, telling him he couldn't fire you because you already quit. You had a lot better job with United Oil, you told him. When he drove off you was standing on the lawn yelling at him—"

"Yelling?"

"Yeah, you were giving him hell, only I couldn't hear you so clear in the house. Then it started raining, and you got down on your hands and knees and dug your fingers into the lawn. I went out and asked what you lost. You said we were about to fall off the world and you wanted me to help you hold on—'' She started to laugh, then cut it short, "I'm sorry, but you did act . . . kind of funny.''

I shook my head, trying to clear it. Dark fragments of memory swirled like storm clouds; I remembered feeling that the earth was tipping away from the sun, pitching me into darkness. I'd been afraid of losing contact and flying off into cold, deep space without Marian there to anchor me. . . .

"Was it a good job?" asked Sandy. "I mean . . . I guess it was, but you mentioned the deal with the other company—''

"I made it up, Sandy. Now let's drop it." The concern in her voice sickened me. I didn't want sympathy; that's why I couldn't go back to the office. I'd mail my resignation; let them believe the story about United Oil. I might even be able to get on there, with a good recommendation—

Oh, sure. Harvey would grab at a chance to recommend me: *"Good man, Maxwell; aside from his drinking problem. Can't blame the boy, of course, considering his domestic situation."* Damn, damn, damn. Nobody would touch me with a ten-foot pole.

An electric shaver whirred, sawing at my nerves. I had a vision of Marian shaving her gently tapered legs. She didn't like me to watch her; shaving was a masculine act that made her feel coarse and indelicate.

I turned to see Sandy with her leg propped on the edge of the bathtub, running a tiny electric shaver along her thick calf. For a moment I watched it chew away the faint stubble, then it dawned on me that it was Marian's shaver. I jerked the cord from the wall plug and the whirring died.

Sandy looked up with her mouth open. "What the hell . . . ?''

"Where'd you get that shaver?"

"Why . . . you gave it to me last night.''

Last night. I'd been almost sure that Marian had taken it with her; apparently I was mistaken.

I held out my hand. "Let's have it.''

She gave it to me, watching my face. I wrapped the cord around the shaver and put it in the medicine cabinet; I'd have to clean it later, when my stomach settled. The air in the bathroom was mushy with the scent of bath soap.

"Did you bring any luggage?" I asked her.

"A suitcase, like you told me."

"Good. I'll help you pack."

She blinked in surprise. "Baby, *wait* a minute . . ."

"Clean up in here first. Then get dressed." I walked to the door. "And stop calling me baby."

I walked into the hall and took a deep breath. It didn't help much; I was sick with the knowledge that I'd thrown away ten years of work Friday night.

I found Sandy's cheap pasteboard suitcase in the bedroom and prowled through the house carrying it open under my arm. Sandy had treated the place like a burlesque runway. I found shoes in the living room, a negligee in the den, and underwear in the basement bar. They were black, sleazy garments that clung to my fingers.

I was nearly finished with the house when I heard a dog barking out back. It wasn't ours; Marian didn't like dogs. I went out and found our neighbor's Dalmatian spraddled on the naked black earth at the edge of the unfinished patio. He was growling at a beagle I'd never seen before.

I yelled, and they ran off. Then I wondered why the hell I bothered. The patio was Marian's idea, another page torn from her futures book. She'd had it started during my last two-month trip around our sales divisions. The night I came home, I'd found her with the contractor who had the job. He wasn't building a patio then. . . .

I went back inside and slammed the door. The next owner could finish the patio. Let him worry about the house and its twenty-five-year mortgage. I couldn't handle the payments without a job.

I'd have to move into a cheaper home in a different neighborhood. I had to start fresh in another job; maybe I'd even go back to pushing doorbells. *Damn.* I missed Marian. I needed her calm, realistic approach to problems; without her I was like a centipede with each leg trying to run in a different direction.

First I had to get rid of Sandy. I walked upstairs and found her wet footprints leading to the bedroom. She hadn't cleaned up the bathroom. In the bedroom, I found Marian's closet open, the clothes disarranged. I felt anger rise inside me.

I found Sandy in the kitchen drinking coffee. She wore the blue nightdress I'd given Marian on our last anniversary. I felt a stab of disappointment that Marian had left it behind; then the disappointment changed to anger. "Stand up," I told Sandy.

She rose slowly, her face blank.

"Now take off the robe."

Her face twisted in confusion. "But you *told* me to wear it yesterday."

I covered the distance between us in two quick steps. I gripped her arm and said: "Slip it off gently. I don't want it damaged." Gradually I tightened my grip until she began to move. "That's it. Now the other arm . . . easy."

When it was off she dropped back in her chair, rubbing her arm. "Your hands are strong, you know that? You oughta see the other marks you gave me." Her lower lip trembled. "I didn't mind them, though. You know why? Because you made me feel like a wife, and I went for that. All of a sudden you change . . ." Her eyes grew shiny and her face became pouchy and ugly.

I watched a tear roll down her cheek and felt my skin crawl. I didn't want her tears. "Isn't your cab here yet?"

"Sure." Her mouth twisted. "It's under the table."

"If it doesn't come you can walk. Now get dressed. I want you out of here when my wife comes back."

"Your *wife?* But you—" She closed her eyes for a minute, then opened them. "You sent her away because you caught her cheating on you."

"I didn't actually *catch* her . . ."

"She didn't deny it, you said."

I didn't want to argue, but the urge to justify myself pulled me in like quicksand. "Sandy, I'd been away for two months. During that time I wasn't exactly a . . . perfect husband myself. Anyway, I don't care what she did. She's coming back.''

"What about your promise?"

"Promise?"

She stood up, and her weak mouth seemed suddenly firm. "You said we'd go to Mexico. You'd sell the house, draw your money out of the bank, sell your stocks . . ."

"Oh, hell. Don't you realize I have no job? The house is mortgaged, I still owe money on the car, I've borrowed against my stocks. Sandy, you're trying to con the wrong man. I'm damn near broke."

Her chin came up at that. "I'm not trying to con you!"

"Then why don't you leave?"

"Because . . . you said you hated your wife because she was a cold, efficient machine. You liked me because I was warm and passionate and . . . and sloppy."

Suddenly I was tired of the conversation. "Listen, whatever happened during those five days, it's ended. I'm a different man. I've turned inside out. What I hated before, I like now. What I liked before, I now hate. You understand?"

"You hate me?"

"It isn't your fault, Sandy. It's just the way it works out."

"Thanks a lot." She walked to the door, then turned to face me. "You should've stayed drunk, Baby."

She walked out and up the stairs, grabbing her suitcase on the way. I watched her disappear into the bedroom, feeling as though I'd just detached a terrier from my leg.

While I waited for her to come down again, the cab arrived. I went out and told him to wait, then went back inside. I paced the long living room, impatient now that I'd decided to get Marian back. She'd be grateful, I thought, though she wouldn't show it. She'd be anxious to please, and I'd accept that. I'd have her make chocolate brownies and bring me coffee in bed. I'd loaf for a day or so, warm and musty under the covers with the soft feel of flannel. We'd make small talk and lazy daytime love. Though she thought there was something perverted about love in the daytime, she wouldn't deny me. Later I'd tell her about the job and we'd decide what to do. . . .

Sandy came down then, clad in a black sequined gown that must have been her working dress. It covered her just a little better than nothing, but I didn't care. I felt almost grateful to her, the way you feel toward a bore when he goes out the door after a long, trying evening. I pressed a twenty into her hand and said, "That's for the cab, Sandy."

She looked down at it sullenly, then stuffed it into her purse and walked out, the gown tight across her haunches. I hurried to the phone and dialed the Regent Hotel. "Give me Mrs. Maxwell's room," I told the operator.

"Just a moment, sir."

I drummed my fingers on the telephone stand while I waited. In my mind I saw Marian sitting in her room. Her small white hands reposed in her lap, palms up. Her nose had a faint blush of red on the end, just where it began to turn up. She'd been crying, or was about to cry. After a moment she rose, picked up her purse, and walked to the door. She paused before the mirror; a small woman fashioned without waste of bone and flesh. Her dark auburn hair was pulled back from her temples, the comb marks straight as plow-furrows on bottomland. On top the hair lay in careful, frozen curls, like a stylized Chinese drawing of the sea. She lifted her hand to touch an imperfection visible only to herself. Suddenly the phone rang . . .

The operator's voice pierced my ear. "Sorry, sir, Mrs. Maxwell checked out yesterday."

My stomach flipped over and a drop of sweat rolled slowly down my back. "Did she . . . leave an address?"

"No sir. Sorry."

I replaced the receiver, tasting a bitterness in my throat. I couldn't think; my mind was like an electrical appliance which had been struck by lightning. It seemed to give off smoke and a faint buzzing sound, but no power.

I heard a noise behind me. I turned to see Sandy standing there.

"I knew she wouldn't be there," she said. "She came here last night."

I could only look at her.

"You . . . sent her away again," said Sandy.

My mouth went dry. I thought of Marian coming home, hoping to be forgiven, finding me in that insane, drunken state and the house ravaged by a four-day orgy. "What . . . what did I say to her?"

"Gee, I don't know. You shoved me into the bathroom when she came. A long time later you came in and said she wouldn't get in our way again."

My face felt tight, as though someone had grabbed the skin at the back of my head and pulled, slitting my eyes and pulling my lips tight across my teeth so that my words came out blurred and fuzzy.

"Was that when I gave you the shaver and the nightdress?"

"Yes." Slowly her eyes grew round. "Baby, you look like you need a drink."

"Oh, Jesus. Jesus Christ." I squeezed my eyes shut and pressed my forehead against the cool, firm wood of the telephone stand. The memory came back all at once, like light returning to a city when the current is restored. It was bright, vivid, and unbearable . . .

The argument had lasted a long time, and we'd moved from room to room. Now we faced each other on the patio, and my voice was hoarse and my breath was ragged. Marian was stiff, sober, and firm as a tree; she'd seen the house, she'd sensed the other woman's presence, and now she was leaving. "This time, Greg, I'll never come back." I screamed curses at her. She regarded me with a cool, quizzical expression that drove my fury higher until there was only hate swirling in my mind. I knocked her down and pried a stone from the patio, lifted it above my head, and smashed it down with all my strength. Afterward, as I pried up more stones, I laughed at the way my hands were shaking.

Sandy's voice came to me from a distant, peaceful land, speaking with a sweetness that curdled my soul. "Let's get drunk, Baby. Don't worry about her. I'll stick with you. Always."

I heard dogs on the patio, fighting again. This time I knew what they were fighting over.

"Hangover." *The Alfred Hitchcock Hour,* December 6, 1962. Directed by Bernard Girard. Teleplay by Lou Rambeau, based on John D. MacDonald's short story "Hangover" (*Cosmopolitan,* July 1956; collected in MacDonald's *End of the Tiger and Other Stories,* Gold Medal, 1966) and on Charles Runyon's short story "Hangover" (*Manhunt,* December 1960). With Tony Randall (Hadley Purvis), Jayne Mansfield (Marian), Dody Heath (Sandra Purvis), Robert P. Lieb (Bill Hunter), Myron Healey (Bob Blake), Tyler McVey (Driscoll), James Maloney (Cushman), June Levant (Saleswoman), William Phipps (Bartender), Chris Roman (Cliff), Richard Franchot (Albert).

I never saw "Hangover," but I could write reams about the events surrounding the story from its conception—based on a real-life drama—to publication in *Manhunt* magazine. It is the Hope Diamond of short stories, with a history permeated with blood, bizarre coincidence, and permutations of evil. Let me give just one example.

At the time my agent, Scott Meredith, informed me of the TV sale, we were living in the Pacific Coast resort village of Zihuatanejo. The TV pay was several times what the original short story had sold for in the magazine, but there was one hitch. The contract had to be signed and notarized.

There was no notary public in Zihuatanejo. The nearest possibility was in Acapulco, a hundred and fifty miles down the coast. The problem was that a hurricane had destroyed all bridges between us and that city. The only boat getting through was from a brewery owned by the president of Mexico; it came once a week bringing beer and other emergency supplies for the fishermen. So I chartered a plane, thus setting the wheels in motion for what may have been the first attempted hijacking of passengers by a pilot.

The plane was small, with a capacity of three passengers plus pilot. In the back sat a young honeymoon couple from Kankakee, Illinois, but the bride had gotten a terrible case of the *turistas* and was getting away from a diet of bully beef and mangoes, which were all we had to eat in Zihuatanejo—oh yes, and fried bananas. Her stomach could hold nothing down, and the groom's tummy was none too stable either. Neither of them spoke Spanish, and they asked me to convey this information to the pilot. I did, noting a strange gleam in his eye but thinking no more about it.

What happened next was like something out of a Paul Bowles novel. It began when we had the pilot fly low over the village that had been wiped out by floodwaters pouring down off the mountains; nothing but a sandy floodplain where several hundred people had lived before. They were still digging down to retrieve the bodies of those buried under the silt. One could see little patches of blackened rubble where the bodies had been burned as they were brought up. No time for an elaborate ceremony—just a few quick words, a dash of holy water, drench the mess with kerosene and give it the torch. Possibly this set the mood for the pilot's attempt at extortion.

He flew away from there and circled far out to sea. The girl behind me was getting green, and her spouse begged me to instruct the pilot not to make any more swoops and dives unless he wanted a very sick woman on his hands. This pilot, a clean-cut Latino-lover type, said that the way to ensure a smooth ride was to pay extra. I took note of the fact that we were no longer flying toward Acapulco, but were circling somewhere out of sight of land. I asked the pilot how much, and he said, "Oh, about a hundred dollars per passenger." I relayed this information to the young man in the backseat. He only laughed and said derisively, "Does he think we're stupid? He wouldn't ditch his own plane." I wasn't so sure, so I turned to the pilot and said, "Let's discuss it when we get on the ground." The pilot looked astonished. Obviously he would have no leverage when we got on the ground. But he was new at the business of blackmailing and unsure of the next step. After a dive and a multiple-gravity pullout, succeeding only in evoking a gush of foul-smelling liquid from the girl, he straightened out and flew at top speed to Acapulco.

When I left him there on the tarmac, he parked as far from the hangar as he could get. The couple threw him a couple of hundred peso notes and staggered away. The pilot looked from the money to the filth in the back of his plane. I told him as I handed him my fare: "Here's a little extra for your service." He took the *toston,* a fifty-centavo piece that even then was nearly worthless, and flung it as far as he could. It tinkled and rolled across the pavement and disappeared into the scrubby jungle surrounding the airport.

And that is only one of the many strange incidents surrounding the story. I didn't get the contract notarized in Acapulco either, but that's another episode.

Charles Runyon

ROBERT BLOCH

A Home Away
from Home

THE TRAIN WAS LATE, and it must have been past nine
o'clock when Natalie found herself standing, all alone, on the
platform before Hightower Station.

The station itself was obviously closed for the night—it was only a
way-stop, really, for there was no town here—and Natalie wasn't
quite sure what to do. She had taken it for granted that Dr. Bracegirdle would be on hand to meet her. Before leaving London, she'd sent
her uncle a wire giving him the time of her arrival. But since the train
had been delayed, perhaps he'd come and gone.

Natalie glanced around uncertainly, then noticed the phone
booth which provided her with a solution. Dr. Bracegirdle's last
letter was in her purse, and it contained both his address and his
phone number. She had fumbled through her bag and found it by
the time she walked over to the booth.

Ringing him up proved a bit of a problem; there seemed to be an
interminable delay before the operator made the connection, and
there was a great deal of buzzing on the line. A glimpse of the hills
beyond the station, through the glass wall of the booth, suggested the

reason for the difficulty. After all, Natalie reminded herself, this was West Country. Conditions might be a bit primitive—

"Hello, hello!"

The woman's voice came over the line, fairly shouting above the din. There was no buzzing noise now, and the sound in the background suggested a babble of voices all intermingled. Natalie bent forward and spoke directly and distinctly into the mouthpiece.

"This is Natalie Rivers," she said. "Is Dr. Bracegirdle there?"

"Who did you say was calling?"

"Natalie Rivers. I'm his niece."

"His what, Miss?"

"Niece," Natalie repeated. "May I speak to him, please?"

"Just a moment."

There was a pause, during which the sound of voices in the background seemed amplified, and then Natalie heard the resonant masculine tones, so much easier to separate from the indistinct murmuring.

"Dr. Bracegirdle here. My dear Natalie, this is an unexpected pleasure!"

"Unexpected? But I sent you a 'gram from London this afternoon." Natalie checked herself as she realized the slight edge of impatience which had crept into her voice. "Didn't it arrive?"

"I'm afraid service is not of the best around here," Dr. Bracegirdle told her, with an apologetic chuckle. "No, your wire didn't arrive. But apparently you did." He chuckled again. "Where are you, my dear?"

"At Hightower Station."

"Oh, dear. It's in exactly the opposite direction."

"Opposite direction?"

"From Peterby's. They rang me up just before you called. Some silly nonsense about an appendix—probably nothing but an upset stomach. But I promised to stop round directly, just in case."

"Don't tell me they still call you for general practice?"

"Emergencies, my dear. There aren't many physicians in these parts. Fortunately, there aren't many patients, either." Dr. Bracegirdle started to chuckle, then sobered. "Look now. You say you're at the station. I'll just send Miss Plummer down to fetch you in the wagon. Have you much luggage?"

"Only my travel case. The rest is coming with the household goods, by boat."

"Boat?"

"Didn't I mention it when I wrote?"

"Yes, that's right, you did. Well, no matter. Miss Plummer will be along for you directly."

"I'll be waiting in front of the platform."

"What was that? Speak up, I can hardly hear you."

"I said I'll be waiting in front of the platform."

"Oh." Dr. Bracegirdle chuckled again. "Bit of a party going on here."

"Shan't I be intruding? I mean, since you weren't expecting me—"

"Not at all! They'll be leaving before long. You wait for Plummer."

The phone clicked off and Natalie returned to the platform. In a surprisingly short time, the station wagon appeared and skidded off the road to halt at the very edge of the tracks. A tall, thin, gray-haired woman, wearing a somewhat rumpled white uniform, emerged and beckoned to Natalie.

"Come along, my dear," she called. "Here, I'll just pop this in back." Scooping up the bag, she tossed it into the rear of the wagon. "Now, in with you—and off we go!"

Scarcely waiting for Natalie to close the door after her, Miss Plummer gunned the motor and the car plunged back onto the road.

The speedometer immediately shot up to seventy, and Natalie flinched. Miss Plummer noticed her agitation at once.

"Sorry," she said. "With Doctor out on call, I can't be away too long."

"Oh yes, the houseguests. He told me."

"Did he now?" Miss Plummer took a sharp turn at a cross-roads and the tires screeched in protest, but to no avail. Natalie decided to drown apprehension in conversation.

"What sort of man is my uncle?" she asked.

"Have you never met him?"

"No. My parents moved to Australia when I was quite young. This is my first trip to England. In fact, it's the first time I've left Canberra."

"Folks with you?"

"They were in a motor smashup two months ago," Natalie said. "Didn't the Doctor tell you?"

"I'm afraid not—you see, I haven't been with him very long." Miss Plummer uttered a short bark, and the car swerved wildly across the road. "Motor smashup, eh? Some people have no business behind the wheel. That's what Doctor says."

She turned and peered at Natalie. "I take it you've come to stay, then?"

"Yes, of course. He wrote me when he was appointed my guardian. That's why I was wondering what he might be like. It's so hard to tell from letters." The thin-faced woman nodded silently, but Natalie had an urge to confide. "To tell the truth, I'm just a little bit edgy. I mean, I've never met a psychiatrist before."

"Haven't you, now?" Miss Plummer shrugged. "You're quite fortunate. I've seen a few in my time. A bit on the know-it-all side, if you ask me. Though I must say, Dr. Bracegirdle is one of the best. Permissive, you know."

"I understand he has quite a practice."

"There's no lack of patients for *that* sort of thing," Miss Plummer observed. "Particularly amongst the well-to-do. I'd say your uncle has done himself handsomely. The house and all—but you'll see." Once again the wagon whirled into a sickening swerve and sped forward between the imposing gates of a huge driveway which led toward an enormous house set amid a grove of trees in the distance. Through the shuttered windows Natalie

caught sight of a faint beam of light—just enough to help reveal
the ornate facade of her uncle's home.

"Oh, dear," she muttered, half to herself.

"What is it?"

"The guests—and it's Saturday night. And here I am, all
mussed from travel."

"Don't give it another thought," Miss Plummer assured her.
"There's no formality here. That's what Doctor told me when I
came. It's a home away from home."

Miss Plummer barked and braked simultaneously, and the station wagon came to an abrupt stop just behind an imposing black
limousine.

"Out with you now!" With brisk efficiency, Miss Plummer
lifted the bag from the rear seat and carried it up the steps, beck-
oning Natalie forward with a nod over her shoulder. She halted at
the door and fumbled for a key.

"No sense knocking," she said. "They'd never hear me." As
the door swung open, her observation was amply confirmed. The
background noise which Natalie had noted over the telephone
now formed a formidable foreground. She stood there, hesitant,
as Miss Plummer swept forward across the threshold.

"Come along, come along!"

Obediently, Natalie entered, and as Miss Plummer shut the
door behind her, she blinked with eyes unaccustomed to the
brightness of the interior.

She found herself standing in a long, somewhat bare hallway.
Directly ahead of her was a large suitcase; at an angle between the
railing and the wall was a desk and chair. To her left was a dark
paneled door—evidently leading to Dr. Bracegirdle's private office, for a small brass plate was affixed to it, bearing his name. To
her right was a huge open parlor, its windows heavily curtained
and shuttered against the night. It was from here that the sounds of
sociability echoed.

Natalie started down the hall toward the stairs. As she did so,
she caught a glimpse of the parlor. Fully a dozen guests eddied
about a large table, talking and gesturing with the animation of

close acquaintance—with one another, and with the contents of the lavish array of bottles gracing the tabletop. A sudden whoop of laughter indicated that at least one guest had abused the Doctor's hospitality.

Natalie passed the entry hastily, so as not to be observed, then glanced behind her to make sure that Miss Plummer was following with her bag. Miss Plummer was indeed following, but her hands were empty. And as Natalie reached the stairs, Miss Plummer shook her head.

"You didn't mean to go up now, did you?" she murmured. "Come in and introduce yourself."

"I thought I might freshen up a bit first."

"Let me go on ahead and get your room in order. Doctor didn't give me notice, you know."

"Really, it's not necessary. I could do with a wash—"

"Doctor should be back any moment now. Do wait for him." Miss Plummer grasped Natalie's arm, and with the same speed and expedition she had bestowed on driving, she steered the girl forward into the lighted room.

"Here's Doctor's niece," she announced. "Miss Natalie Rivers, from Australia."

Several heads turned in Natalie's direction, though Miss Plummer's voice had scarcely penetrated the general conversational din. A short, jolly-looking fat man bobbed toward Natalie, waving a half-empty glass.

"All the way from Australia, eh?" He extended his goblet. "You must be thirsty. Here, take this. I'll get another." And before Natalie could reply, he turned and plunged back into the group around the table.

"Major Hamilton," Miss Plummer whispered. "A dear soul, really. Though I'm afraid he's just a wee bit squiffy."

As Miss Plummer moved away, Natalie glanced uncertainly at the glass in her hand. She was not quite sure where to dispose of it.

"Allow me." A tall, gray-haired, and quite distinguished-looking man with a black mustache moved forward and took the stemware from between her fingers.

"Thank you."

"Not at all. I'm afraid you'll have to excuse the major. The party spirit, you know." He nodded, indicating a woman in extreme décolletage chattering animatedly to a group of three laughing men. "But since it's by way of being a farewell celebration—"

"Ah, there you are!" The short man whom Miss Plummer had identified as Major Hamilton bounced back into orbit around Natalie, a fresh drink in his hand and a fresh smile on his ruddy face. "I'm back again," he announced. "Just like a boomerang, eh?"

He laughed explosively, then paused. "I say, you *do* have boomerangs in Australia? Saw quite a bit of you Aussies at Gallipoli. Of course that was some time ago, before *your* time, I daresay—"

"Please, Major." The tall man smiled at Natalie. There was something reassuring about his presence, and something oddly familiar, too. Natalie wondered where she might have seen him before. She watched while he moved over to the major and removed the drink from his hand.

"Now see here—" the major sputtered.

"You've had enough, old boy. And it's almost time for you to go."

"One for the road—" The major glanced around, his hands waving in appeal. "Everyone *else* is drinking!" He made a lunge for his glass, but the tall man evaded him. Smiling at Natalie over his shoulder, he drew the major to one side and began to mutter to him earnestly in low tones. The major nodded exaggeratedly, drunkenly.

Natalie looked around the room. Nobody was paying the least attention to her except one elderly woman who sat quite alone on a stool before the piano. She regarded Natalie with a fixed stare that made her feel like an intruder on a gala scene. Natalie turned away hastily and again caught sight of the woman in décolletage. She suddenly remembered her own desire to change her clothing

and peered at the doorway, seeking Miss Plummer. But Miss Plummer was nowhere to be seen.

Walking back into the hall, she peered up the staircase.

"Miss Plummer!" she called.

There was no response.

Then from out of the corner of her eye, she noted that the door of the room across the hallway was ajar. In fact, it was opening now, quite rapidly, and as Natalie stared, Miss Plummer came backing out of the room, carrying a pair of scissors in her hand. Before Natalie could call out again and attract her attention, Miss Plummer had scurried off in the other direction.

The people here, Natalie told herself, certainly seemed odd. But wasn't that always the case with people at parties? She crossed before the stairs, meaning to follow Miss Plummer, but found herself halting before the open doorway.

She gazed in curiously at what was obviously her uncle's consultation room. It was a cozy, book-lined study with heavy, leather-covered furniture grouped before the shelves. The psychiatric couch rested in one corner near the wall, and near it was a large mahogany desk. The top of the desk was quite bare save for a cradle telephone, and a thin brown loop snaking out from it.

Something about the loop disturbed Natalie, and before she was conscious of her movement she was inside the room looking down at the desktop and the brown cord from the phone.

And then she realized what had bothered her. The end of the cord had been neatly severed from its connection in the wall.

"Miss Plummer!" Natalie murmured, remembering the pair of scissors she'd seen her holding. *But why would she have cut the phone cord?*

Natalie turned just in time to observe the tall, distinguished-looking man enter the doorway behind her.

"The phone won't be needed," he said as if he'd read her thoughts. "After all, I *did* tell you it was a farewell celebration." And he gave a little chuckle.

Again Natalie sensed something strangely familiar about him, and this time it came to her. She'd heard the same chuckle over the phone, when she'd called from the station.

"You must be playing a joke!" she exclaimed. "You're Dr. Bracegirdle, aren't you?"

"No, my dear." He shook his head as he moved past her across the room. "It's just that no one expected you. We were about to leave when your call came. So we had to say *something.*"

There was a moment of silence. Then, "Where *is* my uncle?" Natalie asked at last.

"Over here."

Natalie found herself standing beside the tall man, gazing down at what lay in a space between the couch and the wall. An instant was all she could bear.

"Messy," the tall man nodded. "Of course it was all so sudden, the opportunity, I mean. And then they *would* get into the liquor—"

His voice echoed hollowly in the room, and Natalie realized the sounds of the party had died away. She glanced up to see them all standing there in the doorway, watching.

Then their ranks parted and Miss Plummer came quickly into the room, wearing an incongruous fur wrap over the rumpled, ill-fitted uniform.

"Oh, my!" she gasped. "So you found him!"

Natalie nodded and took a step forward. "You've got to do something," she said. "Please!"

"Of course you didn't see the others," Miss Plummer said, "since they're upstairs. The Doctor's staff. Gruesome sight."

The men and women had crowded into the room behind Miss Plummer, staring silently.

Natalie turned to them in appeal. "Why, it's the work of a madman!" she cried. "He belongs in an asylum!"

"My dear child," murmured Miss Plummer as she quickly closed and locked the door and the silent starers moved forward. "This *is* an asylum. . . ."

"A Home Away from Home." *The Alfred Hitchcock Hour,* September 27, 1963. Directed by Herschel Daugherty. Teleplay by Robert Bloch, based on his own short story "A Home Away from Home" (*Alfred Hitchcock's Mystery Magazine,* June 1961; collected in Bloch's *Tales in a Jugular Vein,* Pyramid, 1965). With Ray Milland (Dr. Fenwick), Claire Griswold (Natalie Rivers), Virginia Gregg (Miss Gibson), Peter Leeds (Andrew), Beatrice Kay (Sara Sanders), Ben Wright (Dr. Norton), Mary La Roche (Ruth), Connie Gilchrist (Martha), Jack Searle (Nicky Long), Ronald Long (Major), Peter Brooks (Donald), Brendan Dillon (Inspector Roberts), Richard Peel (Officer).

Of all my stories televised on the Hitchcock programs, "A Home Away from Home" probably comes closest to Sir Alfred's slightly Hitchcockeyed view of the world.

That's because I wrote it expressly for a short story contest conducted by *Alfred Hitchcock's Mystery Magazine,* where it won a prize.

Essentially a variation on Poe's "The System of Dr. Tarr and Prof. Fether," the tale is a mere 2500 words long, and hardly contains enough material for dramatizing in a one-hour television format. So when producers Joan Harrison and Norman Lloyd asked me to adapt it for the show, I was faced with a problem. How could I expand the story line and develop the characters while still retaining the elements that made the plot work in its short printed version?

That's a rather pretentious way of saying that I wanted to keep the yarn exciting all the way through, instead of just adding extra scenes for padding. Television's arbitrary program length is like the legendary bed of Procrustes, which either stretched or shortened its unfortunate occupants to make them fit properly within its confines. But it takes more than simple stretching or squashing to make a story work, and my adaptation was no easy task.

If you read the little tale with this in mind, you'll see it wasn't easy for me to enlarge it and maintain the same level of suspense, but I think the dramatization worked.

At least it satisfied me to the point where, years later, I did two novels and a full-length motion picture set, in part, in a similar locale. Perhaps, if the truth were known, such a setting really *is* my home away from home. . . .

Robert Bloch

ELLERY QUEEN

Terror Town

YOUNG SUSAN MARSH, red-haired librarian of the Flora G. Sloan Library, Northfield's cultural pride, steered the old wreck of a Buick around the stanchion blinker in the center of town and headed up Hill Street toward the red-brick town hall, coughing as the smoke came through the floorboards. Susan did not mind. She had discovered that the 1940 sedan only smoked going up steep grades, and the road between town and her little cottage in Burry's Hollow three miles out of Northfield, her usual route, was mostly as level as a barn floor.

The vintage Buick had been given to Susan a few weeks before, in October, by Miss Flora Sloan, Northfield's undisputed autocrat and, to hear some tell it, a lineal descendant of Ebenezer Scrooge.

"But Miss Flora," Susan had exclaimed, her ponytail flying, "why me?"

" 'Cause all that robber Will Pease offered me on her was a measly thirty-five dollars," Miss Flora had said grimly. "I'd rather you had her for nothing."

"Well, I don't know what to say, Miss Flora. She's beautiful."

"Fiddle-de-sticks," the old lady had said. "She needs a ring

264

job, her tires are patchy, one headlight's broken, the paint's scrofulous, and she's stove in on the left side. But the short time I had her, she took me where I wanted to go, Susan, and she'll take you, too. It's better than pedaling a bike six miles a day to the library and back, the way you've had to do since your father passed on." And Miss Flora had added a pinch of pepper: "It isn't as if girls wore bloomers like they used to when *I* was twenty-two."

What Miss Flora had failed to mention was that the heater didn't work, either, and with November nipping up and winter only weeks away, it was going to be a Hobson's choice between keeping the windows open and freezing or shutting them and dying of asphyxiation. But right now, struggling up Hill Street in a smelly blue haze, Susan had a much more worrisome problem. Tom Cooley was missing.

Tommy was the son of a truck farmer in the Valley, a towhead with red hands, big and slow-moving like John Cooley and sorrow-eyed as his mother Sarah, who had died of pneumonia the winter before. Tommy had a hunger for reading, rare in Northfield, and Susan dreamed dreams for him.

"There's not an earthly reason why you shouldn't go on to college, Tommy," Susan had told him. "You're one of the few boys in town who really deserves the chance."

Tommy had said, "Even if Pa could afford it, I can't leave him alone."

"But sooner or later you've got to leave anyway. In a year or so you'll be going into the army."

"I don't know what Pa'll do." And he had quietly switched the subject to books.

There was a sadness about Tommy Cooley, a premature loss of joy, that made Susan want to mother him, high as he towered above her. She looked forward to his visits and their snatches of talk about Hemingway and Thomas Wolfe. Tommy's chores kept him close to the farm; but on the first Monday of every month, rain, snow, or good New England sunshine, he showed up at Susan's desk to return the armful of books she had recommended and go off eagerly with a fresh supply.

On the first Monday in November, there had been no Tommy. When he failed to appear by the end of that week, Susan was sure something was wrong, and on Friday evening she had driven out to the Cooley place. She found the weather-beaten farmhouse locked, a tractor rusting in a furrow, the pumpkins and potatoes unharvested, and no sign of Tommy. Or of his father.

So on Saturday afternoon she had closed the library early, and here she was, bound up Hill Street for Deputy Sheriff Linc Pearce's office on an unhappy mission.

It had to be the county officer, because Northfield's police department was Rollie Fawcett. Old Rollie's policing had been limited for a generation to chalking tires along Main and Hill streets and writing out overtime parking tickets for the one-dollar fines that paid his salary. There was simply no one in Northfield but Linc Pearce to turn to.

Susan wasn't happy about that, either.

The trouble was, to Linc Pearce she was still the female Peter Pan who used to dig the rock salt out of his bottom when old Mr. Burry caught them in his apples. Lengthening her skirts and having to wear bras hadn't changed Linc's attitude one bit. It wasn't as if he were immune to feminine charms; the way he carried on with that overblown Marie Fullerton just before he went into the army, for instance, had been proof enough of *that*. Linc came home quieter, more settled, and he was doing a fine job as Sheriff Howland's deputy in the Northfield district. But he went right back to treating Susan as if they were still swimming raw together in Burry's Creek.

She parked the rattletrap in the space reserved for "Official Cars Only" and marched into town hall with her little jaw set for anything.

Linc went to work on her right off. "Well, if it isn't Snubby Sue," he chuckled, uncoiling all six-foot-three of him from behind his paper-piled desk. "Leave your specs home?"

"What specs?" Susan could see the twitch of a squirrel's whisker at two hundred yards.

"Last time I passed you on the street, you didn't see me at all."

"I saw you, all right," Susan said coldly, and drew back like a snake. "Linc Pearce, if you start chucking me under the chin again—"

"Why, Susie," Linc said, "I'm just setting you a chair."

"Well." Susan sniffed, off guard. "Is it possible you're developing some manners?"

"Yes, ma'am," Linc said respectfully, and he swung her off the floor with one long arm and dropped her into the chair.

"Some day . . ." Susan choked.

"Now, now," Linc said gently. "What's on your mind?"

"Tom Cooley!"

"The silk purse you're working on?" He grinned. "What's Plowboy done now, swiped a library book?"

"He's disappeared," Susan snapped. And she told Linc about Tommy's failure to show up at the library and her visit to the Cooley farm.

Of course, Linc looked indulgent. "There's no mystery about John. He's been away over a month looking to buy another farm as far from Northfield as he can find. John took Sarah's death last winter hard. But Tommy's s'posed to be looking after the place."

"Well, he's not there."

"Probably took off on a toot."

"Leaving a four-thousand-dollar tractor to rust in a half-plowed lot?" Susan's ponytail whisked about like a red flag in a high wind. "Tommy's got too much farmer in him for that, Linc."

"He's seventeen, isn't he?"

"I tell you, I know Tommy Cooley, and you don't!"

Deputy Sheriff Lincoln Pearce looked at her. Then he reached to the costumer for his hat and sheep-lined jacket. "S'pose I'll never hear the end of it if I don't take a look."

Out in the parking space Linc walked all around Susan's recent acquisition. "I know," he said gravely. "It's John Wilkes Booth's getaway car. Where'd you get her?"

"Miss Flora Sloan *presented* her to me three weeks ago when she won that Chevrolet coupé at the bazaar drawing."

Linc whistled. Then he jackknifed himself and got in. "Is it safe? The chances I have to take on this job!"

He went on like that all the way into the valley. Susan drove stiffly, silently.

But as they turned into the Cooley yard, Linc said in an altogether different kind of voice, "John's home. There's his Jeep."

They found John Cooley crouched in a morris chair in his parlor, enormous shoulders at a beaten-down slope. The family Bible lay on his massive knees, and he was staring into space over it.

"Hi, John," Linc said from the doorway.

The farmer's head came about. The bleached gray eyes were dazed.

"My boy's gone, Lincoln." The voice that rumbled from his chest had trouble in it, deep trouble.

"Just heard, John."

"Ain't been home for weeks, looks like." He peered through the dimness of the parlor. "Where's Tommy at, Sue Marsh?"

"I don't know, Mr. Cooley." Susan tried to keep her voice casual. "I was hoping you did."

The farmer rose, looking around as if for a place to put the Bible. He was almost as tall as Linc and half again as broad, a tree of a man struck by lightning.

"When did you see Tom last, John?"

"October the second, when I went off to look for a new place." John Cooley swallowed. "Found me one down in York State, too. Figured to give Tommy a new start, maybe change our luck. But now I'll have to let it go."

"You hold your horses, John," Linc said cheerfully. "Didn't the boy leave you a note?"

"No." The farmer's breathing became noisy. He set the Bible down on the morris chair, as if its weight were suddenly too much.

"We'll find him. Sue, you saw Tom last on the first Monday in October?"

Susan nodded. "It was October the third, I think, the day after Mr. Cooley says he left. Tommy came into the library to return some books and take out others. He had the farm truck, I remember.''

"Truck still here, John?"

"Aya."

"Anything of Tom's missing?"

"His twenty-two."

Linc looked relieved. "Well, that's it. He's gone off into the hills. He'll show up any minute with a fat buck and forty-two kinds of alibis. I wouldn't worry."

"Well, I would," Susan said. She was furious with Linc. "Tommy'd never have left on an extended trip without bringing my library books back first."

"There's female reasoning for you." Linc grinned. But he went over to Cooley and touched the old man's shoulder. "John, you want me to organize a search?"

The shoulder quivered. But all the farmer said was, "Aya."

Overnight, Linc had three search parties formed and the state police alerted. On Sunday morning one party, in charge of old Sanford Brown, Northfield's first selectman, headed west with instructions to stop at every farm and gas station. Rollie Fawcett took the second, going east with identical instructions. The third Linc took charge of himself, including in his party Frenchy Lafont and Lafont's two hound dogs. Frenchy owned the Northfield Bar and Grill across Hill Street from town hall. He was the ace tracker of the county.

"You take her easy, John," Lafont said to John Cooley before they set out. "Me, my dogs, we find the boy. Why you want to go along?"

But the farmer went ahead as if he were deaf, packing a rucksack.

Linc's party disappeared into the heavily timbered country to the north, and they were gone two weeks. They came back bearded, hollow-cheeked, and silent. John Cooley and Frenchy Lafont and his two hounds did not return with them. They showed up ten days later, when the first snowfall made further search useless. Even the dogs looked defeated.

Meanwhile, Linc had furnished police of nearby states with handbills struck off by the Northfield *Times* job press, giving a description of Tommy Cooley and reproducing his latest photograph, the one taken from his high school yearbook. Newspapers, radio and TV stations cooperated. Linc sent an official request to Washington; the enlistment files of the army, navy, marine corps, and air force were combed. Registrars of colleges all over the country were circularized. The FBI was notified.

But no trace of Tommy Cooley—or his hunting rifle—turned up.

Linc and Susan quarreled.

"It's one of those things, I tell you." The cleft between Linc's eyes was biting deep these days. "We haven't been able to fix even the approximate time of his disappearance. It could have been any time between October third and the early part of November. Nobody saw him leave, and apparently no one's seen him since."

"But a grown boy doesn't go up in smoke!" Susan protested. "He's got to be *somewhere*, Linc. He didn't just run away from home. Tommy isn't irresponsible, and if you were half the sheriff's white-haired boy you think you are, you'd find out what happened to him."

This was unreasonable, and Susan knew it. For a thrilling moment she thought Linc was going to get mad at her. But, as usual, he let her down. All he said was, "How about you taking my badge, half-pint, and me handing out library books?"

"Do you think you could locate the right one in the stacks?"

Susan stalked out. After the door banged, Linc got up and gently kicked it.

Once, in mid-December, Susan drove out to the Cooley farm. The rumors about John Cooley were disturbing. He was said to be letting the farm go to seed, mumbling to himself, always poring over his Bible.

She found the rumors exaggerated. The house was dirty and the kitchen piled with unwashed dishes, but the farm itself seemed in good order, considering the season, and the farmer talked lucidly enough. Only his appearance shocked Susan. His ruddy skin had grayed and loosened; his hair had white streaks in it; and his coveralls flapped on his frame.

"I've fetched you a blueberry pie I had in my freezer, Mr. Cooley," she said brightly. "I remember Tommy's saying blueberry's your favorite."

"Aya." Cooley looked down at the pie in his lap, but not as if he saw it. "My Tom's a good boy."

Susan tried to think of something to say. Finally she said, "We've missed you at Grange meetings and church. . . . Isn't it lonesome for you here, Mr. Cooley?"

"Have to wait for the boy," John Cooley explained patiently. "The Lord would never take him from me without a sign. I've had no sign, Susan. He'll come home."

Tommy Cooley was found in the spring.

The rains that year were biblical. They destroyed the early plantings, overflowed ponds and creeks, and sent the Northfield River over its banks to flood thousands of acres of pasture and bottomland. The main highway, between Northfield and the Valley, was under water for several miles.

When the waters sank, they exposed a shallow hole not two miles from the Cooley farm, just off the highway. In the hole lay the remains of John Cooley's son. A county crew repairing the road found him.

Susan heard the tragic news as she was locking the library for the day.

Frenchy Lafont, racing past in his new Ford convertible, slowed down long enough to yell, "They find the Cooley boy's body, Miss Marsh! Ever'body's goin' out!"

How Susan got the aged Buick started in the damp twilight, how she knew where to go, she never remembered. She supposed it was instinct, a blind following of the herd of vehicles stampeding from town onto the Valley road, most of them as undirected as her jalopy. All Susan could think of was the look on John Cooley's gray face when he had said the Lord had given him no sign.

She saw the farmer's face at last, and her heart sank. Cooley was on his knees in the roadside grave, clawing in the muck, his eyes blank and terrible, while all around him people trampled the mud-slimed brush like a nest of aroused ants. Linc Pearce and some state troopers were holding the crowd back, trying to give the bereaved man a decent grieving space; but they need not have wrestled so. The farmer might have been alone in one of his cornfields. His big hands alternately caressed and mauled the grave's mud, as if he would coax and batter it into submission to his frenzy. Once he found a button rotted off his son's leather jacket sleeve, and Linc came over and tried to take it from him; but the big hand became a fist, a mallet, and Linc turned away. The big man put it into the pocket of his coat along with a pebble, a chunk of glass, a clump of grass roots—these were his son, the covenant between them, Mizpah. . . .

Afterward, when the heap under the canvas had been taken away by Art Ormsby's hearse and most of the crowd had crawled off in their cars, Susan was able to come close. They had John Cooley sitting on a stump near the grave now, while men hunted through the brush. They were merely going through the motions, Susan knew: time, the ebbing waters, and the feet of the crowd would have obliterated any clue.

She waited while Linc conferred with a state trooper lieutenant and Dr. Buxton, who was the coroner's physician for Northfield. She saw Dr. Buxton glance at John Cooley, shake his gray head, and get into his car to drive back to town. Then she noticed that the lieutenant was carefully holding a rusty, mud-caked rifle.

When the trooper went off with the rifle Susan walked up to Linc and said, "Well?" They had spoken hardly a word to each other all winter.

Linc squinted briefly down at her and said, "Hello, Sue." Then he looked over at the motionless man on the stump, as if the two were painfully connected in his mind.

"That rifle," Susan said. "Tommy's?"

Linc nodded. "Tossed into the hole with the body. They're going to give it the once-over at the state police lab in Gurleytown, but they won't find anything after all this time."

"How long?"

"Hard to say." Linc's firm lips set tight. "Doc Buxton thinks offhand he's been dead five or six months."

Susan's chest rose, and stayed there. "Linc . . . was it murder?"

"The whole back of his head is smashed in. What else there is we won't know till Doc does the autopsy."

Susan swallowed the raw wind. It was impossible to associate that canvas-shrouded lump with Tommy Cooley's big, sad, eager self, to realize that it had been crumbling in the earth here since last October or early November.

"Who'd want to kill him?" Susan said fiercely. "And why, Linc? Why?"

"That's what I have to find out."

She had never seen him so humorless, his mouth so much like a sprung trap. A wave of warmth washed over her. For the moment Susan felt very close to him.

"Linc, let me help," she said breathlessly.

"How?" Linc said.

The wave recoiled. There was no approaching him on an adult level, in the case of Tommy Cooley as in anything else. Susan almost expected Linc to pat her shoulder.

"It's a man's job," Linc was mumbling. "Thanks all the same."

"And are you the man for it, do you think?" Susan heard herself cry.

"Maybe not. But I'll sure give it a try." Linc took her hand, but she snatched it away. "Now, Susie," he said. "You're all upset. Let me do the sweating on this. With the trail five, six months old . . ."

Susan sloshed away, trembling with fury.

In the weeks that followed, Susan kept tabs on Linc's frustration almost with satisfaction. She got most of her inside information from Dr. Buxton, who was a habitué of the library's mystery shelves, old Flora Sloan, and Frenchy Lafont. Miss Flora's all-seeing eye encompassed events practically before they took place, and Frenchy's strategic location opposite town hall gave him the best-informed clientèle in town.

"Linc Pearce is bellowing around like a heifer in her first season," Miss Flora remarked one day in the library. "But that boy's all fenced in, Susan. There's some things the Almighty doesn't mean for us to know. I guess the mystery of poor Tommy Cooley's one of 'em."

"I can't believe that, Miss Flora," Susan said. "If Linc is fenced in, it's only because it's a very difficult case."

The old lady cocked an eye at her. "Appears to me, Susan, you take a mighty personal interest in it."

"Well, of course! Tommy—"

"Tommy, my foot. You can fool the menfolks with your straight-out talk and your red-hair tempers, Susan Marsh, but you don't fool an old woman. You've been in love with Lincoln Pearce ever since *I* can remember, and I go back to bustles. Why don't you stop this fiddling and marry him?"

"Marry him!" Susan laughed. "Of all the notions, Miss Flora! Naturally, I'm interested in Linc—we grew up together. This is an important case to him—"

"Garbage," Miss Flora said distinctly, and walked out.

Frenchy Lafont said to Susan in mid-May, when she stopped in his café for lunch, "That Linc, he's a fool for dam-sure. You know what, Miss Marsh? Everybody but him know he's licked."

"He's *not* licked, Mr. Lafont!"

The fact was, there was nothing for Linc Pearce or anyone else to grab hold of. The dead boy's skull had been crushed from behind by a blow of considerable force, according to Dr. Buxton. His shoulders and back showed evidences of assault, too; apparently there had been a savage series of blows. But the weapon was not found.

Linc went back to the shallow grave site time after time to nose around in a great circle, studying the road and the brush foot by foot, long after Tommy Cooley was buried in the old Northfield cemetery beside his mother. But it was time wasted. Nor were the state police technicians more successful. They could detect no clue in the dead boy's clothing or rifle. All they could say was that the rifle had not been fired—"Old Aunty Laura's blind cow could see that!" Susan had snapped—so that presumably the boy had been killed without warning or a chance to defend himself. Tommy's rifle had been returned to his father, along with the meaningless contents of his pockets.

No one remembered seeing Tommy after October third. So even the date of the murder was a mystery.

Motive was the darkest mystery of all. It had not been robbery: Tommy's wallet, containing most of the hundred dollars his father had left with him, had been intact in the grave. Linc went into the boy's life and through his effects, questioned and requestioned his friends, his old high school teachers, canvassed every farmer and field hand within miles of the Cooley place. But the killing remained unexplained. The boy had had no enemies, it seemed; he had crossed no one; he had been involved with no girl or woman.

"John," Linc had pleaded with Cooley, "can't you think of anything that might tell why Tommy was murdered? Anything?"

But the farmer had shaken his head and turned away, big fingers gripping his Bible. The Book was now never far from his hand. He plodded about his farm aimlessly in the spring, doing no planting, letting the machinery rust. Once a week or so he drove into Northfield to shop in the supermarket. But he spoke to no one.

One night toward the end of May, as Susan was sitting on her porch after supper, rocking in the mild moonlight and listening to the serenade of the peepers in the pond, the headlights of a car swung into her yard and a tall figure got out.

It couldn't be! But it was. Linc Pearce come to Burry's Hollow. The mountain to Mohamet.

"Susie?"

"Well, if it isn't Lanky Linc," Susan heard herself say calmly. Her heart was thumping like an old well pump.

Linc hesitated at the foot of the porch steps, fumbling with his hat. "Took a chance you'd be home. If you're busy—"

"I'll put my dollies away," Susan said. "For you."

"What?" Linc sounded puzzled.

Susan smiled. "Sit down, stranger."

Linc sat down on the bottom step awkwardly, facing the moon. There were lines in his lean face that Susan had never noticed before.

"How've you been?" Susan said.

"All right," he said impatiently, and turned around. "See here, Susie, it's asinine going on like this. I mean, you and me. Why, you're acting just like a kid."

Susan felt the flames spread from her hair right down to her toes. *"I'm* acting like a kid!" she cried. "Is that what you came here to say, Linc? If it is—"

He shook his head. "I never seem to say the right thing to you. Why can't we be like we used to be, Susie? I mean, I miss that funny little pan of yours, and that carrot top. But ever since this Cooley business started—"

"It started a long time before that," Susan retorted. "And I'd rather not discuss it, Linc, *or* my funny pan, *or* the color of my hair. What about the Cooley case?"

"Susie—"

"The Cooley case," Susan said. "Or do I go to bed?"

"Hopeless. It'll never be solved."

"Because you haven't been able to solve it?"

"Me or anybody else," Linc said, shrugging. "One of those crimes that makes no sense because it never had any. Our theory now is that the Cooley boy was attacked on the road by some psychopathic tramp who buried him in a hurry and lit out for other parts."

"In other words, the most convenient theory possible."

Linc said with elaborate indifference, "It happens all the time."

"And suppose it wasn't a psychopathic tramp?"

"What do you mean?"

"I think it was somebody in Northfield."

"Who?"

"I don't know."

Linc laughed.

"I think you'd better go, Linc Pearce," Susan said distinctly. "I don't like you anymore."

"Now, Susie. . . ."

The phone rang in the house. It was three rings, Susan's signal, and she stamped inside.

"It's for you, Linc," she said coolly. "The bartender over at Frenchy Lafont's."

"Bib Hadley? Should have known better than to tell Bib I was stopping in here on my way home," Linc growled, unfolding himself from the step. "Some drunk acting up, I s'pose. . . . What is it, Bib?"

Discussing me in a bar! Susan thought. She turned away in cold rage.

But then she heard Linc say, "I'll get right on out there, Bib," and hang up.

Something in the way he said it made her turn back.

"What's the matter?" Susan said quickly.

"Another murder."

An icy hand seized her heart.

"Who, Linc? Where?"

"Frenchy Lafont." Linc's voice sounded thick. "Some kids out in a hot rod found his body just off the Valley road. Whole back of his head caved in."

"Like Tommy Cooley," Susan whispered.

"I'll say like Tommy Cooley." Linc waved his long arms futilely. "Bib says they found Frenchy lying in the exact spot where we dug up Tommy's body!"

The Valley road was a wild mess of private cars and Jeeps and farm trucks.

Susan wormed past. In one car Susan saw Miss Flora Sloan. The withered despot of Northfield was driving her new Chevrolet like a demon, the daisies in her straw hat bobbing crazily.

Linc kept his siren going all the way.

We're scared witless, Susan thought.

Two state police cars had set up roadblocks near the site of the new horror. Linc plowed onto the soft shoulder and skidded around into the cleared space. The road in both directions was a double string of lights. Everywhere Susan looked, people were jumping out of cars and running along the road and the shoulders. In a twinkling, the fifty feet of highway between the roadblocks was rimmed with eyes.

Susan almost trod on Linc's heels.

She peeped around his long torso at what lay just off the road on the north side. It sprang at her, brutally detailed, in the police flares. Susan jerked back, hiding her eyes.

She was to remember that photographic flash for the rest of her life: the mound of sandy earth where the grave had been refilled after the removal of Tommy Cooley's body, pebbled, flint-spangled, scabby with weeds; and across it, as on one of Art Ormsby's biers, the flung remains of what had been Frenchy Lafont.

Susan could not see his wound; she could only imagine what it looked like. They had turned him over, so that his face was tilted sharply back to the stars. It did not look the least bit like Frenchy Lafont's face. Frenchy Lafont's face had been dark and vivid, lively with mischief, with beautiful lips over white teeth and a line of vain black mustache. This face looked like old suet. The mouth was a gaping black cavern, the eyes stared like dusty pieces of glass.

"Just like the Cooley kid," one of the troopers was saying.

His voice raised a deep echo, like a far-off growl of thunder. There was more than fear in the growl; there was anger and under the anger, hate. The troopers and Linc looked around, startled.

"Sounds like trouble, Pearce," one of the older troopers muttered to Linc. "They're your people. Better do something."

Linc walked off toward one of the police cars. For a moment Susan almost ran after him; she felt as if she had been left standing naked in the flares.

But the eyes were not on her.

Linc vaulted to the hood of the car and flung his arms wide. The rumble choked and died.

"Neighbors, I knew Frenchy Lafont all my life," Linc said in a quiet way. "Most of you did, too. There isn't a man or woman in Northfield wants more to identify the one who did this and see that he gets what's coming to him. But we can't do it this way. We'll find Frenchy's killer if you'll only go home and give us a chance."

"Like you found the killer of my boy?"

It was John Cooley's hoarse bass voice. He was near the west roadblock, standing tall in his Jeep, his thick arm with the flail of fist at the end like a wrathful judgment. Linc turned to face him.

"Go home, John," Linc said gently.

"Yeah, John, go home!" a shrill voice yelled from behind the other barrier. "Go home and get yourself murdered like Tommy was!"

"That's not helping, Wes Bartlett," Linc said. "Use your head, man—"

But his voice went down under a tidal wave.

"We want protection!"

"Aya!"

"Who's next on the list?"

"Long as *he's* deputy . . ."

"Resign!"

"New sheriff's what we need!"

"Aya! Resign!"

In the roar of the crowd, the clatter of Linc's badge on the hood of the police car was surprisingly loud.

"All right, there's my badge!" Linc shouted. "Now who's the miracle man thinks he can do the job better? I'll recommend him to Sheriff Howland myself. Come on, don't be bashful! Speak up."

He gave them glare for glare. The glares dimmed; the answering silence became uneasy. Something embarrassed invaded the night air.

"Well?" Linc jeered.

Somewhere down the line a car engine started. . . .

Ten minutes later the highway was empty and dark.

Linc jumped off the police car, reached for his badge, and went over to the troopers.

"Nice going, Sheriff," Susan murmured.

But he strode past her to the edge of the burial mound, rock-hard and bitter.

"Let's get to it," he said.

At first they thought it had been a murder in the course of a robbery. Frenchy Lafont's wallet was found untouched on the body, but an envelope with the day's café receipts, which he had been known to have on him earlier in the evening, was missing. The robbery theory collapsed overnight. The envelope of money was found in the night depository box of the First National Bank of Northfield on Main Street when the box was unlocked in the morning.

The weapon was not found. It was the Tommy Cooley case all over again.

Everything about the café owner's murder was baffling. He was a bachelor who lived with his aged mother on the old Lafont place off the Valley road, a mile out of town. His elder brother, a prosperous merchant of Quebec, had not heard from him in months. The brother, in town to make the funeral arrangements and take charge of the mother, could shed no light on the mystery. Old Mrs. Lafont knew nothing.

On the evening of his murder Lafont had left the café shortly before nine, alone, taking the day's receipts with him. He drove off in his new Ford. An hour or so later he was dead some six miles out of town, on the site of the Cooley tragedy. His car was found near the mound. It was towed into the police garage at the Gurleytown barracks and gone over by experts. It yielded nothing but Frenchy Lafont's fingerprints. No blood, no indication of a struggle, no clue of any kind. The fuel tank was almost full.

"He dropped the envelope into the slot at the bank," Linc told Susan, "stopped in at Howie Grebe's gas station to fill up, and drove off west on the Valley road. He must have gone straight to his death. Nothing to show that he was waylaid and held up—nothing was taken, and Frenchy didn't touch the pistol he carried in his glove compartment. Bib Hadley says he was his usual wisecracking self when he left the café."

"You think he had a date with somebody he knew?" Susan asked.

"Well, Hadley says he got a phone call at the café," Linc said slowly, "about eight o'clock that night."

"I hadn't heard that! Who phoned him, Linc?"

"Bib doesn't know. Frenchy answered the call himself."

"Did Bib Hadley overhear anything?"

"No."

"Was Frenchy excited? There must have been something, Linc!"

"Bib didn't notice anything unusual. The call might have had nothing to do with the case."

"Maybe it was some woman Frenchy was fooling with. I've heard stories about him and Logan Street."

Susan colored. Logan Street was a part of Northfield no respectable girl ever mentioned to the opposite sex.

"So far all alibis have stood up." Linc passed his hand over his eyes like an old man. "It's no good thinking, theorizing. I have to *know,* Sue, and there's not a fact I can sink my teeth into."

"But there's got to be a reason for a man's getting the back of his head knocked in!" Susan cried. *"Why* was Frenchy murdered? *Why* was his body dumped on the spot where the murderer had buried Tommy? You can hardly say it was another psychopathic tramp, Linc."

Linc looked at her in a persecuted way. He was glassy-eyed with exhaustion. But he merely said, "Maybe not. Only there doesn't seem to be any more sense in Frenchy's death than in

Tom Cooley's. Look, Susie, I've got work to do, and talk won't help me do it even with you. If you'll excuse me . . ."

"Certainly," Susan said frigidly. "But let me tell you, Linc Pearce, when these murders are solved, it'll be talk and theories and *thinking* that solve them!" And she swept out, thoroughly miserable.

Susan tossed night after night, asking herself unanswerable questions. Why had Tommy Cooley been killed? Why had Frenchy Lafont followed him in death? What was the connection between the two? And—the most frightening question of all— who was going to be the next victim?

A week after Lafont's murder Susan was waiting at the café entrance when Bib Hadley came to open up.

"You must hanker after a cup of my coffee real bad, Miss Marsh," the fat bartender said, unlocking the door. "Come on in. I'll have the urn going in a jiffy."

"What I want, Bib, is information," Susan said grimly. "I'm sick and tired of moping around, waiting to get my head bashed in."

The bartender tied a clean apron around his ample middle. "Seems like every Tom, Dick, and Mary between Northfield and Boston's been in for the same reason. Even had a newspaperman in yesterday from one of the city wire services. Made a special trip just to pump ol' Bib. So get your list in now, Miss Marsh, while Frenchy's brother makes up his mind what to do with this place. What do you want to know?"

"The connection between Tommy Cooley and Frenchy Lafont," Susan said.

"Wasn't any," Bib Hadley said. "Next?"

"But there must have been, Bib! Did Tommy ever work for Mr. Lafont?"

"Nope."

"Did Tommy ever come in here?"

"Tell you the truth, Miss Marsh," the bartender said, lighting the gas under the urn, "I don't believe Frenchy would have known young Tom Cooley if he'd tripped over him in broad day-

light. You know how Frenchy was about teenagers. He'd stand
'em all treat over at Tracy's ice cream parlor, but he wouldn't let
'em come into his own place even for coffee. Gave a good bar a
bad name, Frenchy used to say."

"Well, there was a connection between Tommy and Frenchy
Lafont," Susan said positively, "and these murders won't ever
be solved till it's found."

"And you're going to find it, I s'pose?"

Susan jumped. There he was, in the café doorway, jaws working away like Gary Cooper's in an emotional moment.

"I saw you ambush Bib from my office window," Linc said
bitterly. "Don't you trust me to ask the right questions,
either?"

I don't know why I'm feeling guilty, Susan thought furiously.
This is a free country!

Linc jammed his big foot on the rim of the tub holding the dusty
palm. "You want my badge, too, Sue? Don't you think I've
asked Bib every question you have, and a whole lot more? This is
a tough case. Do you have to make it tougher for me by getting
underfoot?"

"Thanks!" Susan said. "People who won't accept help when
they're stuck from people trying to unstick them are just—just
perambulating *pigheads.*"

"We stopped playing tag in your dad's cow barn long ago,
Sue." Linc said. "When are you going to grow up?"

"I've *grown* up! Oh, how I've grown up, Linc Pearce—and
everybody knows it but you!" Susan screamed. "And do we have
to stand here screaming in front of people?"

"I'm not people," Bib Hadley said. "I ain't even here."

"Nobody's screaming but you." Linc drew himself up so tall
Susan's neck began to hurt. "I thought we knew each other pretty
well, Susie. Maybe we don't know each other at all."

"I'm sure of it!" Susan tried to say it with dignity, but it came
out so choky-sounding she fled past Linc to her jalopy and drove
off down Hill Street with the gas pedal to the floor.

* * *

Two nights later the body of Flora Sloan, autocrat of North-field, was found by a motorcycle trooper just off the Valley high-way. The back of her head had been battered in.

As in the case of Frenchy Lafont, the old lady's body had been tossed onto Tommy Cooley's winter grave. . . .

Flora Sloan had attended a vestry meeting in Christ Church, at which certain parish and financial problems had been argued. As usual, Miss Flora dominated the debate; as usual, she got her way. She had left the meeting in lively spirits when it broke up just before ten o'clock, climbed into her Chevrolet, waved triumphantly at Sanford Brown, who had been her chief antagonist of the evening, and driven off. Presumably she had been bound for the big Sloan house on the western edge of town. But she never reached it; or rather, she had bypassed it, for the Valley road ran by her property.

When her body was found shortly after midnight by the motor-cycle trooper, she had been dead about an hour.

Had Flora Sloan picked someone up, who had forced her to drive to the lonely spot six miles from town and there murdered her? But the old lady had been famous for her dislike of tramps and her suspicion of hitchhikers. She had never been known to give a stranger a lift.

Her purse, money untouched, was found beside her body. A valuable ruby brooch, a Sloan family heirloom, was still pinned to her blue lace dress. The Chevrolet was parked near the grave in almost the identical spot on which Frenchy Lafont's Ford had been abandoned. There were no fingerprints in the car except her own, no clues in the car or anywhere around.

Three nights after Flora Sloan's murder, Sanford Brown, first selectman of Northfield, called a special town meeting. The city fathers, lean old Yankee farmers and businessmen, sat down be-hind the scarred chestnut table in the town hall meeting room un-der an American flag like a panel of hanging judges; and among them—Susan thought they looked dismally like prisoners—sat County Sheriff Howland and his local deputy, Lincoln Pearce.

It was an oppressive night, and the overflow crowd made the

room suffocating. She saw everyone she knew, and some faces she had forgotten.

Old Sanford Brown rapped his gavel hard on the table. A profound silence greeted him.

"Under the authority vested in me," old Brown said rapidly through his nose, "I call this town meetin' to order. As this is special, we will dispense with the usual order of business and get right to it. Sheriff Howland's come down from the county seat at the selectmen's request. Floor's yours, Sheriff."

Sheriff Howland was a large, perspiring man in a smart city suit and a black string tie. He got to his feet, drying his bald head with a sodden handkerchief.

"Friends, when I was elected to office in this county, I looked for the best man I could find to be my deputy in your district. I asked 'round and about and was told there wasn't finer deputy material in Northfield than young Lincoln Pearce. I want you and him to know I have every confidence in his ability to discharge the duties of his office. Linc, you tell these good folks what you told me today."

The buck having been deftly passed to him, Linc rose. His blue eyes were mourning-edged, and he was so pale Susan bled for him.

"I'm no expert on murder, never claimed to be one," Linc began in a matter-of-fact voice, but Susan could see his knuckles whiten on the edge of the table. "However, I've had the help of the best technical men of the state police. And they're as high up a tree as the 'coon of this piece. And that's me."

An old lady chuckled, and several men grinned. *Humility, Linc?* Susan thought in a sort of pain. *Maybe one of these days you'll get around to me. . . .*

"Three people have been beaten to death," Linc said. "One was a boy of seventeen, son of a dirt farmer—quiet boy, Congregationalist, never in trouble. One was a bar-and-grill owner—French-Canadian descent, Roman Catholic, one of the most popular men in town. The third was the last survivor of the family that founded Northfield—rich woman, tightfisted, some said, but we all know her many generosities. She just about ran Northfield all her life. She was a pillar of Christ Episcopal Church, on every important committee, with her finger in every community pie.''

He thinks he has them, Susan thought, glancing about her at the long bony faces. *Linc, Linc . . .*

''The bodies of these three were found in the same spot. So their deaths have to be connected some way. But how? There doesn't seem to be any answer. At least, we haven't been able to find one so far.

''We know nothing about Tommy Cooley's death because of the months that passed before we found his body. Frenchy Lafont was probably lured to his death by a phone call from somebody he knew and wasn't afraid of. Flora Sloan probably picked her killer up as she left the church meeting, which she wouldn't have done unless it was someone she knew. Tommy Cooley's clothing was too far gone to tell us anything, and the rains this spring wiped out any clues that might have been left in his case. But we found dirt on the knees of Frenchy's trousers and Flora Sloan's skirt, so maybe Tommy was made to kneel on that spot just like Frenchy and Miss Flora afterward, and hit a killing blow from behind.''

You can talk and talk, Linc, they won't let you alone anymore, Susan thought. *They won't do anything to you—they'll just ignore you from now on. . . .*

''That's all we have,'' Linc said. ''No connection among the three victims—not one. No motive. Not gain—nothing was taken in any of the three cases as far as we know. Tommy Cooley had nothing to leave anybody; Frenchy Lafont's business and house he left to his eighty-one-year-old mother, and now we're told that Flora Sloan willed her entire estate to charity. No motive—no woman or other man in the case, no jealous husband, wife, or sweetheart. *No motive.*''

Linc stopped, looking down. Susan shut her eyes.

''When someone kills for no reason, he's insane. Three people died because a maniac is loose in our town. It's the only answer that makes sense. If anyone here has a better, for God's sake, let all of us hear it.''

Now the noise came back like a rising wind, and Sanford Brown banged it back to silence. But it was still there, waiting.

"I want to say one more thing."

Susan heard Linc's pride take stubborn voice again. *Linc, Linc, don't you know you've had it? Old Sanford, the selectmen, Sheriff Howland—they all know it. Don't you?*

"I'm not going to hand over my badge unless Sheriff Howland asks for it," Linc went on. "Want it, Sheriff?"

The politician squirmed. "No, Linc, course not—unless the good folks of Northfield feel—"

Poor Linc. Here it comes.

"Let Linc Pearce keep his badge!" a burly farmer shouted from the floor. "The boy's doin' his best. But he's just a boy, that's the trouble. What we need's a committee o' safety. Men with guns to stand watch near the grave site . . . patrol the roads!"

"Mr. Chairman . . ."

Susan slipped out of the meeting room as motions and resolutions winged toward the table from every corner. She caught up with Linc on the steps of the town hall.

" 'Lo, Susie," Linc said with a stiffish grin. "Come after me to watch me digest crow?"

"Committee of safety, men guarding the grave," Susan said bitterly. "What do they expect him to do—walk into their arms? Linc, *please* let me help. You're not beaten yet. Let's you and I talk it over. There must be something you missed! Maybe if we put our heads together—"

"You know something?" Linc put his big hands about her waist and lifted her to his level like a doll. "All of a sudden I want to kiss you."

"Linc, put me down. Don't treat me as if I were a child. Please, Linc."

"My little old Susie."

"And *don't* call me Susie! I loathe it! I've loathed it all my life! Linc, put me down, I say!"

"Sorry." Linc looked genuinely surprised. He deposited her

quietly on the step. "As far as the other thing is concerned, my answer's got to be the same, Sue. They can make up all the committees and posses they want—this is my job and I'll do it by myself or go bust. Can I drive you home?"

"Not *ever!*" And Susan fled to the safety of the old Buick Flora Sloan had given her, where she could burst into tears in decent privacy.

Linc sat in his office long after the last selectman had gone and Rollie Fawcett had darkened the building. He was blackly conscious of the thunderstorm that had sprung up. The rain lashing his windows seemed fitting and proper.

There must be something you missed . . .

Linc was irritated more by the source of the phrase going round in his head than by its persistence. That little fire-eater! She'd singed his tail from the start. Talk about your one-track minds . . .

Suppose she's right?

The thought was like his collar, chafing him raw.

What could he have missed? What? What hadn't he followed up? He'd been over the three cases a hundred times. He couldn't possibly have missed anything. Or had he?

Linc Pearce finally saw it—appropriately enough, during a flash of lightning. The bare office with its whitewashed walls for an instant became bright as day, and in that flash of illumination Linc remembered what he had missed.

It had happened on that first night of the long nightmare. The night Tommy Cooley's body had been found, washed out of its roadside grave by the receding waters of the spring flood. John Cooley had been kneeling in the grave, his hands scrabbling in the mud for some remnant of his son. The pitiful little things he had found and tucked away in the pocket of his checkered red mackinaw— *Suppose one of those things, unknown to Cooley, had been a clue?*

Linc grabbed a slicker and ran.

* * *

The Cooley farmhouse was dark. Linc turned off his lights and ignition, skin prickling at some danger he could not exactly define.

The rain had turned into a tropical downpour. Lightning tore the sky open in quick bursts like cannon salvos, lighting up the shade-drawn windows, the porch with rickety rocking chairs turned to the wall, the open door of the nearby garage. . . .

Cooley's Jeep was not in the garage.

Linc reached for a flashlight and jumped out of his car. He splashed over to the garage and swung his light about. Yes, the farm truck was here, but the Jeep was out.

Linc relaxed. He had not noticed John Cooley at the town meeting, but he must have been there. If he was, with a committee of safety forming, he'd surely be one of the men to be staked out in the brush near Tommy's grave.

Linc went up on the porch and tried the door. It was not locked, and he opened it and stepped into the hall.

"John?" He could be wrong. There might be a dozen explanations for the missing Jeep. "John?"

No one answered. Linc went upstairs and looked into the bedrooms. They were empty.

He went back to John Cooley's old-fashioned bedroom and played his flash about. Of course, the chifforobe. He opened the doors. It was filled with winter garments.

And there was the red mackinaw.

Linc breathed a prayer and put his hand into the right pocket. They were still there, all right.

He took them out one by one, carefully, turning them over in his fingers. The button from young Tom's rotted leather jacket. A pebble. A chunk of dirt-crusted glass . . .

The piece of glass!

It was thick, ridged glass with a curve to it, a roughly triangular piece cracked off from something larger. It was . . . it was . . .

My God! Linc thought.

He went over it again and again, refusing to believe. It couldn't be that simple. The answer to the murders that had happened. The warning of the murder that was going to happen. *The murder of Susan Marsh.*

For a moment of sheer horror, Linc saw her flying red hair, the familiar little face, the snub nose he used to tweak, the brook-water eyes, the impudent mouth that had tormented him all his life.

He saw them all, soiled and still.

A world without Sue . . .

Linc never knew how he got out of the house.

Susan had gone to bed swollen-eyed. But she had been unable to sleep. The mugginess, the storm, the thunder crashes, the lightning bolts bouncing off her pond, made the night hideous. She had never felt so alone.

She crept out of bed, got into a wrapper, and pattered about, clicking switches. She put on every light in the house. Then she went into her tiny parlor and sat there, rigidly listening to the storm.

Oh, Linc, Linc . . .

Her first thought when the crash came and the curtains began blowing about and a cold spray hit her bare feet was that the gale had blown the front door loose.

She looked up.

John Cooley stood in her splintered doorway. He had Tommy's hunting rifle cradled in his arm. In the farmer's eyes Susan saw her death.

"They're watching at the grave," John Cooley said. His voice was all cracked and high, not like his bass at all. "So I can't take you there, Susan Marsh."

"You killed them," Susan said stiffly.

"Get down on your knees, and pray."

He was insane. She saw that now. He had been tottering on the brink ever since Tommy's disappearance, his only son, the child of his beloved Sarah. And he had toppled over when the body was found. Only no one had seen it—not Linc, not she, not anyone.

Linc, Linc.

"Not Tommy," Susan whispered. "You loved Tommy, Mr. Cooley. You wouldn't—couldn't have killed Tommy."

The farmer's twitching face, with its distended eyes, softened into something vaguely human. Tears filled the eyes. The heavy shoulders began to shake.

Oh, dear God, let me find a way to keep him from killing me as he killed Frenchy Lafont and Miss Flora. . . .

"I know you didn't kill Tommy, Mr. Cooley."

With the metal-sheathed butt of Tommy's hunting rifle. That was the weapon that had crushed out their lives. . . . *Dear God . . . I mustn't faint, mustn't . . . those dark smears on the butt . . . get him talking . . . maybe the phone . . . No, no, that would be fatal . . . What can I do! Linc . . .*

"Not Tommy. Somebody else killed Tommy, Mr. Cooley. Who was it? Why don't you tell me?"

The farmer sank into the tapestried chair near the door. The rain beat in on him, mixing with his tears.

"You killed him, Susan Marsh," he wept.

"Oh, no!" Susan cried faintly.

"You, or the Frenchy, or the old woman. I knew from the hunk of glass in the boy's grave. A hunk of headlight glass. Headlight from an old auto. He was run over on the road, hit by an auto from the back . . . from the back. You killed him with an auto and you put him in a dirty hole and piled dirt on him and you ran away. You, or the Frenchy, or the old woman."

Susan wet her lips. "The Buick," she said. "My old Buick."

John Cooley looked up, suddenly cunning. "I found it! Didn't think I would, hey? I looked all over Northfield, and I found the auto it come from. I looked for a smashed headlight, and the auto the old woman gave you was the one the hunk of glass fitted. Was it you run Tommy over? Or the old woman, who run the car before you? Or the Frenchy, who owned the Buick before the old woman bought it?"

"Frenchy Lafont sold that car to Flora Sloan—in October?" Susan gasped.

"Didn't think I'd track that down, hey?" John Cooley said

with a sly chuckle. "Aya! Lafont sold it to the old woman when
he bought his new Ford. And she gave it to you a couple weeks
later when she won a Chevrolet in the Grange bazaar. Oh, I
tracked it all down. I was careful to do proper justice." The eyes
began to stare again; he whimpered. "But which one, which one?
I didn't know which one of you killed Tommy in October, 'cause
nobody knows what day in October he was run over. So I got to
kill you all. That way the Lord's vengeance is mine. The Wrath.
With the boy's gun. I phoned that Lafont, and I says meet me at
the grave, I have to talk to you . . . I walked into the town and I
waited for the old woman to come out of the church, and I stopped
her and made her drive out to the grave. 'Pray, Flora Sloan,' I
says. 'Get down on your murdering knees, sinner, and pray for
your damned soul,' I says. And then I used the Lord's gun butt on
her."

The room was shimmering.

John Cooley was on his feet, the great eyes shining.

"Pray, Susan Marsh," he thundered. "Down on your knees,
girl, and pray for your soul."

Now the steel hand was at the back of her neck, forcing her to
her knees.

*Dear God . . . Linc, you're the one I love, the only one I've
ever . . .*

The last thing Susan saw as she strained against the paralyzing
clutch on her neck was that exultant face, terrible in triumph, and
the rusty blood-caked butt of the rifle held high above it.

She fainted just as Linc Pearce plunged into the room and
hurled himself at the madman.

Susan opened her eyes. She was in her own bed. Linc's long
face was close to hers.

"I thought I heard you say something, Linc, a million years
ago," Susan murmured. "Or maybe it was just now. Didn't you
say something, oh, so nice?"

"I said I love you, Susie—Susan," Linc muttered. "And
something about will you marry me."

Susan closed her eyes again. "That's what I thought you said," she said contentedly.

They never did find out which one had accidentally run over Tommy Cooley, whether Frenchy Lafont or old Miss Flora. They argued about it for years.

"Terror at Northfield." *The Alfred Hitchcock Hour,* October 11, 1963. Directed by Harvey Hart. Teleplay by Leigh Brackett, based on Ellery Queen's short story "Terror Town" (*Argosy,* August 1956). With Dick York (Sheriff Will Pearce), Jacqueline Scott (Susan Marsh), R. G. Armstrong (John Cooley), Gertrude Flynn (Flora Sloan), Dennis Patrick (Frenchy LaFont), Katherine Squire (Mrs. LaFont), Peter Whitney (Bib Hadley).

"'Terror Town" was the only piece of short fiction by Ellery Queen (the cousins Frederic Dannay, 1905–1982, and Manfred B. Lee, 1905–1971) that did not feature the world-famous Ellery Queen detective character. The authors hoped that the story would sell to TV, but the version aired on *The Alfred Hitchcock Hour* kept little beyond the bare bones of Queen's plot and people. Director Harvey Hart and scriptwriter Leigh Brackett revealed early in the film the secret behind the Northfield murders, and added several new scenes and plot elements to punch up the suspense and menace, while eliminating the surprise twists and the strong sense of small-town New England life that distinguished the Queen story. But all in all it was an effectively directed and rather exciting little picture.

Francis M. Nevins, Jr.

JACK RITCHIE

Anyone for Murder?

THE GIRL AT THE CLASSIFIED ADS COUNTER read my submission, chewed on her pencil, and then looked up uncertainly. "You want this put in our paper?"

"Yes. And I would like to have a box number for the replies."

The item I intended to insert in the *Herald Journal* read: *Are you hopelessly tied to your marriage partner? Perhaps there is one ultimate solution to your problem. All correspondence kept strictly confidential. Write Herald Journal, Box No.*

I studied the doubt on her face. "Is there anything wrong?"

The pencil received a few more indentations. "I'm new here. I don't know exactly what the policy of the paper is." She summoned a Mr. Wilson, who was evidently in charge of the section.

He read my sheet of paper. "Are you a lawyer?"

"No."

"I mean . . . aren't you referring to divorce?"

"No."

He cleared his throat. "Just what *do* you mean by 'one ultimate solution'?"

"I prefer to let the ad speak for itself."

And so I was channeled through other hands, ever upward, and finally ushered into the office of J. G. Bingham, advertising manager.

My sheet had preceded me and lay on his desk. He came directly to the point. "I'm afraid you'll have to explain this ad to my satisfaction or this newspaper cannot publish it."

I sighed. "Very well. My name is James Parkerson. I am a professor at the university, and my field is psychology."

He indicated the sheet. "And this has something to do with your field?"

"Yes. I am beginning a paper, and it is my thesis that perhaps ten times as many husbands and wives would be murdered by their mates except for one psychological fact."

"That they are afraid of being caught?"

"That certainly is an important factor, of course. However, it is my contention that equally as important—if not more so—is that people simply cannot bring themselves to the actual act. If they could *delegate* the act of murder—be able to hire someone else for the job—then there would be a tremendous increase in the number of violent deaths."

He frowned. "Do you mean to say that you're actually *advertising* to commit murder? Do you seriously expect people to answer this ad?"

"Of course. People are quite responsive to even the most ridiculous of things. For instance, several years ago an ad appeared in a national magazine consisting of the following words: *This is your last chance. Send one dollar to Box 107.* Just that and nothing more. Absolutely nothing was promised in return and yet thousands of readers sent dollars.

"I specifically chose the words 'one ultimate solution.' The word 'murder' would, of course, frighten away everyone but the insane. I expect my replies to fall into two categories. The first will consist of letters from people who assume that I am a lawyer with some new information about divorce laws. These will not serve for the purposes of my study and I will merely put them aside."

I had been standing, but now I took the chair Bingham indicated. ''The letters in the second category will at first reading appear similar to those in the first, but the *seed* of murder will be there and I am sure that I will be able to detect it. These will be from people to whom the 'one ultimate solution' means something else, and they will be incredulously wondering: *Can it actually be possible? Can this ad really mean what I think it means?* And they will spend a little time and a stamp to cautiously probe.''

Bingham was dubious. ''But when they find out who you are and what your purpose is, won't they shy away immediately?''

''I do not intend to reveal to them who I actually am until my interviews are finished. For all apparent purposes I will be a professional murderer selling my services.''

Bingham thought about it for a full minute and then rubbed his neck. ''All right. I'm not sure I'm doing the right thing, but on the other hand I'm curious myself. We'll run the ad. For how long?''

''For the present, just one day.''

He thought of something else. ''You'd better pick up your replies direct from this office. No telling but what some reporter might be waiting downstairs if you go to your box.''

My ad appeared in that evening's *Herald Journal*. The next day, after my last class at the university, I appeared at Bingham's office to collect my replies.

Bingham appeared uncomfortable as he introduced the solidly built man with him. ''This is Sergeant Larson of the bunco squad. He tells me that one of his jobs is to read the classified ads, especially personals, and to smell out anything fishy.''

''There is absolutely nothing fishy about this,'' I said firmly. ''Perhaps you'd better explain to the sergeant what I am doing.''

Larson cut in. ''He already has. But I'd like to check this out for myself. Let's see your wallet. Take out your money first.''

I did as I was told and he examined the billfold. ''Well, at least you've got Parkerson's wallet. I'll drop in at the university to make certain that you really are who you say you are.''

Bingham handed me a small pack of envelopes. ''These came in the mail this morning.''

There were only six of them. I was a bit disappointed.

Larson watched me put them in my pocket. ''Are some of those from people who you think might want to have their husbands or wives murdered?''

''I haven't read them yet, but I believe so.''

He put forward one hand. ''Let's have the letters.''

I ignored the extended palm. ''Certainly not. These are addressed to me. They are my personal correspondence.''

He scowled. ''Look, professor, don't you want to *prevent* murder?''

''Of course. And ultimately my work will contribute to that direction. But first one must diagnose the extent of the disease before one can go about treating it. And besides, don't you see that none of these people will murder until they can actually hire someone? And while they are negotiating with me, they are at least temporarily neutralized.''

Sergeant Larson accepted that reluctantly. ''But when you're through negotiating, we want those names. We'd like to talk those people out of the notions they have.''

I agreed. ''It might be a breach of confidence, but on the other hand, I do see your point. When I am through you shall receive the names.''

I drove home and was about to enter my study when my wife, Doris, stopped me. ''Dear, have you been thinking about what we'll do on your sabbatical year?''

''We'll stay right here,'' I said. ''I'd like to do work on a new project of mine.''

She sighed. ''You work too hard, dear. I've been reading about those round-the-world trips on tramp steamers. Most of them take a limited number of passengers. Wouldn't that be a nice way to spend the year?''

I was impatient to get at my letters. "Doris, what is your reason for wanting to travel?"

"Why, to see new people, I imagine."

"Really? But don't you agree that people all over the world are basically pretty much alike?"

"Well . . . yes."

"In that case, Doris, what is the purpose of spending a lot of money to verify a fact which you already know?"

I went into my study, opened the six letters, and read them. Four fell positively into Category One. The remaining two were the ones in which I was interested.

I reread the first.

Dear Sir:

I have just seen your most interesting advertisement in this evening's *Herald Journal.*

It ocurred to me that perhaps you do not know the possibilities of 'one ultimate solution.' Or do you?

If you wish to exchange letters, please insert the following ad in the *Herald Journal:* Lost. Collie dog. Male. Answers to name of Regis.

The letter was unsigned.

I studied the typewritten sheet of paper. The *o*'s and *e*'s were clogged, and the rest of the type could have used a thorough brushing. The ribbon, too, was faded and should have been replaced. Except for the redundancy of "collie dog," and the spelling "ocurred," the letter seemed literate enough.

Or was that spelling correct? I glanced about for my desk dictionary, but didn't see it. I rose and went to the doorway. "Doris, how would you spell 'occurred'?"

She thought a moment. "O-c-u-r-r-e-d."

That still didn't sound right to me. "Where is the dictionary?"

"It's on the secretary in the living room, dear."

I fetched the dictionary and returned to my study. The word was spelled with two *c*'s.

I turned to the second letter in Category Two. It, also, was typewritten—without salutation or signature—and quite brief.

Mac's Bar. 21st and Wells. Tonight. 8 P.M. Order Scotch. Untie and retie right shoelace.

Simple enough, I thought, and I would certainly keep the appointment.

I picked up the phone, called the *Herald Journal,* and had the ad concerning Regis, the lost collie, inserted in tomorrow's newspaper.

When I hung up, my eyes wandered to the dictionary and then back to the first of the two letters. I stared at it for about five minutes and then took a blank sheet of paper to the typewriter.

I inserted it and typed: *It occurred to me that the quick brown fox jumps over the lazy dog.* And also, *It occurred to me that six quick movements by the enemy will jeopardize the five gunboats.*

I studied the words. They were dark and clear. No clogging of the *o*'s and *e*'s. I smiled sheepishly and crumpled the paper. Really, it was ridiculous what thoughts occasionally occurred to the human mind.

After supper, I put on my topcoat. "I'm going back to the university for a little while, dear. Have some work to do. No telling when I'll be back."

"All right, dear," she said. "By the way, did you notice that I cleaned your typewriter keys and put on a new ribbon?"

I paused in the process of putting on my hat. "When did you do that?"

"This morning, dear."

I left the house. It was drizzling.

Millions of people misspell "occurred," I reflected somewhat aggressively as I turned the ignition key of my car. They either use one "c" or one "r," or both. And typewriter keys are cleaned and new ribbons put on . . .

The motor caught and I drove on to Mac's Bar.

I found an empty stool at the bar and ordered a Scotch. I untied and retied my right shoelace and then gazed expectantly about the place for someone to step forward.

No one did.

I glanced at the wall clock. Exactly eight. Perhaps he, or she, was late.

Ten minutes later an average-size man entered Mac's Bar. I downed my drink and then, in a clear, carrying voice, ordered another Scotch. I untied and retied my right shoelace. The new patron ignored me.

I waited patiently for the next person to enter the tavern.

Eight persons later, I decided to give up. Besides, I had succeeded in tying a completely unworkable knot in my right shoelace.

When I entered my house, Doris appeared to be asleep upstairs. I finished a large bag of potato chips I vaguely remembered purchasing at Mac's Bar, and then went to bed. I had a bit of difficulty negotiating the stairs.

In the morning I had a splitting headache. It was entirely possible that I was allergic to potato chips. I managed to untie the knot in my shoelace, and at breakfast I took nothing but coffee.

Doris looked worried. "Catching the flu?"

"Possibly." I finished my black coffee, took two aspirins, and left the house.

At the university, my morning classes dragged on interminably, and it was a profound relief to me when the noon hour finally came.

I managed to eat something at the faculty cafeteria and then decided that a stroll about the campus might do me good. I paused near the Memorial Union to light my pipe. As I glanced over the match flame, I saw a tall, well-dressed man approach.

He smiled slightly. "How do you feel this morning?"

I had never seen him before, and the condition of my health was clearly none of his business.

He glanced down at my shoes. "I see that you got the knot untied."

I stared at him. "Were you . . . ? Did *you* send me that . . . ?"

He nodded. "Yes. And I was at Mac's Bar last night."

I bristled. "Then why the devil didn't you come forward? Especially before I purchased those potato chips."

"Because I am a very cautious man, and this is a cautious matter." He studied me. "What did you mean by one ultimate solution?"

I had not quite regained my temper. "Try me," I said bluntly.

He smiled faintly. "Murder?"

I hesitated, but then said, "Correct."

His eyes went over me again. "Just how much would you charge to murder my wife?"

I selected a number offhand. "Ten thousand dollars."

The amount did not seem to disturb him in the least. "Just how would you go about doing it?"

"We would, of course, arrange that you have an alibi, and I would shoot your wife at that particular time. You would not be involved."

He nodded. "Very simple, and therefore it should work, Professor Parkerson."

I was slightly disconcerted. "How did you know my name?"

"I followed you to your home last night and to the university this morning. I made it my business to find out who you are. And somehow, Professor, I simply do not believe that a man in your position would turn to murder, either as a profession or a hobby."

"Sir," I said stiffly. "Do you or do you not want me to murder your wife?"

"I am not married. Just what *are* you up to, Professor?"

"That is *my* business."

His eyes flickered. "I think I'll report this to the police. They might be interested."

"I already have clearance with the police. At least on the sergeant level."

"Or perhaps I should take my information to some newspaper reporter? He might find the story worthwhile."

That dismayed me considerably. While I wanted the publicity of a two-line ad for one day, I did not want the publicity of a feature story. That would certainly frighten away all my prospective clients for the present and the future.

He pressed again. "Shall I go to a newspaper with my information?"

I sighed. "No."

We sat down on a nearby bench and I told him about my project. He was thoughtful when I finished.

"Have you received any replies to your ad?"

"Six, so far."

He was silent for a few moments and then said, "Professor Parkerson, when you get the names of your clients—those in the second category—would you pass them on to me?"

"To you? Why?"

"I will pay you five hundred dollars for each name—providing, of course, that I ultimately do business with the client."

A light flickered in my brain. "Why do *you* want those names?"

He smiled. "One of the difficulties of my profession is establishing contact with prospective clients. I of course cannot advertise for them. But you can."

I blurted the unnecessary question. "Your profession is *murder?*"

"Possibly we could work out some percentage arrangement instead," he said. "Let us say fifteen percent of anything I receive?"

I stood up. "I believe that it is now *my* turn to summon the police."

He shrugged. "What could you possibly prove? I would deny that we ever had this conversation. And my name and fingerprints do not appear in police records anywhere." His eyes seemed to glitter. "You don't seem to realize how *big* we can make this. Your 'research' needn't be confined to just one locality. You can make it nationwide. A veritable Kinsey report—in volume, at least. And your profession is a perfect legitimate front."

"Never. Absolutely never."

He was not perturbed. "I'll give you a little time to think it over, Professor. And remember that there are probably hundreds of other psychologists who might jump at the chance I'm offering you."

I watched him cross the street and get into a sleek 1963 convertible.

After my last class of the day, I drove home in my 1946 sedan.

Doris was sorting a mass of clothes. "For the rummage sale at church, dear."

I looked over the garments. "What is my brown suit doing there? That's the one I wore when we were married."

"It's worn, dear. I didn't know you were sentimental about it."

"I am not sentimental. But there is still a lot of good wear in it. Put the suit back into the closet."

"All right, dear. But you really don't have to be married and buried in the same suit these days."

I regarded her speculatively. Why did she choose that particular expression? Married and buried.

I shrugged and went into the study. I reached for a sheet of paper. The population of the United States is approximately 186,000,000. Suppose one hundred thousand of those people wanted to get rid of their mates—surely a conservative figure. But why limit the field to husbands and wives? After all, there are uncles, aunts, nephews, nieces, friends. . . .

Suppose one could establish contact with just five thousand of them? And suppose one would average five thousand dollars per individual? That would come to twenty-five million dollars. And fifteen percent of twenty-five million was—

I crumpled the paper abruptly and tossed it away. I turned to a stack of tests, and doggedly set about marking them.

* * *

On Thursday afternoon I went to the *Herald Journal*. In box number 1183 I found an envelope in response to my ad about Regis, the lost collie.

I read the note.

Dear Sir:

I have seen the ad concerning Regis, your lost collie dog.

I think it is time we met. I suggest the Leoni Restaurant at the corner of 27th and Gerald at eight in the evening. Friday.

I shall be wearing a rose chiffon scarf and expect you to have a bachelor's-button boutonniere. I shall say, "Regis," and you will respond with, "Black collar."

I reread the words. That the writer was a woman was now definitely established. And this time the typewritten words were clear and dark.

The Leoni Restaurant? Oh, yes. I remembered the place. Doris and I had dined there a year ago. Or was it two?

I thought about that for a while and then continued home. When I entered the house, I said, "Doris, it's been some time since we went out to dinner. Suppose we make it Leoni's this Friday evening?"

She looked up from her magazine. "I'm sorry, dear. But that's my Women's Club night. I'd cancel, but I'm chaplain this year and really ought to be there. When one becomes an officer in an organization, one must assume certain responsibilities, and attendance is one of them."

I put my hat back on. "I'm going outside for a short walk."

"But you just came in, dear."

"Nevertheless, I am going for a walk."

It was dark and windy outside. Was it possible that Doris was just playing some kind of trick on me? But how could she know about my project? It is my policy to be secretive about my work until I am fully into it. This saves the embarrassment of withdrawal, should the field prove to be an impossible one.

Or was it actually possible that Doris seriously entertained the fantastic notion of getting rid of me?

We'd been married ten years and, I had thought, happily. Of course ours had been the quiet life, but certainly Doris must be acclimated to something like that. I had deliberately married "in service," so to speak. Her father had been a professor of Romance languages and her mother an associate professor in zoology. Her re-creation of the ecology of a pond is still the standard exhibit in that department.

Should I confront Doris and demand an explanation?

I shook my head. No. I had to find out just how far she really intended to go.

Should I wear a beard or something of that order when I met her at Leoni's? I'd see Professor Tibbery of the drama department tomorrow and see what he could do for me.

A long convertible slowed down, passed me, and then drew to a stop at the curb. The tall stranger who made murder his business got out of the car and waited for me.

"Well, Professor, have you made up your mind to play along?"

A new chain of thoughts came to my mind. Why do people kill? For profit, of course. For passion. *And* in self-defense.

My eyes widened at the idea. Would I be morally justified in having Doris murdered before she had the chance to murder me? Should I hire someone to do the job for me? Like this man standing before me? I closed my eyes and wrestled with cold logic and warm emotion.

No. I couldn't have Doris killed. I had married her for better or worse, though this was considerably worse than I had expected.

"Well, Professor," the stranger said again. "Are you ready to do business?"

I opened my eyes. "We have absolutely no business to discuss."

He tilted his head slightly for ten seconds of appraisal and then reached inside his topcoat. He produced a card and handed it to me. "I shall be at the Westland Hotel for one more day. And let me remind you that there are other psychologists who might jump at this opportunity."

"Feel free to help yourself."

When the taillights of his automobile disappeared around the corner, I took the card to the nearest lamplight. It contained no information besides the name. Charles A. Hasker. Was that his real name? If he truly did not have a record with the police, that could very well be. However, it really did not matter. I would inform Sergeant Larson where Hasker could be reached.

Perhaps the police could do nothing about him at the moment, but on the other hand they would be informed of his existence and profession, and he could be watched. Eventually he would be apprehended.

When I reached home, I found my neighbor, Professor Conner, waiting at the chessboard.

Why he continually chooses to drop in, I do not know. We have little in common. His field is zoology. I introduced the *divertissement* of chess because it is preferable to his conversation.

At eleven, he consumed two of Doris' tuna-salad sandwiches and departed.

On Friday, after supper, Doris went upstairs to dress for Women's Club. When she came down, she kissed me lightly. "I don't know exactly when I'll get back, dear. The subject for discussion tonight is Castro, and there's no telling how many resolutions we'll pass."

I regarded her moodily. "Have you forgotten anything? Like a rose chiffon scarf?"

"It's in my purse, dear. Do you mind if I take the car tonight?"

"I thought Professor Bronson's wife usually picked you up?"

"I told her not to. Frankly I'd like a little freedom of movement. Otherwise I always have to leave when she does."

When she left, I opened the closet and fetched the makeup Professor Tibbery had given me earlier in the day.

I reviewed his directions and propped up a mirror. Why in the world would Doris want to kill me? *Why?* For money? Ridiculous. Our assets were modest indeed.

For my life insurance? It was a fairly tidy amount, yet not so great that it should constitute a temptation. Was there another man? I smiled at that. There was absolutely not one iota of evi—

I sat without moving for fully a minute.

Why did Professor Conner appear at our home so often? Was he really interested in chess? Why did Doris always serve those confounded tuna-salad sandwiches? They are definitely not *my* favorite.

And Conner is a bachelor. His interest is vertebrate zoology. Certainly a man who specializes in the lower vertebrates would eventually aspire to the higher. . . .

I glared at my now bearded reflection and then put on my pair of green-tinted sunglasses. On the way out of the house I stopped at the refrigerator and removed the bachelor's-button boutonniere from its concealment behind the dill-pickle jar.

I arrived at Leoni's at approximately eight and stood immediately inside the entrance, aggressively exhibiting my boutonniere.

Leoni's was a modest establishment containing about a dozen tables and a similar number of booths. My eyes searched the room. None of the women at the tables was wearing a rose chiffon scarf. I could not, however, see into the booths.

I remained standing where I was for five minutes and had about determined to make a personal inspection of the booths when a woman of about twenty-five rose from one of the tables and approached me.

She spoke somewhat tentatively. "Regis?" She stared at me warily.

I blinked. "You are not wearing a rose chiffon scarf."

"But I *am.*"

Then I remembered my green-tinted glasses. I flushed slightly and removed them. Yes, she was wearing a rose chiffon scarf.

And I had never seen her before in my life.

"Black collar," I said weakly.

She led me to her table and I listened to her story. She wanted to get rid of her husband, but would not disclose the motive. Probably money, I thought, but I couldn't have cared less.

We quickly settled for a fee of ten thousand dollars and I made an appointment to meet her once again when we would thrash out details. But, of course, I had not the slightest intention of seeing her again. I would give her name and address to Sergeant Larson and leave it to him to dissuade her from murder.

As far as I was concerned, this was the end of my current project. Instead, I would devote my sabbatical year to constructing a personality silhouette of Certified Public Accountants. After all, that had been my second choice.

I went to the nearest bar and ordered a Scotch and soda. I felt a sense of exhilaration which, I suppose, is normal to any man when he discovers that his wife does not want to kill him.

I lingered over three more Scotches, and at ten-thirty I left. It was about three miles to my house, a gibbous moon had risen, and I felt like walking.

The residential streets were quite silent and deserted, and so it happened that I noticed the automobile which passed me four blocks from my home.

It was my own sedan, and Doris was probably returning from Women's Club. The car pulled to the curb approximately one block ahead of me.

Ah, Doris had seen me, and was waiting.

But then something else occurred to me. I was still wearing the beard. How had she recognized me? And in the moonlight?

I frowned as I approached the car.

What I had taken for a rather bulky shadow in the front seat now parted. There were two people in the car. I stopped and stared into the window. Doris . . . and Professor Conner!

The two faces coldly returned my stare and conveyed the message that what was happening here was clearly none of my business.

My wife's voice came uncharacteristically hard. "Got nose trouble, mister? Move on."

I moved on.

At the corner I turned and immediately crouched behind the cover of a hedge to peer back. I had not been mistaken. They resumed their embrace. And in *my* car!

I timed them by my watch. Ten minutes. Fifteen. There was no indication when they would cease. I rose and marched toward the light of a public phone booth a block away.

How much would Hasker charge to permanently dispose of Doris? *And* Professor Conner? Probably some outrageous sum. Even with a fifteen-percent discount, I doubted if I could afford it.

Or perhaps he would do it for nothing, if he and I became partners.

"Anyone for Murder?". *The Alfred Hitchcock Hour,* March 13, 1964. Directed by Leo Penn. Teleplay by Arthur Ross, based on Jack Ritchie's short story "Anyone for Murder?" (*Alfred Hitchcock's Mystery Magazine,* January 1964). With Barry Nelson (James Parkerson), Patricia Breslin (Doris Parkerson), Edward Andrews (Bingham), Dick Dawson (Robert Johnson), Robert Jacquin (Connelley), Richard X. Slattery (Detective Barker), David Fresco (Waiter).

Wisconsin-based Jack Ritchie (1922–1983) was that rarest of literary birds, a professional writer of short stories. Between 1953 and his recent death, he sold more than five hundred tales, most of them to the mystery magazines. Two of his early stories in the tough-guy manner of *Manhunt* and similar fifties crime pulps were adapted into thirty-minute *Alfred Hitchcock Presents* episodes; and another pair, including "Anyone for Murder?" into segments of *The Alfred Hitchcock Hour.* As you've seen, it's a gem of a tale, combining radical storytelling economy and bizarre humor in the distinctive Ritchie vein, and even though I've never seen the telefilm version, I can't see how director Leo Penn and scriptwriter Arthur Ross could have gone wrong with it if they followed Ritchie's blueprint.

Francis M. Nevins, Jr.

JAMES YAFFE

One of the Family

EVER SINCE THE BEGINNING OF WINTER the big worry in Joan Porter's life had been what to do when the nurse left. Little Bruce was three months old now, and Mrs. Finney couldn't stay with him much longer. She was an infant nurse, and plenty of other newborn infants were clamoring for her services. She had agreed to remain in the Porter home only until they found some older, less highly trained woman to take over the job.

But this wasn't so easy. Joan had made up her mind that just anybody wouldn't do. After all, this woman would be Bruce's constant companion for the next two or three years, maybe even longer. And all the psychology books emphasized how important those two or three years could be. Why, the wrong kind of influence at this early age might mar the child's whole life.

What a relief it was, then, when Harry came home one night and told Joan the wonderful news. "You know who called me up at the office this afternoon? Frieda, of all people! Frieda—you remember, I've told you all about her—she was my old nurse when I was a kid; she was with me till I was six years old. Well, she read about Brucie in the New Rochelle papers, and she wants to know if we'd like her to take care of him."

It was a real miracle. Joan certainly did remember what Harry had told her about his old nurse Frieda—her funny German accent, her warm affectionate temperament, her firmness when Harry was naughty, her little lullabies and her wonderful bedtime stories, her fussiness over his personal appearance, her pride at his childish accomplishments.

Harry didn't even know Frieda's last name—she had been married, but her husband was dead for many years and Harry had no idea who he had been. All Harry knew was that she was his Frieda. How many times he had said, "If I can look back to a happy childhood, and if I'm a reasonably well-balanced man today, I think I owe most of it to Frieda." And how many times Joan had dreamed of finding just such a perfect nurse for her own little boy.

Frieda arrived the following Monday morning, and Harry and Joan met her at the New Rochelle station.

Right away Joan knew everything was going to be all right. Frieda was a heavily built woman in her early sixties, with large features, thick grayish hair, and a brown, lined face. But there was nothing coarse about her looks in spite of their plainness. Joan saw compassion in her eyes, as well as the usual German briskness and efficiency. And there was something oddly sad and delicate about her smile. She wore a plain gray coat, slightly shabby but still respectable. On her head was a sensible, somewhat old-fashioned hat. Her shoes were heavy and solid and they suggested a complete absence of female vanity.

The two women warmed up to each other immediately. "Mrs. Porter," Frieda said, holding Joan at arm's length on the station platform. "So this is my little Harry's wife. I always knew he would marry a fine pretty girl, that one." Harry blushed and said that Frieda made him feel like six years old again. Joan laughed, shook Frieda's hand warmly, and took her arm to help her into the car.

All during the ride they told stories about "their Harry," while Harry made feeble protests from the driver's seat.

As they pulled up to the house, Frieda began to grow excited.

"I cannot wait to see him," she said. "The little baby. I must know is he as handsome as his papa was."

Harry parked the car, and Frieda said some nice things about the house. But her excitement was growing—she couldn't conceal that the main thing on her mind was the baby. This pleased Joan very much.

Finally they were upstairs in the nursery and Frieda was looking down at Bruce in his playpen. For a long time she didn't say anything. Then her voice came, low and trembling. "He is beautiful. He is the most beautiful baby that ever was."

Joan looked at her and saw with a little pang of sympathy that there were tears in Frieda's eyes. "Mrs. Porter, how do I thank you?" Frieda said. "It is like the old days once more."

On a sudden impulse Joan reached out and put her arms around the old lady. "You don't have to thank me," she said. "From now on you're going to be just like one of the family."

Joan's instinct was justified. Frieda quickly proved to be what Westchester matrons call "a perfect jewel." With her two suitcases, which apparently contained all the clothes and possessions she had in the world, she moved into the maid's room adjoining the nursery, and within a week it was hard to imagine how the household had ever managed to run without her.

Most important, of course, was her devotion to Bruce. Quietly, without any fuss, she took over all the duties of tending for him. She fed him—and far less of the strained food was lost on his chin than in the days when Joan used to feed him. She washed him—and it was amazing how little squirming and squealing he did under her magic touch. She had an uncanny instinct, almost a second sight, for knowing when his diapers needed changing. And she seemed to get endless delight out of cooing at him, humming to him, tickling him, and bringing a smile to his face.

At the same time she didn't monopolize him. She was that most astounding phenomenon, a nurse who didn't consider herself infinitely more important in the child's life than his own mother. When the time came for Joan to take over the cooing and tickling,

Frieda always stepped into the background, without the trace of a sour look. And if Joan asked to do the washing or the feeding, Frieda simply let her do it, and never went through the usual repertoire of grunts and sneers and superior sniffs.

In addition to all this, Frieda was perfectly willing to help out with the housework. She did the cleaning right along with Joan. She even insisted on being allowed to take turns with the cooking. "I know you are a good cook," Frieda said, "but I too have much experience with cooking. And sometimes a nice young couple that's in love, you like to sit together at the table, with a couple of candles maybe, and look in the eyes and don't have to worry if the roast is burning."

Joan laughed and said, "You sound as if you're talking from first-hand knowledge. I'll bet when you were first married—"

Frieda gave a rueful little smile. "No, no, it was not like this for me, Mrs. Porter. My husband was not like my little Harry. He was a Prussian, you understand—" She laughed and changed the subject, and Joan never asked her again.

"I don't know what I'd do without Frieda." That was how Joan summed it up to her mother one month after Frieda's arrival. It was Frieda's afternoon off, and Joan and her mother were sitting in the nursery, drinking coffee and watching Bruce crawl around in his playpen. "In fact," Joan went on, "I sometimes think it's too good to be true."

"It *is* too good to be true," her mother said. "That's the way it always goes with these possessive old nurses. The minute they move in, they start taking things over. Before you know it, they won't let you touch your own baby."

"But Frieda's not like that at all. She's not the least bit possessive. She wants to see Bruce happy. Nothing pleases her more than when I'm playing with him. If you knew how sweet she is—"

"Oh, I'm sure of it." Mother raised her chin in that imperious way of hers. "They're always sweet as honey at the start. Little by little they make themselves indispensable. And when the time comes, watch out! You can't do this, you can't do that, baby has to take his nap now, baby can't be disturbed, baby doesn't want to see you. In the end you're lucky if they don't lock you out of the nursery.''

But Joan just smiled and patted her mother's hand. ''Well, one thing you'll have to admit. It's better to have a possessive nurse who really loves your child than *this* kind of nurse.'' She motioned at the afternoon newspaper, which was folded on the arm of her chair.

''What kind of nurse?'' Mother said.

''Didn't you read it in the paper yet? This terrible case out in San Francisco.'' Joan opened the paper and read the story aloud.

It was about a family in San Francisco whose infant boy had died a month and a half before. The doctor had thought it was one of those mysterious viral infections that sometimes carried infants off, and the baby had been buried in the regular way. But just recently some relative in the family, an old-maid aunt who lived with them, convinced the authorities to exhume the body and do a post-mortem—and sure enough, they discovered the baby had been poisoned. Now they were looking for the baby's old nurse, a woman who had been discharged shortly before the tragedy. This nurse had always been very fussy and didn't like anyone but her touching the baby. But the most suspicious thing of all was that the day before the baby's death, she had actually locked the nursery door and refused to let the mother and aunt come in at feeding time. This, in fact, was the reason she had been discharged.

There wasn't any proof against the woman, of course, but already the newspapers were beginning to refer to her as Nurse Butcher. . . .

''Now that's a dreadful thing,'' Joan's mother said with a shudder. ''But it doesn't change my opinion any. These old nurses always think they know better than the mother, and believe me that's— Joan, look out!'' She gave a little scream. ''He's going to get his fingers caught in the bars of the playpen!''

''He won't hurt himself, Mother. You have to let a baby experiment; otherwise, he'll be timid and self-conscious all his life.''

''That's something out of your ridiculous psychology books, I suppose! Well, I don't intend to sit by quietly and watch *my* grandson break his fingers! All right, Brucie baby, all right, all right, don't cry, Grandma's here. . . ."

It was just two days later that Bruce got the first of his stomach attacks. He started crying in the middle of the night. Joan woke up sharply and realized even from her bedroom that this wasn't his usual cry. By the time she reached the nursery, Frieda was already there, bending over him and whispering to him comfortingly.

They called Dr. Flowers. Under ideal circumstances he wasn't the doctor Joan would have chosen—he was very old and a little bit too vague and easygoing for her taste. But he had been Harry's family doctor for years, and he would have been hurt if Harry had called in anybody else.

"Nothing to worry about, my dear, nothing at all," said old Dr. Flowers in his high droning voice. "Just a little stomach upset, that's all. I've called the pharmacy; they're sending out a prescription. Meanwhile keep him warm and quiet, and that strong young fellow of yours'll be good as new by morning."

It was two more mornings before he was good as new. During that time he alternated fits of choking and retching with long periods of lying on his back, staring dully at the ceiling. Joan could hardly think straight during those two days, she was so frantic. The only thing that enabled her to get through the ordeal was Frieda. Frieda was a miracle of efficiency—she took care of the baby, gave him his medicine, sang him to sleep, eased his pain, cleaned up after his vomitings, kept the house running smoothly, calmed Joan's nerves, and dealt with Harry's appetite. And yet there was never a moment when she wasn't cheerful, quiet, and unobtrusive. She didn't act like some bossy Trained Nurse, forever "managing" things.

At last Bruce was wriggling and giggling again, just like normal. And Joan got ready to throw herself down on her bed and sleep for a week. But not before she took Frieda's hand and squeezed it quickly and murmured, "Thank you."

The next day the household was back to its regular routine. At six in the evening Frieda was upstairs putting the baby to bed, and Harry and Joan were downstairs having a cocktail before dinner.

"Oh, look," Joan said, glancing through the second section of the evening paper, "here's some more about that case out in California—that Nurse Butcher, they call her."

"A lot of sensationalism," Harry said. "It says here the new hydrogen bomb could wipe out a whole city, and everybody gets all excited over some dull little murder out in San Francisco."

"Well, it's only natural. Killing a little baby like that—it's so brutal."

Harry looked up at her, amused. "And why is it more brutal to kill one little baby than a whole city full of people, including thousands of babies?"

"I don't know. It just is. It's only logical." Obscurely dissatisfied with her reasoning, Joan looked down at the paper quickly and began to read the story.

A few minutes later she gave an odd little laugh.

"What's the joke?" Harry said.

"It's just a funny coincidence. When the police searched the house where that baby died, they found a bottle hidden behind the dresser in the nurse's room. The bottle was still half full of arsenic. So now they're looking for her. They want to arrest her for murder."

"Okay, but where's this funny coincidence you mentioned?"

"Well, they give her description here in the paper. 'In her sixties. Stout and heavy. About five-foot-three. Gray hair. Dark complexion. Wears plain, cheap clothes. Speaks with a German accent.' " Joan stopped reading and looked up at him. "Don't you see? That description sort of—well, it fits Frieda."

Harry stared at her a moment. Then he threw back his head and burst out laughing.

Joan lowered her eyes and grew red. "I don't see what you're laughing about. I only said it was a coincidence."

"Sure, sure. Shirley Holmes Porter is on the case. Poor Frieda—we only happen to have known her for more than twenty-five years; she only happens to have practically raised me single-handed. But that's all right, she's got gray hair and a German accent, so we'd better start sniffing our food for the telltale odor of bitter almonds.'' He laughed some more. ''Darling, you're all worn out, you've had a rough time the last few days, and you're not thinking clearly. Don't you see, that description in the paper fits nine out of every ten German nursemaids who ever lived! Go into Central Park any morning of the week, and I'll make you a bet that every other bench will have at least one old lady on it who fits that description.''

Already Joan was feeling a little peeved at herself. So she took a peeved tone with him. ''I didn't say I thought this meant anything, did I? I was simply pointing out a coincidence, and now you treat me like a mental incompetent.''

''Darling, I'm sorry.'' He came up to her and kissed her gravely on the forehead. ''I certainly wouldn't want to imply that you're a mental incompetent. Or a mental anything else.''

After that he didn't refer to the matter again. Except once, during dinner, he made his face very solemn and took a long significant sniff at the salad. Then he winked at her, maddeningly.

Well, that's the end of it, Joan told herself. That silly idea was out of her head once and for all.

But sometimes it isn't as easy to get an idea out of your head as it was to get it in there in the first place. Anyway, that's how it had always been with Joan. Odd notions and suspicions came to her out of nowhere, and even though she knew how absurd they were, she just couldn't be satisfied until she had followed them up and proved to herself that there was nothing in them. For instance, back in college, when she was first engaged to Harry, and somebody mentioned that he had been seen with that Natalie Taylor from South Carolina—Joan had tortured herself for days, and finally told Harry she was breaking the engagement, and said the most awful things to him. She still remembered her humiliation when she found out that Natalie Taylor was his first cousin, and the only reason he had taken her out that night was because his mother asked him to.

It's the same thing now, Joan told herself. She was simply letting her imagination run away with her.

And yet, the very next morning, while she and Frieda were cleaning up the master bedroom, she found herself moving—as if against her own will—toward that dangerous subject.

"You know, Frieda," she said, as they stood across the bed from each other and shook out a sheet, "you've never told us much about your life during the last twenty years . . . since you took care of Harry. I don't want to pry, goodness knows, but since you're practically one of the family, we *are* interested. . . ."

Was it still her imagination, or did Frieda's good-humored smile tighten up a little at this question? "My life is not interesting, Mrs. Porter. After I stop working for my Harry's mama, I went to the Atkins, these were friends of his mama on West End Avenue—"

"Oh, I know about the Atkins, of course. You were with them for almost seven years. And after that you were with that artist and his family. Harry has told me all about that; he says you used to send him birthday cards regularly all that time. It's *after* the artist that I'm curious about, Frieda. You wrote Harry that you were going to give up nursing and live out West with your married daughter. That was ten years ago, and he didn't hear from you since."

Frieda was busy tucking in the blankets. "It did not work out with my married daughter, Mrs. Porter. The house was too small, and I was not sympathetic with her husband, that no-good Carl. I am there one year, and they move to Saint Louis. They ask me to move with them, but I say no, I will to nursing go back. And so this is what I do." She lifted her chin and gave a stiff laugh. "So this is not very interesting, is it?"

"Whom did you work for out West?"

"I work for many people, Mrs. Porter."

"But the last ones you worked for, what were *their* names?"

"Their names?" Frieda fluffed up the pillow vigorously for a moment. "Their name is—Munster. Mr. and Mrs. William Munster."

Joan noted that this wasn't anything like the name of those people in San Francisco whose baby had died. "Was that out in San Francisco?"

"No. It was a small city, Bakersfield. I have never been to San Francisco."

Joan took a breath.. Then she brought out her next question, trembling a little. "And their baby—this Mr. and Mrs. Munster— was it a little boy, too?"

Frieda seemed to relax. She smiled. "Oh, yes. It is always a little boy. I am great friends with them always, little boys. I think I do the bathroom now, Mrs. Porter." She was gone before Joan could ask another question.

For the rest of the morning Joan thought about this conversation. Frieda's manner had been evasive. There was no doubt about that, it wasn't Joan's imagination at all. And why on earth should she want to conceal the details of her life these last few years if there wasn't something to conceal?—perhaps something dreadful?

Lots of reasons, Joan answered herself. Personal and private reasons. People have a right to their privacy, don't they? Why should they pour out their life history to every nosy Westchester housewife who comes along? Mind your own business, Joan told herself firmly.

Softly, insinuatingly, a small inner voice said to her: Bruce is your baby; *that's* your business; that's the only business that really matters.

And a few days later three things happened that brought all her submerged suspicions right back up to the surface.

The first thing happened at breakfast. On the back page of the *Times* she ran across a small item about Nurse Butcher.

"Listen to this, Harry," she said, trying to keep her voice casual. "You know that San Francisco murder case we were talking about the other day? Well, they've got some more information about the nurse who's supposed to have done it. This ticket seller from the railroad station remembers seeing her the day after the baby's funeral. He says he sold her a coach ticket to New York. That's a three- or four-day trip by train, and this murder happened about six weeks ago—that's just about a week before Frieda got in touch with you and asked for the job, isn't it?''

Harry lowered his half of the paper slowly and gave a sigh. ''And exactly what is *that* supposed to mean?''

''I don't say it means anything—''

''Oh, you don't, do you? What else have you been saying, I'd like to know? My God, honey, use a little common sense, will you? Hundreds of people take the train to New York every day. Besides, that woman may not have been going to New York at all. She could just as easily have got off at Chicago, or never taken the train in the first place. I don't understand how you can be so silly.''

''I know it, I know I'm silly. Only—in the second part of this story they give a quotation from a big psychiatrist. They asked him if he had any theory as to why this Nurse Butcher poisoned that baby. And listen to what he says—he says she is undoubtedly a victim of a common type of psychosis that attacks women of middle age who have no children, or whose children have neglected them. Such women, as a result of their frustration, grow to feel great resentment against younger women with small babies. They feel that it is unjust for such women to be happier than themselves, and often they will resort to extreme and violent methods to punish these young mothers for this fancied injustice.''

''Very ingenious,'' Harry said. ''If there's one type of person I hate, it's a breakfast-table psychiatrist.''

''Harry,'' Joan pushed on despite his sarcasm, ''I have to know once and for all! I have to be sure, otherwise I'll never have another moment's peace. Frieda told me her last employers were a Mr. and Mrs. William Munster in Bakersfield, California. Well, I'm going to send a telegram to my brother Eddie in Los Angeles—he's a lawyer, he's got ways of looking things up—and ask him to get in touch with these Munster people and wire me right back. And another thing—I'm going to ask Eddie if the papers out there have printed a picture of this nurse. If they have, I'm going to ask him to send it to me. I *know* it's silly," she said, forestalling his objections, "but I have to do it!"

So right after breakfast she did it—while Frieda was out in the backyard hanging up the wash.

That same afternoon, the second thing happened. Frieda was outside with the baby carriage, and Joan suddenly felt an intense desire to search Frieda's room, to see if there was anything there which might set her mind at ease. She knew this was a terrible thing to do; she hated snoopy people—"but it's for Bruce's sake," she told herself.

As it turned out she didn't have to search the room. Because the moment she stepped into it, her eye was caught by something on the dresser. It was a bottle, a large bottle about three-quarters full of a thick brownish liquid. Joan went up to it and took it in her hands, but there was no label on it, nothing at all to indicate what it contained. Quickly she unscrewed the top and smelled it. The liquid, whatever it was, had no smell at all.

A little later, when Frieda and Bruce came back to the house, Joan spoke up thoughtfully. "I was passing your room, Frieda, and your door was open and I happened to notice this bottle on the dresser. I was wondering—is it something out of our medicine cabinet?"

Frieda didn't seem at all perturbed by this question. She went right on taking off the baby's little sweater. "Yes, it is medicine, Mrs. Porter, but not from the medicine cabinet. It is my own."

"Something you take yourself?"

"No, no. It is not for me. It is for the baby."

The easy cheerfulness with which she said this made Joan turn cold. "But I don't remember Dr. Flowers prescribing anything like that."

"It is not from Dr. Flowers. He knows nothing, that one. This is my own medicine, something I use when I am a girl in Germany. If my baby don't feel so good, he has a little cold or a bad stomach maybe, I will give him this. Much better it works than the medicine Dr. Flowers gives him.''

"Frieda—'' Joan couldn't keep the panic out of her voice, "You're not to give any of that to Bruce!''

"But Mrs. Porter, I cannot understand. It is very good for him. I give this medicine to all of my babies.''

"Don't you dare give any of it to Bruce!'' Joan could feel the tears rushing to her eyes. "Don't you dare, do you hear me!''

She saw the look of hurt and bewilderment on Frieda's face. "Mrs. Porter, I would do nothing to hurt my baby. Don't you know this, how much I love him?''

A wave of shame came over Joan. "Frieda—I don't know what— I'm sorry!'' She gasped out the last word, then turned and ran off to her room.

When she saw Frieda at dinner that night, both were as calm and amiable as ever. Neither of them said a word about the incident.

And then, around ten o'clock, the third thing happened. Frieda was upstairs asleep, and Joan and Harry were watching television, when the phone rang. It was Western Union. Joan had received an answer from her brother Eddie in Los Angeles. The girl read it to her over the phone:

CALLED CONTACTS IN BAKERSFIELD. LOOKED UP TOWN REC-ORDS, PHONE BOOKS, TAX ROLLS. NOBODY NAMED WILLIAM MUNSTER LIVING THERE LAST FIVE YEARS. WILL DIG UP PIC-TURE, SEND SPECIAL DELIVERY.

Even Harry was a little shaken by this. He kept frowning and saying, "I don't get it. Why should she lie to you? What reason would she have?''

There was an edge of hysteria in Joan's voice as she answered him. "I can think of one good reason!''

Harry went on frowning. "We'll talk to her about it in the morning. I'm sure there's some perfectly reasonable explanation. Besides, when you get that photograph you'll see how silly all this is. My God, I've known Frieda since I was a boy! She's always been like one of the family."

"One of the family," Joan said.

But they didn't talk to Frieda about it in the morning. During the night Bruce got sick again, and his suffering drove everything else out of their minds.

Dr. Flowers said it was the same trouble as before. "A simple upset stomach, nothing at all to get concerned about. There's probably something he's allergic to. Just as soon as this little siege is over, I'll run a series of tests."

By this time Joan had no faith at all in Dr. Flowers. The idea gripped her that Bruce would only be safe if she never left his side or let him out of her sight. She canceled all her dates and committee meetings, took over Bruce's washing and feeding, moved a cot into the nursery, and spent the second night of his illness with him.

Every single time he turned over or sighed she was out of her cot, bending over his crib.

Frieda offered to help many times. "You are working too hard. You are not used to this. Go and sleep, I will take care of him." But Joan refused all Frieda's offers, hastily at first, then more and more firmly. And she steeled herself against that confused, disappointed look which came over the old woman's face.

One time, after Bruce had an especially violent fit of retching, Frieda made another offer to help, and Joan lashed out at her furiously, "Go away! We don't want your help! We can do without your kind of help!"

She apologized a moment later. She explained that she was tired and worried and didn't know what she was saying. But even the smile with which Frieda accepted this apology couldn't cover up the pain in her eyes.

On the third night of Bruce's illness, Harry called up and said he couldn't come home for dinner; he had to stay in New York with some out-of-town buyers.

"Darling, when will you get here?"

The fear must have sounded in her voice. He answered her with a reassuring laugh. "Now why are you so upset? I'll be back around midnight. If Brucie gets any worse, call Dr. Flowers."

She hung up and hurried back to the nursery. Bruce was alone, just as she had left him.

Slowly the twilight faded into darkness. Slowly and agonizingly the night passed. Joan prepared Bruce's dinner herself. But she kept Frieda in the kitchen with her while she was doing so. She told Frieda that she needed her help, but when it actually came to the point, she wouldn't let Frieda touch a thing. Then she went upstairs to the nursery and fed Bruce, and Frieda stood in the doorway and watched but didn't come any closer.

Then Frieda and Joan had their own dinner. All Joan would eat was a sandwich she made herself and a glass of milk. Frieda offered to cook something for her, but she shook her head hard. "I'm not really hungry," she said. "And I don't want to leave Bruce by himself too long."

After that, as they ate, the women exchanged hardly a word. Once Frieda made a remark about the old days in Germany, another time about all the signs Bruce was showing of being a superior child. Infallible conversation-starters usually. But tonight Joan couldn't begin to respond.

When they went up to the nursery and sat with Bruce, they perched on chairs at opposite sides of the crib and watched him as he slept. Again they exchanged hardly a word.

"He is getting better, I think," Frieda said once. "He was more comfortable today." She hesitated, then went on, "You agree, yes, he was comfortable today?"

Joan didn't answer.

Later Frieda gave a little laugh and spoke again. "That Dr. Flowers, he knows nothing of little babies. It is a good thing we don't have to depend on him, I think."

Joan looked up sharply, wondering what Frieda meant by that remark. But she didn't say anything.

The night wore on. The two women cast thick shadows across the room in the light of the small night-lamp. Once in a while, when she knew Frieda wasn't looking, Joan stared at her hard, trying to understand what this old woman was really like. Was she what she seemed to be, innocent old Frieda, the conventional German nanny devoted to her charge? Or were the thoughts in that wrinkled head deeper and blacker and more muddied, full of undercurrents of jealousy, frustration, and suppressed violence? Joan just couldn't tell. One minute Frieda's face seemed the incarnation of evil, the next it was everything sweet and simple and comforting in this world—

How do you ever know about anybody? Joan asked herself. Faces, ordinary faces, the faces that seem the warmest and fondest and that mean the most to you—can you ever be sure what's behind them? For a moment, with a thrill of horror, it seemed to Joan that life was a nightmare, the whole world a pack of grinning devils. . . .

Downstairs the doorbell rang. Joan started and looked at her watch: 11:30. "Frieda, answer the door, will you?"

Frieda left the room. A minute later she was calling up the stairs. "It is from the post office. A letter, special delivery."

Joan went downstairs and took the letter from Frieda's hand, trying not to show her excitement. She turned away slightly so that Frieda couldn't watch her opening it. Then, with trembling fingers, she tore open the envelope. A folded newspaper clipping dropped into her hand. At the top of the clipping, in heavy print, was a caption: "Mrs. Oscar Baumgartner—Police are looking for this woman in connection with the death of—"

Joan didn't have to read any further. The picture underneath the caption was a little blurred and a little dark, but it was still clear enough.

It was Frieda's picture.

There couldn't be any doubt of it.

Then she noticed that Frieda was no longer standing by her side.

The first clutch of panic froze Joan to the spot.

Then it was gone, and a terrible cry burst out of her.

"Bruce!"

She was climbing the stairs, she was running up the hall. The nursery door was shut. She yanked it open, gasped at what she saw . . .

Frieda was stooping over the crib. In one of her hands was a spoon. In the other hand was the bottle Joan had seen on Frieda's dresser, the bottle of brownish liquid. In her softest, most soothing voice, Frieda was whispering to Bruce, "All right, my baby, now you swallow this and it will stop the pain; it will make you feel nice again. Frieda tells you so—" Bruce was awake now, looking up at her solemnly. He smiled and stretched out his hand. She brought the spoon up to his lips.

Joan dashed forward, lunged at Frieda, pulled the spoon from her hand. The brownish liquid spattered over Bruce's crib, the bottle fell to the floor with a crash. Bruce started to cry.

"Murderess!" Joan shouted at Frieda. "Butcher! Nurse Butcher!"

Frieda took a step toward her. Her mouth was twisted to one side.

"Stay away from us!" Joan shouted, her voice hoarse and exhausted. "Stay away from my baby!"

And then it was a whirl in her head—Frieda's twisted mouth, Bruce's cries, the roaring in her ears, the night-lamp growing brighter and brighter. The last thing she knew was the tight clutch of Frieda's bony fingers on her arm. . . .

She was lying on her back. Harry's face was looking down at her.

It was a mist at first; she thought she must be dreaming it. Then it grew sharper; she became aware of the familiar pattern of wallpaper, the feel of her own bed under her.

Suddenly Joan started up with a cry. "Bruce!"

Harry's hand was on her shoulder, easing her gently down on the pillow. "He's all right, honey. He's sleeping now."

"But Frieda—"

"Frieda's in her room."

"In her room!" Once more Joan tried to sit up. "But Harry, she's not *alone*? She'll try again—she wants to kill him—"

Harry gave a troubled sigh. "Yes—she told me what happened before I got home. She told me those things you said to her. Joan, darling." He leaned forward. "It was all in the papers tonight, I read it on the train from the city. The killer of that baby has been caught. She's made a full confession. Frieda had nothing to do with it."

Joan stared up at him, taking in his words slowly.

"But Harry . . . that picture in the newspaper . . . that was Frieda's picture. . . ."

"Yes, Frieda was that baby's nurse, all right. She had her suspicions that somebody was trying to harm him. That's why she locked the door at feeding time."

"But she lied to me! Telling me she worked for those Munsters—"

"Don't you see, darling? She was frightened. When she read in the papers that the baby was dead, and that she was wanted for murder, she was afraid to say anything. The facts looked so bad against her—somebody had carefully seen to that. She thought the police would never believe her story. After all," —Harry lowered his eyes nervously—"she couldn't expect the police to know how kind and gentle she is. The way the rest of us should have known."

"But she was feeding that stuff to Bruce. . . . And the way she grabbed me before I fainted—"

Harry smiled wearily. "She told you what the stuff was. Her own favorite home medicine. She used to pour it down my throat twice a week when I was a kid. As for the way she grabbed hold of you—she saw you falling, and she was trying to help you."

"Trying to help me." A painful shudder began to shake Joan's body. "But, Harry, if she really was that baby's nurse—what about the bottle of arsenic they found in her room?"

"It was put there to implicate her. By the real killer."

"The real killer?"

Harry sighed again. "It was the baby's old-maid aunt. It was just as that psychiatrist said—a frustrated middle-aged woman with no children of her own, full of resentment against women more fortunate than her. That's why she pestered them to have the body exhumed a month after the funeral; that's why she tried to get Frieda blamed for the crime. It wasn't enough for her to take out her resentment on the baby's mother. She had to do something terrible to Frieda, too—because Frieda, who wasn't even related to the baby, had so much of his love.''

"So much of his love." Joan repeated the words slowly, feeling at last the full horror of what she had done.

She sat up.

"I'm going to her."

Frieda was in her room, packing a suitcase. She looked up as Joan entered. Her eyes were red, her face was gray and old.

Joan went up to her, and spoke as earnestly and intently as she could. "Frieda, I apologize. Please forgive me. Please stay here with Bruce and us."

Frieda's lips trembled. It was a few moments before she could stop the trembling. And then she managed a smile of great sweetness and sadness. "I do not blame you for anything, Mrs. Porter. A mother must protect her baby. But I think it is better I go now."

"We want you so much, Frieda. You're just like one of the family. That's really true—"

But Frieda was shaking her head slowly. "One of the family," she said, so lightly and softly, without a touch of bitterness. "No, this is not so. This is how we fool ourselves, women like me. We are never one of the family. We are in the house. We look after the baby. Everybody speaks politely to us. But for us there is no family anymore." She paused a moment, then gave a quiet smile. "I will give it up, I think, the nursing. I have a little money. I will find somewhere a place to live, and there I will live, and that will make me happy." She lowered her head, and quickly went on with her packing.

That night Joan couldn't fall asleep. She lay on her back in the darkness. Finally she spoke.

"I'll never forget what I did to her—no, never."

"Of course you will," Harry said from the twin bed. "You're upset now. But after a while, as time goes by—believe me, honey, people always forget these things."

Joan thought this over a moment. Then she spoke in a flat, even voice. "You're right," she said. "That's the most terrible part."

"One of the Family." *The Alfred Hitchcock Hour*, February 8, 1965. Directed by Joseph Pevney. Teleplay by Oscar Millard, based on James Yaffe's short story "One of the Family" (*Ellery Queen's Mystery Magazine*, May 1956). With Lilia Skala (Frieda), Kathryn Hays (Joyce Dailey), Jeremy Slate (Dexter Dailey), Olive Deering (Christine Callendar).

I remember being very pleased. The TV version stuck to the original story line, and made the surprise ending more dramatic by bringing it onstage from offstage. (This was my suggestion, when I sold them the story.) And my characters always seem more interesting to me when I see them brought to life by good actors.

James Yaffe

HELEN NIELSEN

Death Scene

THE WOMAN WHO HAD DRIVEN IN with the black Duesenberg fascinated Leo Manfred. She stood well, as if she might be a model or a dancer. Her ankles were arched and her calves firm. Leo wriggled out from under the car he was working on in order to examine her more closely.

She was dressed all in white—white hat with a wide, schoolgirl brim; white dress, fitted enough to make her body beckon him further; white shoes with high, spiked heels.

But it was more than the way she dressed and the way she stood. There was something strange about her, almost mysterious, and mystery didn't go well in the grease-and-grime society of Wagner's Garage. Leo got to his feet.

Carl Wagner, who was half again Leo's thirty years, and far more interested in the motor he'd uncovered than in any woman, blocked the view of her face. But her voice, when she spoke, was soft and resonant.

"Mr. Wagner," she said, "can you tell me when my automobile will be ready?"

Automobile—not car. Leo's active mind took note.

By this time Wagner was peering under the hood with the enthusiasm of a picnicker who had just opened a boxed banquet.

"It's a big motor, Miss Revere," he answered, "and every cylinder has to be synchronized. Your father's always been very particular about that."

"My father—" She hesitated. There was the ghost of a smile. It couldn't be seen, but it was felt—the way some perfumes, Leo reflected, are felt. "My father is very particular, Mr. Wagner. But it's such a warm day, and I don't feel like shopping."

Carl Wagner wasted neither words nor time. The fingers of one hand went poking into the pocket of his coveralls and dug up a set of keys at the same instant that he glanced up and saw Leo.

"My helper will take you home," he said. "You can tell your father that we'll deliver the car just as soon as it's ready."

If Leo Manfred had believed in fate, he would have thought this was it; but Leo believed in Leo Manfred and a thing called opportunity.

Women were Leo's specialty. He possessed a small black book containing the telephone numbers of more than 57 varieties; but no one listed in his book was anything like the passenger who occupied the backseat of the boss's new Pontiac as it nosed up into the hills above the boulevard.

Leo tried to catch her face in the rearview mirror. She never looked at him. She stared out of the window or fussed with her purse. Her face was always half lost beneath the shadow of the hat. She seemed shy, and shyness was a refreshing challenge.

At her direction, the Pontiac wound higher and higher, beyond one new real estate development after another, until, at the crest of a long private driveway, it came to a stop at the entrance of a huge house. Architecturally, the house was a combination of Mediterranean and late Moorish, with several touches of early Hollywood. Not being architecturally inclined, Leo didn't recognize this; but he did recognize that it must have cost a pretty penny when it was built, and that the gardener toiling over a pasture-size lawn couldn't have been supplied by the Department of Parks and Beaches.

And yet, there was a shabbiness about the place—a kind of

weariness, a kind of nostalgia, that struck home as Leo escorted his passenger to the door.

"I know this house!" he exclaimed. "I've seen pictures of it. It has a name—" And then he stared at the woman in white, who had been given a name by Carl Wagner. "Revere," he remembered aloud. "Gordon Revere."

"Gavin Revere," she corrected.

"Gavin Revere," Leo repeated. "That's it! This is the house that the big film director Gavin Revere built for his bride, Monica Parrish. It's called—"

The woman in white had taken a key out of her purse.

"Mon-Vere," she said.

Leo watched her insert the key into the lock of the massive door and then, suddenly, the answer to the mystery broke over him.

"If you're Miss Revere," he said, "then you must be the daughter of Monica Parrish. No wonder I couldn't take my eyes off you."

"Couldn't you?"

She turned toward him, briefly, before entering the house. Out of her purse she took a dollar bill and offered it; but Leo had glimpsed more than a stretch of long, drab hall behind her. Much more.

"I couldn't take money," he protested, "not from you. Your mother was an idol of mine. I used to beg dimes from my uncle—I was an orphan—to go to the movies whenever a Monica Parrish was playing."

Leo allowed a note of reverence to creep into his voice.

"When you were a very small boy, I suppose," Miss Revere said.

"Eleven or twelve," Leo answered. "I never missed a film your mother and father made—"

The door closed before Leo could say more; and the last thing he saw was that almost smile under the shadow of the hat.

Back at the garage, Carl Wagner had questions to answer.

"Why didn't you tell me who she was?" Leo demanded. "You knew."

Wagner knew motors. The singing cylinders of the Duesenberg were to him what a paycheck and a beautiful woman, in the order named, were to Leo Manfred. He pulled his head out from under the raised hood and reminisced dreamily.

"I remember the first time Gavin Revere drove this car in for an oil change," he mused. "It was three weeks old, and not one more scratch on it now than there was then."

"Whatever happened to him?" Leo persisted.

"Polo," Wagner said. "There was a time when everybody who was anybody had to play polo. Revere wasn't made for it. Cracked his spine and ended up in a wheelchair. He was in and out of hospitals for a couple of years before he tried a comeback. By that time everything had changed. He made a couple of flops and retired."

"And Monica Parrish?"

"Like Siamese twins," Wagner said. "Their careers were tied together. Revere went down, Parrish went down. I think she finally got a divorce and married a Count Somebody—or maybe she was the one who went into that Hindu religion. What does it matter? Stars rise and stars fall, Leo, but a good motor . . ."

Twelve cylinders of delight for Carl Wagner; but for Leo Manfred, a sweet thought growing in the fertile soil of his rich, black mind.

"I'll take the car back when it's ready," he said.

And then Wagner gave him one long stare and a piece of advice that wasn't going to be heeded.

"Leo," he said, "stick to those numbers in your little black book."

For a man like Leo Manfred, time was short. He had a long way to travel to get where he wanted to go, and no qualms about the means of transportation. When he drove the Duesenberg up into the hills, he observed more carefully the new developments along the way. The hills were being whittled down, leveled off, terraced, and turned into neat pocket-estates as fast as the tractors could make new roads and the trucks haul away surplus dirt. Each estate sold for $25,000 to $35,000, exclusive of buildings, and he would have needed an adding machine to calculate how much the vast grounds of Mon-Vere would bring on the open market.

As for the house itself—he considered that as he nosed the machine up the steep driveway. It might have some value as a museum or a landmark—Mon-Vere Estates, with the famous old house in the center. But who cared about relics anymore? Raze the house and there would be room for more estates. It didn't occur to Leo that he might be premature in his thinking.

He had showered and changed into his new imported sports shirt; he was wearing his narrowest trousers, and had carefully groomed his mop of near-black hair. He was, as the rearview mirror reassured him, a handsome devil, and the daughter of Gavin Revere, in spite of a somewhat ethereal quality, was a woman—and unless all his instincts, which were usually sound, had failed him, a lonely woman. Celebrities reared their children carefully, as if they might be contaminated by the common herd, which made them all the more susceptible to anyone with nerve and vitality.

When Leo rang the bell of the old house, it was the woman in white who answered the door, smiling graciously and holding out her hand for the keys. Leo had other plans. Wagner insisted that the car be in perfect order, he told her. She would have to take a test drive around the grounds. His job was at stake—he might get fired if he didn't obey the boss's orders.

With that, she consented, and while they drove Leo was able to communicate more of his awe and respect and to make a closer evaluation of the property, which was even larger than he had hoped. Not until they returned and were preparing to enter the garage did he manage to flood the motor and stall the car.

"It must be the carburetor," he said. "I'll have a look."

Adjusting the carburetor gave him additional time and an opportunity to get his hands dirty. They were in that condition when a man's voice called out from the patio near the garage.

"Monica? What's wrong? Who is that man?"

Gavin Revere was a commanding figure, even in a wheelchair.

A handsome man with a mane of pure white hair, clear eyes, and strong features. The woman in white responded to his call like an obedient child.

When the occasion demanded, Leo could wear humility with the grace of his imported sports shirt. He approached Revere in an attitude of deep respect. Mr. Revere's car had to be in perfect condition. Would he care to have his chair rolled closer so that he could hear the motor? Would he like to take a test drive? Had he really put more than 90,000 miles on that machine himself?

Revere's eyes brightened, and hostility and suspicion drained away. For a time, then, he went reminiscing through the past, talking fluently while Leo studied the reserved Monica Revere at an ever-decreasing distance. When talk wore thin, there was only the excuse of his soiled hands. The servants were on vacation, he was told, and the water in their quarters had been shut off. The gardener, then, had been a day man.

Leo was shown to a guest bath inside the house—ornate, dated, and noisy. A few minutes inside the building was all he needed to reassure himself that his initial reaction to the front hall had been correct: the place was a gigantic white elephant built before income taxes and the high cost of living. An aging house, an aging car—props for an old man's memories.

Down the hall from the bathroom he found even more interesting props. One huge room was a kind of gallery. The walls were hung with stills from old Revere-Parrish films—love scenes, action scenes, close-ups of Monica Parrish. Beauty was still there—not quite lost behind too much makeup; but the whole display reeked of an outdated past culminating in a shrine-like exhibition of an agonized death scene—exaggerated to the point of the ridiculous—beneath which, standing on a marble pedestal, stood a gleaming Oscar.

Absorbed, Leo became only gradually aware of a presence behind him. He turned. The afternoon light was beginning to fade, and against it, half-shadow and half-substance, stood Monica Revere.

"I thought I might find you here," she said. She looked toward the death scene with something like reverence in her eyes. "This was his greatest one," she said. "He comes here often to remember."

"He" was pronounced as if in reference to a deity.

"He created her," Leo said.

"Yes," she answered softly.

"And now both of them are destroying you."

It was the only way to approach her. In a matter of moments she would have shown him graciously to the door. It was better to be thrown out trying, he thought. She was suddenly at the edge of anger.

"Burying you," Leo added quickly. "Your youth, your beauty—"

"No, please," she protested.

Leo took her by the shoulders. "Yes, please," he said firmly. "Why do you think I came back? Wagner could have sent someone else. But today I saw a woman come into that garage such as I'd never seen before. A lovely, lonely woman—"

She tried to pull away, but Leo's arms were strong. He pulled her closer and found her mouth. She struggled free and glanced back over her shoulder toward the hall.

"What are you afraid of?" he asked. "Hasn't he ever allowed you to be kissed?"

She seemed bewildered.

"You don't understand," she said.

"Don't I? How long do you think it takes for me to see the truth? A twenty-five-year-old car, a thirty-year-old house, servants on 'vacation.' No, don't deny it. I've got to tell you the truth about yourself. You're living in a mausoleum. Look at this room! Look at that stupid shrine!"

"Stupid!" she gasped.

"Stupid," Leo repeated. "A silly piece of metal and an old photograph of an overdone act by a defunct ham. Monica, listen. Don't you hear my heart beating?" He pulled her close again. "That's the sound of life, Monica—all the life that's waiting for you outside these walls. Monica—"

There was a moment when she could have either screamed or melted in his arms. The moment hovered—and then she melted. It was some time before she spoke again.

"What is your name?" she murmured.

"Later," Leo said. "Details come later."

The swiftness of his conquest didn't surprise Leo. Monica Revere had been sheltered enough to make her ripe for a man who could recognize and grasp opportunity.

The courtship proved easier than he dared hope. At first they met, somewhat furtively, at small, out-of-the-way places where Monica liked to sit in a half-dark booth or at candlelit tables. She shunned popular clubs and bright lights, and this modesty Leo found both refreshing and economical.

Then, at his suggestion, further trouble developed with the Duesenberg, necessitating trips to Mon-Vere, where he toiled over the motor while Gavin Revere, from his wheelchair watched, directed, and reminisced. In due time Leo learned that Revere was firmly entrenched at Mon-Vere. "I will leave," he said, "in a hearse and not before—"which, when Leo pondered on it, seemed a splendid suggestion.

A man in a wheelchair. The situation posed interesting possibilities, particularly when the grounds on which he used the chair were situated so high above the city—so remote, so rugged, and so neglected. The gardener had been only for the frontage. Further inspection of the property revealed a sad state of disrepair in the rear, including the patio where Revere was so fond of sunning himself and which overlooked a sheer drop of at least two hundred feet to a superhighway someone had thoughtfully constructed below. Testing the area with an old croquet ball found in the garage, Leo discovered a definite slope toward the drop, and only a very low and shaky stucco wall as an obstacle.

Turning from a minute study of this shaky wall, Leo found Monica, mere yards away, watching him from under the shadow of a wide-brimmed straw hat. He rose to the occasion instantly.

"I hoped you would follow me," he said. "I had to see you

alone. This can't go on, Monica. I can't go on seeing you, hearing you, touching you—but never possessing you. I want to marry you, Monica—I want to marry you now.''

Leo had a special way of illustrating ''now'' that always left a woman somewhat dazed. Monica Revere was no exception. She clung to him submissively and promised to speak with Gavin Revere as soon as she could.

Two days later, Leo was summoned to a command performance in the gallery of Mon-Vere. The hallowed stills surrounded him; the gleaming Oscar and the grotesque death scene formed a background for Gavin Revere's wheelchair. Monica stood discreetly in the shadows. She had pleaded the case well. Marriage was agreeable to Gavin Revere—with one condition.

''You see around us the mementos of a faded glory,'' Revere said. ''I know it seems foolish to you, but aside from the sentimental value, these relics indicate that Monica has lived well. I had hoped to see to it that she always would; but since my accident I am no longer considered a good insurance risk. I must be certain that Monica is protected when I leave this world, and a sick man can't do that. If you are healthy enough to pass the physical examination and obtain a life insurance policy for fifty thousand dollars, taken out with Monica Revere named as beneficiary, I will give my consent to the marriage. Not otherwise.

''You may apply at any company you desire,'' he added, ''provided, of course, that it is a reputable one. Monica, dear, isn't our old friend, Jeremy Hodges, a representative for Pacific Coast Mutual? See if his card is in my desk.''

The card was in the desk.

''I'll call him and make the appointment, if you wish,'' Revere concluded, ''but if you do go to Hodges, please, for the sake of an old man's pride, say nothing of why you are doing this. I don't want it gossiped around that Gavin Revere is reduced to making deals.''

His voice broke. He was further gone than Leo had expected—which would make everything so much easier. Leo accepted the card and waited while the appointment was made on the phone. It was a small thing for Leo to do—to humor an old man not long for this world.

While he waited, Leo mentally calculated the value of the huge ceiling beams and hardwood paneling, which would have to come out before the wreckers disposed of Gavin Revere's faded glory.

Being as perfect a physical specimen as nature would allow, Leo had no difficulty getting insurance. Revere was satisfied. The marriage date was set, and nothing remained except discussion of plans for a simple ceremony and honeymoon.

One bright afternoon on the patio, Leo and Monica—her face shaded by another large-brimmed hat—and Gavin Revere in his wheelchair, discussed the details. As Revere talked, recalling his own honeymoon in Honolulu, Monica steered him about. The air was warm, but a strong breeze came in from the open end of the area where the paving sloped gently toward the precipice.

At one point, Monica took her hands from the chair to catch at her hat, and the chair rolled almost a foot closer to the edge before she recaptured it. Leo controlled his emotion. It could have happened then, without any action on his part. The thought pierced his mind that she might have seen more than she pretended to see the day she found him at the low wall. Could it be that she too wanted Gavin Revere out of the way?

Monica had now reached the end of the patio, and swung the chair about.

"Volcanic peaks," Revere intoned, "rising like jagged fingers pointing Godward from the fertile, tropical Paradise . . ."

Monica, wearied, sank to rest on the shelf of the low wall. Leo wanted to cry out.

"A veritable Eden for young lovers," Gavin mused. "I remember it well . . ."

Unnoticed by Monica, who was busy arranging the folds of her skirt, the old wall had cracked under her weight and was beginning to bow outward toward the sheer drop. Leo moved forward quickly. This was all wrong—Monica was his deed to Mon-Vere. All those magnificent estates were poised on the edge of oblivion.

The crack widened.

"Look out—"

The last words of Leo Manfred ended in a kind of eerie wail, for in lunging forward, he managed somehow—probably because Gavin Revere, as if on cue, chose that instant to grasp the wheels of the chair and push himself about—to collide with the chair and thereby lose his balance at the very edge of the crumbling wall.

At the same instant, Monica rose to her feet to catch at her wind-snatched hat, and Leo had a blurred view of her turning toward him as he hurtled past in his headlong lunge into eternity.

At such moments, time stands as still as the horrible photos in Gavin Revere's gallery of faded glory; and in one awful moment Leo saw what he had been too self-centered to see previously— Monica Revere's face without a hat and without shadows. She smiled in a serene, satisfied sort of way; and in some detached manner of self-observation he was quite certain that his own agonized features were an exact duplication of the face in the death scene.

Leo Manfred was never able to make an accurate measurement; but it was well over two hundred feet to the busy superhighway below.

In policies of high amounts, the Pacific Coast Mutual always conducted a thorough investigation. Jeremy Hodges, being an old friend, was extremely helpful. The young man, he reported, had been insistent that Monica Revere be named his sole beneficiary; he had refused to say why. "It's a personal matter," he had stated. "What difference does it make?" It had made no difference to Hodges, when such a high commission was at stake.

"It's very touching," Gavin Revere said. "We had known the young man such a short time. He came to deliver my automobile from the garage. He seemed quite taken with Monica."

Monica stood beside the statuette, next to the enlarged still of the death scene. She smiled softly.

"He told me that he was a great fan of Monica Parrish when he was a little boy," she said.

Jeremy handed the insurance check to Gavin and then gallantly kissed Monica's hand.

"We are all fans . . . and little boys . . . in the presence of Monica Parrish," he said. "How do you do it, my dear? What is your secret? The years have taken their toll of Gavin, as they have of me, but they never seem to touch you at all."

It was a sweet lie. The years had touched her—about the eyes, which she liked to keep shaded, and the mouth, which sometimes went hard—as it did when Jeremy left and Gavin examined the check.

"A great tragedy," he mused. "But as you explained to me at rehearsal, my dear, it really was his own idea. And we can use the money. I've been thinking of trying to find a good script."

Monica Parrish hardly listened. Gavin could have his dreams; she had her revenge. Her head rose proudly.

"All the critics agreed," she said. "I was magnificent in the death scene."

"Death Scene." *The Alfred Hitchcock Hour,* March 8, 1965, Directed by Harvey Hart. Teleplay by James Bridges, based on Helen Nielsen's short story "Death Scene" (*Ellery Queen's Mystery Magazine,* May 1963). With James Farentino (Leo Manfred), Vera Miles (Nicky Revere), John Carradine (Gavin Revere), Buck Taylor (Dancer), Leonard Yorr (Bill Wagner), Virginia Aldridge (Susan Revere).

"Death Scene" was presented in the last season of the Hitchcock series. In order to go out with flying colors, top talent went into the production: a flawless cast, an ingenious adaptation, and an added twist-on-my-twist ending. I loved it!

Helen Nielsen

EDWARD D. HOCH

Winter Run

JOHNNY KENDELL WAS FIRST out of the squad car, first into the alley with his gun already drawn. The snow had drifted here, and it was easy to follow the prints of the running feet. He knew the neighborhood, knew that the alley dead-ended at a ten-foot board fence. The man he sought would be trapped there.

"This is the police!" he shouted. "Come out with your hands up!"

There was no answer except the whistle of wind through the alley, and something which might have been the desperate breathing of a trapped man. Behind him, Kendell could hear Sergeant Racin following, and knew that he too would have his gun drawn. The man they sought had broken the window of a liquor store down the street and had made off with an armload of gin bottles. Now he'd escaped to nowhere and had left a trail in the snow that couldn't be missed, long running steps.

Overhead, as suddenly as the flick of a light switch, the full moon passed from behind a cloud and bathed the alley in a blue-white glow. Twenty feet ahead of him, Johnny Kendell saw the man he tracked, saw the quick glisten of something in his up-raised hand. Johnny squeezed the trigger of his police revolver.

Even after the targeted quarry had staggered backward, dying, into the fence that blocked the alley's end, Kendell kept firing. He didn't stop until Sergeant Racin, aghast, knocked the gun from his hand, kicked it out of reach.

Kendell didn't wait for the departmental investigation. Within forty-eight hours he had resigned from the force and was headed west with a girl named Sandy Brown whom he'd been planning to marry in a month. And it was not until the little car had burned up close to three hundred miles that he felt like talking about it, even to someone as close as Sandy.

"He was a bum, an old guy who just couldn't wait for the next drink. After he broke the window and stole that gin, he just went down the alley to drink it in peace. He was lifting a bottle to his lips when I saw him, and I don't know what I thought it was—a gun, maybe, or a knife. As soon as I fired the first shot I knew it was just a bottle, and I guess maybe in my rage at myself, or at the world, I kept pulling the trigger." He lit a cigarette with shaking hands. "If he hadn't been just a bum, I'd probably be up before the grand jury!"

Sandy was a quiet girl who asked little from the man she loved. She was tall and angular, with a boyish cut to her dark brown hair, and a way of laughing that made men want to sell their souls. That laugh, and the subdued twinkle deep within her pale blue eyes, told anyone who cared that Sandy Brown was not always quiet, not really boyish.

Now, sitting beside Johnny Kendell, she said, "He was as good as dead anyway, Johnny. If he'd passed out in that alley, they wouldn't have found him until he was frozen stiff."

He swerved the car a bit to avoid a stretch of highway where the snow had drifted over. "But I put three bullets in him, just to make sure. He stole some gin, and I killed him for it."

"You thought he had a weapon."

"I didn't think. I just didn't think about anything. Sergeant Racin had been talking about a cop he knew who was crippled by a holdup man's bullet, and I suppose if I was thinking about anything it was about that."

"I still wish you had stayed until after the hearing."

"So they could fire me nice and official? No thanks!"

Johnny drove and smoked in silence for a time, opening the side window a bit to let the cold air whisper through his blond hair. He was handsome, not yet thirty, and until now there'd always been a ring of certainty about his every action. "I guess I just wasn't cut out to be a cop," he said finally.

"What *are* you cut out for, Johnny? Just running across the country like this? Running when nobody's chasing you?"

"We'll find a place to stop and I'll get a job and then we'll get married. You'll see."

"What can you do besides run?"

He stared out through the windshield at the passing banks of soot-stained snow. "I can kill a man," he answered.

The town was called Wagon Lake, a name that fitted its past better than its present. The obvious signs of that past were everywhere to be seen: the old cottages that lined the frozen lakefront, and the deeply rutted dirt roads which here and there ran parallel to the modern highways. But Wagon Lake, once so far removed from everywhere, had reckoned without the coming of the automobile and the postwar boom which would convert it into a fashionable suburb less than an hour's drive from the largest city in the state.

The place was Midwestern to its very roots, and perhaps there was something about the air that convinced Johnny Kendell. That, or perhaps he was only tired of running. "This is the place," he told Sandy while they were stopped at a gas station. "Let's stay awhile."

"The lake's all frozen over," she retorted, looking dubious.

"We're not going swimming."

"No, but summer places like this always seem so cold in the winter, colder than regular cities."

But they could both see that the subdivisions had come to Wagon Lake along with the superhighways, and it was no longer just a summer place. They would stay.

For the time being they settled on adjoining rooms at a nearby motel, because Sandy refused to share an apartment with him until they were married. In the morning, Kendell left her the task of starting the apartment hunt while he went off in search of work. At the third place he tried, the man shook his head sadly. "Nobody around here hires in the winter," he told Kendell, "except maybe the sheriff. You're a husky fellow. Why don't you try him?"

"Thanks, maybe I will," Johnny Kendell said, but he tried two more local businesses before he found himself at the courthouse and the sheriff's office.

The sheriff's name was Quintin Dade, and he spoke from around a cheap cigar that never left the corner of his mouth. He was a politician and a smart one. Despite the cigar, it was obvious that the newly arrived wealth of Wagon Lake had elected him.

"Sure," he said, settling down behind a desk scattered casually with letters, reports, and Wanted circulars. "I'm looking for a man. We always hire somebody in the winter, to patrol the lake road and keep an eye on the cottages. People leave some expensive stuff in those old places during the winter months. They expect it to be protected."

"You don't have a man yet?" Kendell asked.

"We had one, up until last week." Sheriff Dade offered no more. Instead, he asked, "Any experience in police work?"

"I was on the force for better than a year back East."

"Why'd you leave?"

"I wanted to travel."

"Married?"

"I will be, as soon as I land a job."

"This one just pays seventy-five a week, and it's nights. If you work out, though, I'll keep you on come summer."

"What do I have to do?"

"Drive a patrol car around the lake every hour, check cottages, make sure the kids aren't busting them up—that sort of thing."

"Have you had much trouble?"

"Oh, nothing serious," the sheriff answered, looking quickly away. "Nothing you couldn't handle, a big guy like you."

"Would I have to carry a gun?"

"Well, sure!"

Johnny Kendell thought about it. "All right," he said finally. "I'll give it a try."

"Good. Here are some applications to fill out. I'll be checking with the people back East, but that needn't delay your starting. I've got a gun here for you. I can show you the car and you can begin tonight."

Kendell accepted the .38 revolver with reluctance. It was a different make from the one he'd carried back East, but they were too similar. The very feel and weight and coldness of it against his palm brought back the memory of that night in the alley.

Later, when he went back to the motel and told Sandy about the job, she only sat cross-legged on her bed staring up at him. "It wasn't even a week ago, Johnny. How can you take another gun in your hand so soon?"

"I won't have it in my hand. I promise you I won't even draw it."

"What if you see some kids breaking into a cottage?"

"Sandy, it's a job! It's the only thing I know how to do. On seventy-five a week we can get married."

"We can get married anyway. I found a job myself, down at the supermarket."

Kendell stared out the window at a distant hill dotted here and there with snowy spots. "I told him I'd take the job, Sandy. I thought you were on my side."

"I am. I always have been. But you killed a man, Johnny. I don't want it to happen again, for any reason."

"It won't happen again."

He went over to the bed and kissed her, their lips barely brushing.

That night, Sheriff Dade took him out on the first run around the lake, pausing at a number of deserted cottages while instructing him in the art of checking for intruders. The evening was cold, but there was a moon which reflected brightly off the surface of the frozen lake. Kendell wore his own suit and topcoat, with only the badge and gun to show that he belonged in the sheriff's car. He knew at once that he would like the job, even the boredom of it, and he listened carefully to the sheriff's orders.

"About once an hour you take a swing around the lake. That takes you twenty minutes, plus stops. But don't fall into a pattern with your trips, so someone can predict when you'll be passing any given cottage. Vary it, and of course, check these bars along here too. Especially on weekends we get a lot of underage drinkers. And they're the ones who usually get loaded and decide to break into a cottage."

"They even come here in the winter?"

"This isn't a summer town anymore. But sometimes I have a time convincing the cottagers of that."

They rode in silence for a time, and the weight of the gun was heavy on Johnny Kendell's hip. Finally, he decided what had to be done. "Sheriff," he began, "there's something I want to tell you."

"What's that?"

"You'll find out anyway when you check on me back East. I killed a man while I was on duty. Just last week. He was a bum who broke into a liquor store, and I thought he had a gun so I shot him. I resigned from the force because they were making a fuss about it."

Sheriff Dade scratched his balding head. "Well, I don't hold that against you. Glad you mentioned it, though. Just remember, out here the most dangerous thing you'll probably face will be a couple of beered-up teenagers. And they don't call for guns."

"I know."

"Right. Drop me back at the courthouse and you're on your own. Good luck."

An hour later, Kendell started his first solo swing around the lake, concentrating on the line of shuttered cottages which stood like sentinels against some invader from the frozen lake. Once he stopped the car to investigate four figures moving on the ice, but they were only children gingerly testing skates on the glossy surface.

On the far side of the lake he checked a couple of cottages at random. Then he pulled in and parked beside a bar called the Blue Zebra. It had more cars than the others, and there was a certain Friday night gaiety about the place even from outside. He went in, letting his topcoat hang loosely over the badge pinned to his suit lapel. The bar was crowded and all the tables were occupied, but he couldn't pinpoint any underage group. They were young men self-consciously trying to please their dates, beer-drinking groups of men fresh from their weekly bowling, and the occasional women nearing middle age that one always finds sitting on bar stools.

Kendell chatted a few moments with the owner and then went back outside. There was nothing for him here. He'd turned down the inevitable offer of a drink because it was too early in the evening, and too soon on the job to be relaxing.

As he was climbing into his car, a voice called to him from the doorway of the Blue Zebra. ''Hey, Deputy!''

''What's the trouble?''

The man was slim and tall, and not much older than Kendell. He came down the steps of the bar slowly, not speaking again until he was standing only inches away. ''I just wanted to get a look at you, that's all. I had that job until last week.''

''Oh?'' Kendell said, because there was nothing else to say.

''Didn't old Dade tell you he fired me?''

''No.''

''Well, he did. Ask him why sometime. Ask him why he fired Milt Woodman.'' He laughed and turned away, heading back to the bar.

Kendell shrugged and got into the car. It didn't really matter to him that a man named Milt Woodman was bitter about losing his job. His thoughts were on the future, and on Sandy, waiting back at the motel . . .

She was sleeping when he returned to their rooms. He went in quietly and sat on the edge of the bed, waiting until she awakened. Presently her blue eyes opened and she saw him. "Hi. How'd it go?"

"Fine. I think I'm going to like it. Get up and watch the sunrise with me."

"I have to go to work at the supermarket."

"Nuts to that! I'm never going to see you if we're both working."

"We need the money, Johnny. We can't afford this motel, or these two rooms, much longer."

"Let's talk about it later, huh?" He suddenly realized that he hadn't heard her laugh in days, and the thought of it made him sad. Sandy's laughter had always been an important part of her.

That night passed much as the previous one, with patrols around the lake and frequent checks at the crowded bars. He saw Milt Woodman again, watching him through the haze of cigarette smoke at the Blue Zebra, but this time the man did not speak. The following day, though, Kendell remembered to ask Sheriff Dade about him.

"I ran into somebody Friday night—fellow named Milt Woodman," he said.

Dade frowned. "He try to give you any trouble?"

"No, not really. He just said to ask you sometime why you fired him."

"*Are* you asking me?"

"No. It doesn't matter to me in the least."

Dade nodded. "It shouldn't. But let me know if he bothers you any more."

"Why should he?" Kendell asked, troubled by the remark.

"No reason. Just keep on your toes."

The following night, Monday, Johnny didn't have to work. He decided to celebrate with Sandy by taking her to a nearby drive-in where the management kept open all winter by supplying little heaters for each car.

Tuesday night, just after midnight, Kendell pulled into the

parking lot at the Blue Zebra. The neoned jukebox was playing something plaintive and the bar was almost empty. The owner offered him a drink again, and he decided he could risk it.

"Hello, Deputy," a voice said at his shoulder. He knew before he turned that it was Milt Woodman.

"The name's Johnny Kendell," he said, keeping it friendly.

"Nice name. You know mine." He chuckled a little. "That's a good-looking wife you got. Saw you together at the movie last night."

"Oh?" Kendell moved instinctively away.

Milt Woodman kept on smiling. "Did Dade ever tell you why he fired me?"

"I didn't ask him."

The chuckle became a laugh. "Good boy! Keep your nose clean. Protect that seventy-five a week." He turned and went toward the door. "See you around."

Kendell finished his drink and followed him out. There was a hint of snow in the air, and tonight no moon could be seen. Ahead, on the road, the twin taillights of Woodman's car glowed for a moment until they disappeared around a curve. Kendell gunned his car ahead with a sudden urge to follow the man, but when he'd reached the curve himself the road ahead was clear. Woodman had turned off somewhere.

The rest of the week was quiet, but on Friday he had a shock. It had always been difficult for him to sleep days, and he often awakened around noon after only four or five hours' slumber. This day he decided to meet Sandy at her job for lunch, and as he arrived at the supermarket, he saw her chatting with someone at the checkout counter. It was Milt Woodman, and they were laughing together like old friends.

Kendell walked around the block, trying to tell himself that there was nothing to be concerned about. When he returned to the store, Woodman was gone and Sandy was ready for lunch.

"Who was your friend?" he asked casually.

"What friend?"

"I passed a few minutes ago and you were talking to some guy. Seemed to be having a great time."

"Oh, I don't know, a customer. He comes in a lot, loafs around."

Kendell didn't mention it again. But it struck him over the weekend that Sandy no longer harped on the need for a quick marriage. In fact, she no longer mentioned marriage at all.

On Monday evening, Kendell's night off, Sheriff Dade invited them for dinner at his house. It was a friendly gesture, and Sandy was eager to accept at once. Mrs. Dade proved to be a handsome blond woman in her mid-thirties, and she handled the evening with the air of someone who knew all about living the good life at Wagon Lake.

After dinner, Kendell followed Dade to his basement workshop. "Just a place to putter around in," the sheriff told him. He picked up a power saw and handled it fondly. "Don't get as much time down here as I'd like."

"You're kept pretty busy at work."

Dade nodded. "Too busy. But I like the job you're doing, Johnny. I really do."

"Thanks." Kendell lit a cigarette and leaned against the workbench. "Sheriff, there's something I want to ask you. I didn't ask it before."

"What's that?"

"Why did you fire Milt Woodman?"

"He been giving you trouble?"

"No. Not really. I guess I'm just curious."

"All right. There's no real reason for not telling you, I suppose. He used to get down at the far end of the lake, beyond the Blue Zebra, and park his car in the bushes. Then he'd take some girl into one of the cottages and spend half the night there with her. I couldn't have that sort of thing going on. The fool was supposed to be guarding the cottages, not using them for his private parties."

"He's quite a man with the girls, huh?"

Dade nodded sourly. "He always was. He's just a no-good bum. I should never have hired him in the first place."

They went upstairs to join the ladies. Nothing more was said about Woodman's activities, but the next night while on patrol Kendell spotted him once again in the Blue Zebra. He waited down the road until Woodman emerged, then followed him around the curve to the point where he'd vanished the week before. Yes, he'd turned off into one of the steep driveways that led down to the cottages at the water's edge. There was a driveway between each pair of cottages, so Kendell had the spot pretty much narrowed down to one of two places, both big rambling houses built back when Wagon Lake was a summer retreat for the very rich.

He smoked a cigarette and tried to decide what to do. It was his duty to keep people away from the cottages, yet for some reason he wasn't quite ready to challenge Milt Woodman. Perhaps he knew that the man would never submit meekly to his orders. Perhaps he knew he might once again have to use the gun on his hip.

So he did nothing that night about Milt Woodman.

The following day Sheriff Dade handed him a mimeographed list. "I made up a new directory of names and addresses around town. All the houses are listed, along with the phone numbers of the bars and some of the other places you check. Might want to leave it with your wife, in case she has to reach you during the night." Dade always referred to Sandy as Kendell's wife, though he must have known better. "You're still at that motel, aren't you?"

"For a while longer," Kendell answered vaguely.

Dade grunted. "Seen Woodman around?"

"Caught a glimpse of him last night. Didn't talk to him."

The sheriff nodded and said no more.

The following evening, when Johnny was getting ready to go on duty, Sandy seemed more distant than ever.

"What's the matter?" he asked finally.

"Oh, just a hard day, I guess. All the weekend shopping starts on Thursday."

"Has that guy been in again? The one I saw you talking to?"

"I told you he comes in a lot. What of it?"

"Sandy—" He went to her, but she turned away.

"Johnny, you're different, changed. Ever since you killed that man, you've been like a stranger. I thought you were really sorry about it, but now you've taken this job so you can carry a gun again."

"I haven't had it out of the holster!"

"Not yet."

"All right," he said finally. "I'm sorry you feel that way. I'll see you in the morning." He went out, conscious of the revolver's weight against his hip.

The night was cold, with a hint of snow again in the air. He drove faster than usual, making one circuit of the lake in fifteen minutes, and barely glancing at the crowded parking lots along the route. The words with Sandy had bothered him, more than he cared to admit. On the second trip around the lake, he tried to pick out Woodman's car, but it was nowhere to be seen. Or was his car hidden off the road down at one of those cottages?

He thought about Sandy some more.

Near midnight, with the moon playing through the clouds and reflecting off the frozen lake, Johnny drove into town, between his inspection trips. There wasn't much time, so he went directly to the motel. Sandy's room was empty, the bed smooth and undisturbed.

He drove back to the lake, this time seeking lights in the cottages he knew Woodman used. But all seemed dark and deserted. There were no familiar faces at the Blue Zebra, either. He accepted a drink from the manager and stood by the bar sipping it. His mood grew gradually worse, and when a college boy tried to buy a drink for his girl, Kendell chased them out for being underage. It was something he had never done before.

Later, around two, while he was checking another couple

parked down a side road, he saw Woodman's familiar car shoot past. There was a girl in the front seat with him, a concealing scarf wrapped around her hair. Kendell let out his breath slowly. If it was Sandy, he thought that he would kill her.

"Where were you last night?" he asked her in the morning, trying to keep his voice casual. "I stopped by around midnight."

"I went to a late movie."

"How come?"

She lit a cigarette, turning half away from him before she answered. "I just get tired of sitting around here alone every night. Can't you understand that?"

"I understand it all right," he said.

Late that afternoon, when the winter darkness had already descended over the town and the lake, he left his room early and drove out to the old cottages beyond the Blue Zebra. He parked off the road, in the hidden spot he knew Woodman used, and made his way to the nearer of the houses. There seemed nothing unusual about it, no signs of illegal entry, and he turned his attention to the cottage on the other side of the driveway. There, facing the lake, he found an unlatched window and climbed in.

The place was furnished like a country estate house, and great white sheets had been draped over the furniture to protect it from a winter's dust. He'd never seen so elaborate a summer home, but he hadn't come to look at furniture. In the bedroom upstairs he found what he sought. There had been some attempt to collect the beer bottles into a neat pile, but they hadn't bothered to smooth out the sheets.

He looked in the ashtray and saw Sandy's brand. All right, he tried to tell himself, that proved nothing. Not for sure. Then he saw on the floor a crumpled ball of paper, which she'd used to blot her lipstick. He smoothed it out, fearing, but already knowing. It was the mimeographed list Sheriff Dade had given him just two days before, the one Sandy had stuffed into her purse.

All right. Now he knew.

He left it all as he'd found it and went back out the window.

Even Woodman would not have dared leave such a mess for any length of time. He was planning to come back, and soon—perhaps that night. And he wouldn't dare bring another girl, when he hadn't yet cleaned up the evidence of the last one. No, it would be Sandy again.

Kendell drove to the Blue Zebra and had two quick drinks before starting his tour of duty. Then, as he drove around the lake, he tried to keep a special eye out for Woodman's car. At midnight, back at the bar, he asked the manager, "Seen Milt around tonight?"

"Woodman? Yeah, he stopped by for some cigarettes and beer."

"Thanks."

Kendell stepped into the phone booth and called the motel. Sandy was not in her room. He left the bar and drove down the road, past the cottage. There were no lights, but he caught a glimpse of Woodman's car in the usual spot. They were there, all right.

He parked farther down the road, and for a long time just sat in the car, smoking. Presently he took the .38 revolver from his holster and checked to see that it was loaded. Then he drove back to the Blue Zebra for two more drinks.

When he returned to the cottage, Woodman's car was still there. Kendell made his way around to the front and silently worked the window open. He heard their muffled, whispering voices as he started up the stairs.

The bedroom door was open, and he stood for a moment in the hallway, letting his eyes grow accustomed to the dark. They hadn't yet heard his approach.

"Woodman," he said.

The man started at the sound of his name, rising from the bed with a curse. "What the hell!"

Kendell fired once at the voice, heard the girl's scream of terror, and fired again. He squeezed the trigger and kept squeezing it, because this time there was no Sergeant Racin to knock the

356   Edward D. Hoch

pistol from his hand. This time there was nothing to stop him until
all six shots had been blasted into the figures on the bed.

Then, letting the pistol fall to the floor, he walked over and
struck a match. Milt Woodman was sprawled on the floor, his
head in a gathering pool of blood. The girl's body was still under
the sheet, and he approached it carefully.

It wasn't Sandy.

It was Mrs. Dade, the sheriff's wife.

This time he knew they wouldn't be far behind him. This time
he knew there'd be no next town, no new life.

But he had to keep going. Running.

"Off Season." *The Alfred Hitchcock Hour,* May 10, 1965. Directed by William
Friedkin. Teleplay by Robert Bloch, based on Edward D. Hoch's short story
"Winter Run" (*Alfred Hitchcock's Mystery Magazine,* January 1965). With
John Gavin (Johnny Kendell), Indus Arthur (Sandy), Tom Drake (Sheriff
Dade).

"Winter Run," televised under the title "Off Season," was the final new
show to be done on *The Alfred Hitchcock Hour* before the series ended its run. It
was the first of my stories ever to be adapted for television. I was so pleased by
the prospect that I viewed it quite uncritically, not even minding a slight change
in the story's final scene. The script, after all, was by Robert Bloch, one of the
top writers in the business. I remember meeting Bloch at a party in New York a
year or two later, however, and he told me his original script had been quite
faithful to my story. He blamed the director for some last-minute changes in it.
Whatever the circumstances, I was pleased by the final result.

Edward D. Hoch